W9-CCH-735

THE CROWDFUNDING HANDBOOK

THE

CROWDFUNDING HANDBOOK

Raise Money for Your Small Business or Start-Up With Equity Funding Portals

CLIFF ENNICO

⚡AMACOM

AMERICAN MANAGEMENT ASSOCIATION
New York • Atlanta • Brussels • Chicago • Mexico City • San Francisco • Shanghai • Tokyo
Toronto • Washington, D.C.

Bulk discounts available. For details visit: www.amacombooks.org/go/specialsales
Or contact special sales: Phone: 800-250-5308 / Email: specialsls@amanet.org
View all the AMACOM titles at: www.amacombooks.org
American Management Association: www.amanet.org

This publication is designed to provide accurate and authoritative information in regard to the subject matter covered. It is sold with the understanding that the publisher is not engaged in rendering legal, accounting, or other professional service. If legal advice or other expert assistance is required, the services of a competent professional person should be sought.

Names: Ennico, Clifford R., author.
Title: The crowdfunding handbook : raise money for your small business
  or start-up with equity funding portals / Cliff Ennico.
Description: New York, NY : AMACOM, [2016]
Identifiers: LCCN 2016001361| ISBN 978-0814433607 (pbk.) | ISBN
  9780814433614(ebook)
Subjects: LCSH: Crowd funding. | Venture capital. | New business
  enterprises--Finance. | Small business--Finance.
Classification: LCC HG4751 .E56 2016 | DDC 658.15/224--dc23 LC record available at http://
lccn.loc.gov/2016001361

© 2016 Clifford R. Ennico
All rights reserved.
Printed in the United States of America.

This publication may not be reproduced, stored in a retrieval system, or transmitted in whole or in part, in any form or by any means, electronic, mechanical, photocopying, recording, or otherwise, without the prior written permission of AMACOM, a division of American Management Association, 1601 Broadway, New York, NY 10019.

The scanning, uploading, or distribution of this book via the Internet or any other means without the express permission of the publisher is illegal and punishable by law. Please purchase only authorized electronic editions of this work and do not participate in or encourage piracy of copyrighted materials, electronically or otherwise. Your support of the author's rights is appreciated.

About AMA

American Management Association (www.amanet.org) is a world leader in talent development, advancing the skills of individuals to drive business success. Our mission is to support the goals of individuals and organizations through a complete range of products and services, including classroom and virtual seminars, webcasts, webinars, podcasts, conferences, corporate and government solutions, business books, and research. AMA's approach to improving performance combines experiential learning—learning through doing—with opportunities for ongoing professional growth at every step of one's career journey.

Printing number
10 9 8 7 6 5 4 3 2

To the seven strong women who shaped my character and made me what I am today:

Almerinda Ruggiero Ennico (1893–1976)

Matilda "Tillie" Wagner Frenz (1898–1983)

Edna Fredericka Wagner (1902–1990)

Maria Ennico White (1910–1992)

Maria Elena (Helen) Ennico (1911–1999)

Elizabeth (Betty) Urland Ennico (1916–2012)

Ruth Frenz Ennico (1928–2014)

LIMIT OF LIABILITY / DISCLAIMER OF WARRANTY

The publisher and the author make no representations or warranties with respect to the accuracy or completeness of the contents of this work and specifically disclaim all warranties, including without limitation warranties of fitness for a particular purpose. No warranty may be created or extended by sales or promotional materials. The advice and strategies contained herein may not be suitable for every situation. This work is sold with the understanding that the publisher and the author are not engaged in rendering financial, regulatory, investment, or other professional services. While the author is engaged in rendering legal services, he is providing only legal information in this book, not actual advice or guidance upon which any particular reader can rely. If professional assistance is required, the services of a competent professional person should be sought. Neither the publisher nor the author shall be liable for damages arising herefrom. The fact that an organization or website is referred to in this work as a citation and/or a potential source of further information does not mean that the author or the publisher endorses the information the organization or website may provide or recommendations it may make. Further, readers should be aware that websites listed in this work may have changed or disappeared between when this work was written and when it is read.

Legal counsel should be consulted before offering or selling securities. A violation of either state or federal securities laws may result in civil and/or criminal penalties. The U.S. Securities and Exchange Commission may from time to time change its existing regulations permitting crowdfunded offerings of securities. Any such changes may cause the content of this book to become inaccurate. The author and publisher do not undertake to revise, amend, or update this book with new information or inform the reader of any changes.

CONTENTS

PART 1

THE BASICS OF CROWDFUNDING

PART 2

LAUNCHING A SUCCESSFUL TITLE III CROWDFUNDED OFFERING, STEP BY STEP

Chapter 7. After Your Successful Crowdfunded Offering Is Completed 83

PART 3

COMMUNICATING WITH YOUR CROWD

Chapter 8. Keeping Your Crowd Under Control 95

Chapter 9. Going Back for Seconds: Launching Multiple Crowdfunded Offerings 106

PART 4

CONSIDERATIONS FOR INVESTING IN A CROWDFUNDED OFFERING OR SETTING UP A FUNDING PORTAL

Chapter 10. Should You Invest in a Crowdfunded Offering? 113

Chapter 11. Should You Set Up a Funding Portal? 130

PART 5

BACKGROUND ESSENTIALS: CROWDFUNDING HISTORY, LAW, AND REGULATIONS

Chapter 12. Federal Regulation of Private Offerings of Securities Prior to the JOBS Act 143

CONTENTS

INTRODUCTION

Since the dawn of the digital era, entrepreneurs have dreamed of being able to raise capital on the Internet.

Until 2012, they couldn't do so legally, because federal and state securities laws in the United States prohibited businesses from raising capital using "general solicitation" and "general advertising" methods such as newspaper ads, television and radio commercials, email blasts, Internet advertising, and social media websites. To be able to issue securities in exchange for investment, entrepreneurs were required to register an initial public offering (IPO) with the federal government, a process that typically takes months and costs hundreds of thousands of dollars in legal, accounting, and other fees they can't afford.

In 2012, that changed with the passage of the federal Jumpstart Our Business Startups (JOBS) Act, which allowed entrepreneurs and start-up companies for the first time to raise capital using "general solicitation" and "general advertising" in two specific situations:

1. They could use these methods as long as they sold their securities only to "accredited investors" (extremely wealthy and sophisticated people who arguably don't need the protection of the securities laws).

2. They were authorized to sell their securities to the public through "crowd-funding portals" registered with the U.S. Securities and Exchange Commission (SEC).

Since the mid-2000s, a number of crowdfunding websites (most prominently Kickstarter.com, Indiegogo.com, and RocketHub.com) have helped individuals and companies raise money from the public to finance specific projects (such as a new book or film, an invention, or even in vitro fertilization treatments). However, these early crowdfunding websites could not offer securities in exchange for investment. Under the JOBS Act, companies can now use crowdfunding sites to offer their stock, bonds, and other securities to the public without having to make an IPO and without violating securities laws.

In October 2015, after two years of public comment, the SEC handed down Regulation Crowdfunding, a document of almost seven hundred pages spelling out the rules under which entrepreneurs and their companies can use crowdfunding websites to raise capital and sell their securities.

If you are an entrepreneur with an amazing idea but no money to launch it, if you are a start-up or early-stage company looking to raise capital through crowdfunding, or if you are a lawyer, accountant, or other adviser to entrepreneurs and early-stage companies, *The Crowdfunding Handbook* is for you. In the chapters that follow, you will learn, step by step, how to:

- Determine if a crowdfunded offering is right for your company

- Set up your company to maximize the odds of crowdfunding success

- Figure out how much money you need to raise via crowdfunding and what type of securities you should offer to the "crowd"

- Prepare the documents necessary to offer your securities to the crowd

- Find and deal with the crowdfunding websites (called portals) that will host your crowdfunded offering

- Make changes to your offering or pull the plug on it before the offering is finalized

- Market and promote your offering online and off-line

- Manage your investor crowd once the offering is over

If you are an investor looking to find the next Facebook or Twitter while they are still off the radar screen and invisible to other investors, *The Crowdfunding Handbook* is also for you. In the chapters that follow, you will learn how to read the documents entrepreneurs are required to prepare to promote their companies, communicate with company founders, make intelligent investment choices, and (perhaps) become a player in the companies you invest in.

Over the years, a number of books have been published on the crowdfunding phenomenon, but the vast majority of these were written before the JOBS Act was passed, and they do not discuss how to use crowdfunding to raise capital for a start-up business. While there are one or two books in print describing the JOBS Act and its implications for the process of raising capital, they were published well before the Regulation Crowdfunding rules were passed. They were not written by lawyers, and they did not give step-by-step guidance on how to navigate these new rules.

The Crowdfunding Handbook is one of the first—if not the first—practical guide for entrepreneurs and start-ups that want to raise capital through crowdfunding, providing them with the information and tools they need to launch a successful offering of securities on the Internet and setting the standard for all future books on this topic.

This book is divided into five parts.

Since some readers may not be familiar with the crowdfunding process, Part 1 offers an overview of the basics and describes how crowdfunding had evolved prior to the JOBS Act.

Part 2, the heart of the book, provides a step-by-step guide to launching a crowdfunded offering of securities. It contains specific information and tips on:

- Making sure your company can legally raise capital through crowdfunding

- Creating the right legal entity for a crowdfunded offering and incorporating in the right state

- Selecting the right security (stock, bonds, or something more creative) to offer the crowd

- Preparing a term sheet for the offering and selling it to the crowdfunding portals that will host the offering

- Setting the terms of the offering and changing them if necessary while the offering is in progress

- Preparing the offering documents that will sell your company to investors

- Marketing your offering online and off-line

- Closing your offering and getting your money from the portal

- Understanding your legal responsibilities once the offering is completed

- Managing your crowd and keeping your investors happy so you still have time to run your company

Part 3 gives advice on communicating with crowdfunding investors, including making changes to your business plan and launching multiple crowdfunded offerings.

Part 4 contains information for two specific types of players in the coming market for crowdfunded securities:

1. People who wish to invest in crowdfunded securities but who need to know the rules and limits on their investments

2. Entrepreneurs who wish to set up crowdfunding portals to help other companies raise capital through crowdfunded offerings of securities

Finally, for readers who need to know more than the basics, Part 5 tracks the history of federal and state securities laws prior to the JOBS Act, summarizes the JOBS Act's key provisions, and contains a detailed description of the rules in Regulation Crowdfunding.

For those readers looking for specific information, a road map to *The Crowdfunding Handbook* is provided at the end of the Introduction.

An appendix section to *The Crowdfunding Handbook* contains numerous forms and other documents that will help entrepreneurs create successful crowdfunded offerings. These include:

- The official text of Form C, the SEC's required disclosure and reporting form for offerings under Regulation Crowdfunding, along with the question-and-answer version of Form C

- Sample incorporation documents for a company seeking to raise capital via crowdfunding

- Sample term sheets for several types of offerings

- A sample risk-factors section (required by the JOBS Act and Regulation Crowdfunding) describing the pitfalls inherent in a crowdfunded offering of securities

- A sample questionnaire by which entrepreneurs and funding portals can determine if an investor is accredited

With the help of *The Crowdfunding Handbook*, any reader should be able to take advantage of this new and exciting way to raise the capital he or she needs to launch a successful venture. All you need now is a compelling idea for a new venture, a detailed business plan, and the courage to see it through.

THE ROAD MAP: WHERE TO FIND DETAILED DISCUSSION OF REGULATION CROWDFUNDING

Title III of the JOBS Act added a new Section 4(a)(6) to the Securities Act of 1933 to permit companies to engage in crowdfunded offerings of securities without having to go through the public offering registration process. The exemption is subject to many conditions, which are described in detail in Chapter 13.

Title III also added the new Section 4A to the Securities Act, containing numerous hoops that issuers, funding portals, and investors will need to jump through in order to launch a successful crowdfunded offering. Regulation Crowdfunding, which implemented these requirements, contains almost seven hundred pages of new regulations, which are too numerous and detailed to be described in a single chapter.

Accordingly, the author has spread discussion of Regulation Crowdfunding over several chapters to help issuers and their professional advisers identify the rules and regulations that apply at each stage of the crowdfunded offering process, as follows:

- Rules on an issuer's eligibility for Title III crowdfunded offerings are described in Chapter 3.

- Rules on the documents and financial statements that must be prepared and filed with the SEC and the funding portal before an issuer launches a crowdfunded offering are described in Chapter 5.

- Rules on advertising and publicity during a crowdfunded offering, and changes in the offering terms made while the offering is pending, are described in Chapter 6.

- Rules on an issuer's responsibilities to investors after a crowdfunded offering has been completed are described in Chapter 7.

- Rules for investors in crowdfunded offerings are described in Chapter 10.

- Rules for funding portals are described in Chapter 11 but briefly, because this is a book primarily for issuers and their professional advisers, not entrepreneurs looking to set up funding portals under Title III; some resources for those folks are listed in the "Suggestions for Further Reading" section near the end of this book.

Part 1

THE BASICS OF CROWDFUNDING

CHAPTER 1

What Is Crowdfunding?

Most business start-ups have relied at some point on the friends-and-family offering to raise the capital needed to create new businesses—to make the products, provide the services, and launch the innovations that make the global economy exciting and dynamic and provide the foundation for human progress.

Since historically few other people (to say nothing of reluctant banks after the 2008 financial crisis) have been willing to risk their hard-earned money on speculative start-ups, most entrepreneurs and company founders, having exhausted their credit cards and personal savings, have been forced to borrow money or seek investment from their friends, college roommates, family members, teachers, mentors, and anyone else who would listen to their pitch. The near-universal popularity of friends-and-family offerings can be explained by two basic facts of human nature:

1. Friends and family members will frequently offer you money out of love and affection (or, less charitably, to get you out of their hair), not necessarily for the purely economic motive of seeking a return on their investment.

2. Friends and family members are less likely than other people to sue you and force you into bankruptcy if the you-know-what hits the fan and the start-up fails to achieve liftoff.

Historically, the pool of available capital from friends and family has been extremely limited for most entrepreneurs, and the success of these offerings often depended on who your friends and family were. If they were rich or well connected, you were more likely than not to get the capital you needed to launch your business. If your friends and family were poor, well . . .

But that is about to change. In a big way.

Taking the Friends-and-Family Offering to the Next Level

The past decade has seen an explosive growth in Internet-based social media platforms, such as Facebook, Twitter, Instagram, Pinterest, Snapchat, Google+, and LinkedIn. While these platforms are significantly different from each other, all have one basic thing in common: they are designed to help people exponentially expand their network of friends and family by building a personal network of followers, fans, hangers-on, groupies, posses, and significant others so that it becomes larger than the friends and family who share entrepreneurs' DNA or who actually know them in the flesh.

Thanks to these platforms, millions of people throughout the world have discovered that they have more in common with someone in a remote foreign country than they do with their next-door neighbors. The author himself, a relative novice on social media, has about four hundred friends on Facebook and almost two hundred on Twitter. I admit to knowing personally only a handful of them. Each week I receive invitations to friend other people on Facebook, and I wonder how in the devil these people found me, and why they care about my "friendship." I sometimes wonder whether the people who use cartoon caricatures or famous artwork as their Facebook photos are real people or computer algorithms.

It was only a matter of time before entrepreneurs, visionaries, and dreamers started thinking about tapping into these expanded social media networks to raise capital for their projects, their businesses, and other aspects of their lives.

But there was a problem.

Since the 1930s, the U.S. Securities and Exchange Commission (SEC) had imposed severe restrictions on an entrepreneur's ability to raise capital using "general solicitation" or "general advertising." The idea was that you had to actually know people, and know them fairly well, before you hit them up for money.

I have had personal experience with these limitations. Back in the early 1990s, I and a couple of partners decided to produce a television show based on a novel idea: entrepreneurs from around the country would pitch their ideas before a panel of venture capitalists, lawyers, and industry experts and have their business plans critiqued before a live television audience.

Sound familiar? Fans of the popular network television show *Shark Tank* might be surprised to know that my show, *MoneyHunt*, ran on PBS for seven years before it folded when the Internet bubble burst in 2001 (to see some old episodes, search on YouTube for "Cliff Ennico" or "MoneyHunt television show").

Because I was not only the host of the show but the legal expert on the management team, I spent countless hours speaking to securities lawyers, SEC staffers, and others trying to get the answer to a simple question: what can entrepreneurs say, and not say, on television about their efforts to raise capital? In the early 1990s, the answer was "nothing," and each guest on *MoneyHunt* was instructed in no uncertain terms not to say anything about raising money in order to avoid a cease-and-desist order from the SEC and other securities regulators. If a guest blurted out "we are looking to raise $1 million for 20 percent of our company," we had to stop taping and rerecord that segment to avoid being sued by the government. Not a happy outcome for a show devoted to the entrepreneurial life.

Enter crowdfunding.

The term *crowdfunding*, in its most general sense, means raising money for something from a group of people that is large and relatively undefined: the crowd. Crowdfunding has been around in one form or another since the mid-2000s, but only in late 2015 have crowdfunding techniques been legally approved for companies looking to raise capital.

Crowdfunding offers entrepreneurs who are not yet ready to exploit more traditional avenues of capital raising—such as venture capitalists and angel investors—to tap into their ever-expanding social networks on Facebook, LinkedIn, Twitter, and elsewhere to raise money for their businesses. It also gives them the limited ability to advertise and promote their offerings, even on television, without violating SEC rules and regulations.

Even more significant, crowdfunding offers investors chances to tap into start-up and early-stage companies that aren't yet on the radar screens of larger and better-informed investors, and (perhaps) get a piece of the next Facebook before the marketplace finds out about it and media attention drives up the price of the company's shares.

Of course, whenever the U.S. government loosens the rules in one area of the law, it tightens them somewhere else, and crowdfunding is no exception. As a condition for allowing entrepreneurs freer access to the capital markets, the SEC has imposed lots of conditions designed to ensure that unsophisticated investors do not lose their shirts buying into companies that aren't ready for prime time. Some of these conditions may pose insurmountable barriers to many companies and investors who want to take full advantage of crowdfunded investments.

This book is a guide for entrepreneurs, investors, and others to the new crowdfunding rules, with tips and advice on how to best take advantage of them.

The Different Types of Crowdfunding

There are three basic types of crowdfunding for companies looking to raise capital. With project crowdfunding, those who contribute invest in a specific project (such as a new book or film) but do not receive securities in a company. Accredited-investor crowdfunding allows high-net-worth individuals and organizations to invest in a company and receive securities (usually but not always preferred stock or convertible debt) in return. Title III of the JOBS Act, and the SEC regulations adopted in October 2015, have opened social media crowdfunding or equity crowdfunding to the general public, enabling them to participate in offerings of securities by start-up and early-stage companies as long as their total investments in such securities do not exceed specified amounts.

This book focuses on social media crowdfunding, but first a few words to explain the three types.

Project Crowdfunding, Including Gift Crowdfunding

Until now, most crowdfunding activity has been limited to project crowdfunding and gift crowdfunding.

In project crowdfunding, an individual or company solicits money from the crowd for a project of some kind and gives investors something tangible or intangible in return but not securities in a company.

Let's say I decided to write a book—a novel, for example, with vampires and zombies competing to have sex with remaining live humans on a reality television show after a nuclear holocaust (yes, yes, I know it's been done to death, but it's just an example—please go with it). I submit it to several traditional publishers, but no one is interested.

I get a brilliant idea: I decide to seek crowdfunding for my new book. I create a crowdfunding campaign on Kickstarter, IndieGoGo, RocketHub, or another crowdfunding platform, describe the book in detail (perhaps with a sample chapter and other information that would be included in a book proposal), and ask for money. For $25, an investor would get an autographed copy of the book on its release. For $100, an investor gets to participate in a webinar in which I will discuss the book and my inspiration for it, answer questions, and so forth. For $1,000, an investor gets an invitation to my book-launch party at an exclusive New York City restaurant or nightclub. You get the idea.

As part of the campaign, I would set a minimum total amount I will accept for the project, for example, $25,000. If I raise the $25,000 through the crowdfunding campaign, then I accept the investments, write and publish the book (either in print format or as an e-book), and fulfill my promises to the investors (send the autographed copies, host the webinar and the launch party). If my campaign doesn't reach $25,000 by a certain date, then the investors get their money back (without interest), and I turn to my next project.

This is an example of project crowdfunding. Authors, inventors, other creative types, and companies looking to test-market products have been using this method of crowdfunding for almost a decade. Because project crowdfunding does not involve investment in a company, or in securities as defined by federal and state securities laws, it has not been regulated by the SEC.

A variation on project crowdfunding is gift crowdfunding, in which the investor doesn't expect anything in return except the opportunity to have a positive impact on the world in some way. Examples of gift crowdfunding include:

- People without health insurance looking to finance a much-needed surgical procedure

- Infertile couples looking to finance in vitro fertilization procedures (in a recent crowdfunding campaign, a couple asked for money to help conceive a baby and gave investors the opportunity to participate in naming the baby by voting from a list developed by the couple and their parents)

- Not-for-profit or charitable organizations looking to raise tax-deductible donations for specific projects

In most gift crowdfunding campaigns, investors do not expect to receive anything in return for their money except the opportunity to feel good about themselves and the world in general. If a gift crowdfunding investor is looking to deduct her investment on her taxes as a charitable contribution, however, she needs to invest in a bona fide public charity registered with the Internal Revenue Service (IRS) under Section 501(c)(3) of the federal Internal Revenue Code. My vampire/zombie novel wouldn't qualify, nor would the infertile couple seeking to have a baby.

Like project crowdfunding, gift crowdfunding does not involve an investment in a company or securities and accordingly is not regulated (except perhaps by the IRS and state attorneys general, which to some extent regulate fund-raising activities by charitable organizations).

◆ ◆ ◆

In April 2012, Congress passed the Jumpstart Our Business Startups (JOBS) Act of 2012, which was signed into law by President Barack Obama later in the year.

The overall purpose of the JOBS Act was to ease restrictions on capital raising for early-stage companies. The JOBS Act contained six sections, or titles, making significant changes to the federal securities laws. All six titles are summarized in Chapter 13 of this book, but two titles of the JOBS Act are of particular interest for this book.

Accredited-Investor Crowdfunding (Title II Crowdfunding)

Title II of the JOBS Act created a new exemption for private offerings of securities (those not required to be registered with the SEC) in the United States. Prior to the JOBS Act, companies were not allowed to advertise or promote private offerings of securities at all, with certain very narrow exceptions. Under Title II (and a follow-up SEC release issued in July 2013), companies were allowed to do so as long as:

- They weren't raising more than $1 million over a twelve-month period

- They allowed only accredited investors (extremely sophisticated or rich people who could afford to lose their entire investments in the company) to buy securities in the company

The concept of an accredited investor is discussed in more detail in Chapter 10. Title II offerings are discussed at length in Chapter 13.

Social Media or Equity Crowdfunding (Title III Crowdfunding)

Title III of the JOBS Act, the primary subject of this book, allows entrepreneurs and start-up companies to sell securities in their companies using crowdfunding techniques, even if investors who participate in the offering are not accredited investors.

Title III is the heart of the JOBS Act, containing the provisions that will allow crowdfunded offerings of securities on the Internet. On October 23, 2013, the SEC issued a lengthy release (nearly seven hundred pages) spelling out the rules for how Title III crowdfunded investments can and cannot be accomplished: the proposed Regulation Crowdfunding. After two years of public comment and debate, the SEC approved the final version of Regulation Crowdfunding on October 30, 2015. The new rules will become effective May 16, 2016.

Under the regulations, it doesn't matter how many people invest in a Title III crowdfunded offering, or who they are, as long as:

- If the investor's net worth and annual income are both less than $100,000, he or she does not invest more than $2,000 or 5 percent of his or her net worth or income (whichever is greater) in crowdfunded offerings of securities during a rolling twelve-month period

- If the investor's net worth or annual income is $100,000 or more, he or she does not invest more than 10 percent of his or her net worth or income (whichever is less) in crowdfunded offerings of securities during a rolling twelve-month period

The SEC's goal in drafting this limitation is to ensure that investors in crowd-funded offerings can afford to lose their entire investments if the company they're investing in collapses, files for bankruptcy, or otherwise fails to live up to its promise. As a practical matter, this means that most ordinary folks will be legally allowed to participate in only a handful of crowdfunded investments under Title III of the JOBS Act. As has always been the case, wealthy people will be allowed to invest more in these types of offerings.

The regulations also require that Title III crowdfunded offerings be made through a funding portal, not to the securities-issuing companies directly. A funding portal is a financing intermediary that registers with the SEC for the sole purpose of facilitating crowdfunded offerings of securities. It can be a free-standing company or a division or affiliate of a registered broker-dealer exchanging in a full range of securities-related activities. Brief profiles of several companies that are expected to register as funding portals under Title III appear in the section "Suggestions for Further Reading" near the end of this book.

The regulations put the burden squarely on the funding portals to ensure that crowdfunded offerings go smoothly and comply with all federal laws and regulations. Among other things (discussed in Chapter 11), a funding portal must:

- Be registered with the SEC and be a member of the Financial Industry Regulatory Authority (FINRA)

- Handle all documents for each crowdfunded offering and make them available to investors online

- Scrutinize all offering statements and other documents submitted by companies to ensure legal compliance

- Determine whether investors in crowdfunded offerings are either accredited investors or have satisfied the SEC's limits on investment in private offerings

- Handle all funds received from investors in crowdfunded offerings and make sure the investors get their money back if an offering fails to raise the desired amount of capital

Additionally, a funding portal is liable to investors (along with the portal's directors, officers, and employees) if it fails to use "reasonable care" in reviewing a company's offering documents or fails to adopt a "reasonable policy" to avoid false or misleading statements made by companies in those documents.

Who Should Be Reading This Book?

There are three key groups of players in a crowdfunded offering of securities: the companies seeking financing (called issuers), the investors, and the funding portals that connect the two. While I have included some information for investors in Chapter 10, and some information for people looking to start funding portals in Chapter 11, this book is primarily for the kinds of people I have served as a lawyer and consultant for more than thirty-five years: entrepreneurs looking to start new companies, entrepreneurs with existing companies that need capital to grow to the next level, and the accountants, financial advisers, business development consultants, and other professionals who work with them.

Despite my profession, I have attempted to write this book in plain English. No prior knowledge of accounting, entrepreneurial finance, or securities law is required. If you are planning to launch a crowdfunded offering, however, you will need to read a few additional books about business and financial planning, accounting, cash-flow management, maintaining good relations with investors, and other relevant topics. A number of excellent ones are listed in the "Suggestions for Further Reading" section near the end of the book (and no, I have not written all of them).

Social media crowdfunding under Title III of the JOBS Act is not for everyone.

While theoretically any start-up or early-stage company can register with a funding portal to solicit crowdfunded investments, as a practical matter many companies will not be able to do so because the funding portals will be programmed to screen out companies that are not ready to offer their securities to the public.

In order to launch a Title III crowdfunded offering, a company must:

- Have a written business plan, with clearly defined strategies for developing and marketing the company's products and services, dealing with competition, and financing its operations

- Have access to (and the ability to afford) lawyers, accountants, and other professionals who can transform the company's business plan into an "offering document" meeting the requirements of the SEC's Regulation Crowdfunding and in the form of the SEC's new Form C (a copy of which appears as Appendix 1 at the end of this book; these so-called "Form C Disclosures" are discussed in Chapter 5)

- Have incorporated either as a corporation or limited liability company (LLC) in the state where the company has its principal place of business (the different forms of legal organization, and the advantages and disadvantages of each for crowdfunded offerings, are discussed in Chapter 4)

- Have built its management team to the point where investors will have confidence in them

- (Preferably) have accepted loans or investments from one or two angel investors

- (Most important) have strategies or procedures in place to communicate with a large crowd of investors on an ongoing basis if the company's offering is successful (this is discussed in Chapter 8)

In this book, readers will be neither encouraged to seek nor discouraged from seeking crowdfunded investment for their companies. Crowdfunded offerings of securities have advantages and disadvantages, but they require a certain amount of discipline and attention to detail, more so than traditional private offerings of securities. If managed properly, they can be a wonderful way to raise capital that wouldn't be available from any other source and can introduce your company to talent and networking opportunities that would not otherwise be possible.

If managed poorly, they can lead to disgruntled investors, class-action lawsuits against your company and its founders (including you), and other unpleasantness. I have tried throughout this book to balance the positive and the negative aspects of crowdfunded investments with a focus on teaching readers how to handle them the right way—that is, in such a way as to maximize the chance your company will reap the benefits while doing as much as possible to avoid the pitfalls and dangers.

Where This Book Will Take You

This book is organized into five parts:

- Chapters 1 and 2 explain what crowdfunding is and how it evolved.

- Chapters 3 through 7 lay out the steps necessary to launch a successful Title III crowdfunded offering.

- Chapters 8 and 9 discuss how to deal with a crowd of investors if your Title III crowdfunded offering is successful.

- Chapters 10 and 11 present pros and cons for individuals considering investing in such an offering and/or setting up a funding portal.

- Chapters 12 and 13 summarize the federal laws and SEC regulations relating to private offerings of securities and explain how the two collided in the federal JOBS Act and the SEC's regulation of Title II and Title III crowdfunded offerings.

Several appendices appear at the end of this book, including form documents and term sheets for different types of crowdfunded offerings.

A Word About Legal and Tax Information

There is a big difference between legal information and legal advice.

While this book will discuss at length the federal laws and regulations governing crowdfunded offerings of securities, any legal and tax information in this book is for educational purposes only and is not to be relied on as legal or tax advice, which can only be given by a lawyer or tax professional who is licensed to practice in your state.

A Few Words Before We Launch

The author is an attorney in private practice who has spent most of his career representing business start-ups, early-stage companies, and the people who invest in them. While I have helped hundreds of clients put together friends-and-family offerings over the years, I have never worked for the SEC or any other government agency and therefore was not privy to any inside information regarding the discussions and debates leading up to the JOBS Act, Regulation Crowdfunding, or any other law governing crowdfunded offerings of securities. I also confess that I have never launched a funding campaign on Kickstarter, IndieGoGo, RocketHub, or any other crowdfunding website. Although, boy, am I tempted.

The SEC's Regulation Crowdfunding was finalized in October 2015, shortly before this book was going into print, and it is possible there have been subsequent developments that are not covered in these pages. The reader is encouraged to subscribe to some of the websites listed in the "Suggestions for Further Reading" section near the end of this book to keep track of current developments in this fast-evolving field of entrepreneurial finance.

Subject to the foregoing, as we lawyers say, *The Crowdfunding Handbook* is entirely my doing, and I am solely responsible for its contents.

CHAPTER 2

The Evolution of Crowdfunding

In the seventeenth and eighteenth centuries, many book publishers sold their offerings by means of subscriptions, what the industry today calls advance-sale copies. The publisher would solicit advance purchases from subscribers, print the exact number of books for which it received subscriptions, and mention the subscribers on the title page of the book. Many companies today use similar crowdfunding methods to test the market for new product and service offerings.

According to Wikipedia, the American Committee for the Statue of Liberty in New York Harbor ran out of funds for the statue's pedestal in 1884. Incensed that the statue might not be completed, newspaper publisher Joseph Pulitzer urged the American public to donate money toward the pedestal in his newspaper the *New York World*. Pulitzer raised over $100,000 in six months. More than one hundred twenty-five thousand people contributed to the cause; most donations were one dollar or less.

These are early examples of crowdfunding.

The Friends-and-Family Offering

In a way, companies looking to raise capital have always relied to some extent on a form of crowdfunding: hitting up friends, family members, neighbors, old college roommates, and people they know for loans, gifts, or contributions to help get their businesses (or their lives) off the ground. The reward for such investors was frequently intangible (love, affection, helping your slacker kid buy his way into a job, or the right to reserve a restaurant table on New Year's Eve).

What made such friends-and-family offerings difficult, of course, was that most people's networks were relatively small and tightly confined. Also, you had to approach each person one on one and establish a personal rapport with each of them. To network successfully in the pre-Internet world, you had to take time to get to know someone before you asked him for a favor or for money. If your network was rich and well connected, life was good. If it wasn't, well . . .

Intermediate Steps: Microlending and Peer-to-Peer Lending

That began to change in the early 2000s with the concept of microlending, pioneered by Dr. Mohammed Yunus in Bangladesh. In 1976, Yunus launched a research project with his graduate students in Bangladesh. His goal was to give banking opportunities to low-income people, eliminate the exploitation of the poor, and create opportunities for self-employment. His initial loan was $27 to forty-two women who lived in a village sustained by bamboo production. After this successful loan, Yunus was able to secure a loan from the government to lend small amounts to the poor. Within five years, the program had more than thirty thousand members, and in 1983, the program transformed into Grameen Bank. The bank now has more than eight million borrowers; 97 percent of the money goes to women-operated businesses.

Yunus and Grameen Bank (www.muhammadyunus.org and www.grameenfoundation.org) were awarded the Nobel Peace Prize in 2006 for their efforts in economic and social development, and they have been the inspiration for a number of microlending sites in the United States.

In 2005, Kiva.org (unaffiliated with Grameen Bank) became the first microlending website. It gave individuals the ability to lend small amounts of money to entrepreneurs in poor, rural areas across the globe. What makes Kiva so attractive is that lenders are given pictures and a profile for each loan. They see whom the loan is going to, what it will be used for, and the terms of repayment.

Kiva has field partners in various world regions that help document the stories and distribute the loans to individuals. This unique system personalizes the process and gives investors not only more information about their borrowers but confirmation that their investment is having a meaningful impact on the borrower and his or her community.

In 2006, Prosper.com launched the first peer-to-peer lending site in the United States. The concept was similar to Yunus's microfinance vision and Kiva's microlending model. On the website, an individual submits a request for funding, which includes a story, a picture, and his or her credit score. You might find people who are trying to refinance debt, fund a vacation, or start a business.

The difference between Prosper and earlier forms of microfinance is that this was the first time the process existed outside of developing countries. U.S. entrepreneurs looking for funding typically have had more financial options than developing nations. What makes Prosper's concept attractive to borrowers is that the interest rates are generally less than those a bank might offer. Additionally, it gives credit-strapped consumers alternatives to traditional bank loans.

In 2007, LendingClub.com launched the second peer-to-peer lending site in the United States. In line with its goal of creating an alternative to banks, it offered borrowers and investors great rates. The concept of the site is similar to that of Prosper.com. Recently, Lending Club surpassed Prosper in loan funding ($353 million versus $255 million).

Microlending has proven extremely successful in traditional societies, where people tend to live in the same tightly knit communities their entire lives. In such communities, everyone knows everyone else, and there is a culture of shame for any individual who does not live by the rules and pay back debts promptly. Someone who takes the money and runs is likely to become a pariah in her village or town.

In highly mobile America, where people change jobs and residences frequently—often so quickly that they seem never to set down roots anywhere—the microlending concept has had greater difficulty taking off. In a culture that tolerates and forgives bankruptcy and other indiscretions, worships risk taking, and believes that success often results from lessons learned from multiple failures, the idea that you should suffer for not paying your debts on time seems—well, a bit antiquated. And as for feeling shame about anything—as they used to say in Brooklyn, fuhgeddaboudit (today the denizens of Brooklyn would say "chill, dude," which amounts to much the same thing).

The Social Media Revolution

What really made crowdfunding (and crowdlending, for that matter) more viable, of course, was the introduction of social media networks, such as Facebook and Twitter, in the mid-2000s. Originally viewed as online Rolodexes that would help people keep track of business contacts and far-flung family members, social media platforms have revolutionized the concept of a personal network.

Today it is not uncommon for even relatively unknown entrepreneurs to have hundreds of friends on Facebook or thousands of followers on Twitter. Social media has, in fact, changed the concept of a personal network from a group of people one knows and stays in frequent contact with to something more akin to a fan club, a "posse," or—to use a marketing term—an affinity group.

Your social media contacts are not necessarily friends or family; they are just people who, for one reason or another, are interested in you and want to keep up with what you're doing. But in large enough numbers they can be a rich source for financing projects of all types.

Here's a mantra I will be repeating throughout this book: success in crowdfunding (of any kind) depends on your ability to develop, manage, grow, and leverage a large following on social media. Because that's where your crowd will come from.

Kickstarter.com and Project Crowdfunding

In 2009, Kickstarter launched as a new way to fund creativity. The company also helped bring a new term to the forefront—*crowdfunding*—which allows a large group of people to pool their money to help fund an idea. Kickstarter took this concept and built a model that helps creative minds get funding from their peers. Projects range from documentaries to smart watches.

As I pointed out in Chapter 1, most crowdfunding activity involving social media networks has so far been limited to either project crowdfunding or gift crowdfunding.

In project crowdfunding, an individual or company solicits money from the crowd for a project of some kind and gives investors something either tangible or intangible in return but not securities in a company. For example, a rock band might solicit contributions to record its next CD.

In gift crowdfunding, an individual or company makes a donation or gift without any expectation of return, except perhaps for a charitable deduction if the crowdfunding is being done by a charitable organization registered with the IRS under Section 501(c)(3) of the U.S. Internal Revenue Code. For example, a church might use crowdfunding to raise money for a mission overseas.

Today there are numerous crowdfunding platforms in the United States, dominated by the big ten:

1. Kickstarter.com (the industry pioneer, accepts creative projects only)

2. IndieGoGo.com (accepts creative, personal, and charitable projects)

3. Gofundme.com (the largest, with more than three hundred thousand campaigns since its inception, accepts personal and charitable projects and local fund-raising efforts)

4. YouCaring.com (personal projects only)

5. Kiva.org (international microloans only)

6. Causes.com (not-for-profit fund-raiser for grassroots campaigns only)

7. GiveForward.com (medical expenses only)

8. CrowdRise.com (charitable projects only)

9. DonorsChoose.org (school donations only)

10. FirstGiving.com (charitable projects only)

Angel Investor Social Media Websites

Independent from project and gift crowdfunding, a number of social media sites have cropped up in recent years to help identify angel investor communities and put them in touch with start-up and early-stage companies. These sites, emboldened by Title II of the JOBS Act and the SEC's July 2013 release removing the prohibition on "general solicitation" and "general advertising" from offerings to accredited investors, have given life to a new type of venture financing vehicle, called an online syndicate, which allows angel investors (virtually all of whom are accredited investors under the SEC rules) to quickly assemble a group of investors over the Internet for a targeted start-up company.

Currently, the most prominent website in this field is AngelList (http://angel.co), with 159 investor syndicates and 4,865 early-stage companies looking for capital online.

Such websites are ideally positioned to become portals for the facilitation of accredited investor crowdfunding offerings under Title II of the JOBS Act (described in detail in Chapter 13).

Intrastate Crowdfunding Under State Law

It took a long time (from October 2013 to October 2015) for the SEC to finalize its crowdfunding regulations under Title III of the JOBS Act. During that time, a number of U.S. states decided they didn't want to wait for the final SEC regulations.

Just about every state has some sort of intrastate exemption for securities offerings by local companies. Generally, if your company is organized and located in the state, makes offers and sales only to people who reside in the same state, and complies with other restrictions (which vary from state to state; for example, limiting the number of purchasers or the dollar amount of the offering), your offering is exempt from federal and state securities laws.

In the two years before final passage of the SEC's crowdfunding regulations, no less than 29 states—including Alabama, Georgia, Idaho, Indiana, Kansas, Maine, Maryland, Massachusetts, Michigan, Oregon, Texas, Vermont, Washington, and Wisconsin—and the District of Columbia amended their intrastate offering exemptions to allow crowd-funding for offerings of securities that take place within their borders.

In all these states, an intrastate crowdfunded offering would need to comply with all restrictions imposed by the SEC's Rule 147 relating to intrastate offerings (the text of which can be found at www.law.cornell.edu/cfr/text/17/230.147). For example:

- The issuer must be organized and located in the state (in Wisconsin, the majority of the issuer's full-time workers must also work in Wisconsin).

- All prospective purchasers must reside in the state (in Texas, the offering must also be completed in Texas).

- The issuer must file an offering notice with the state securities regulator on a prescribed form.

In some states (including Texas and Wisconsin), the offering must also comply with all restrictions in the SEC's Regulation Crowdfunding.

Small businesses with social media followings that are largely limited to a single state should consider making a crowdfunded offering under their state's intrastate rules rather than following the cumbersome procedures involved in launching an interstate offering under the SEC's Regulation Crowdfunding.

The downside? Even one out-of-state purchaser in an intrastate offering can blow the exemption, so issuers will need to make 100 percent sure that all purchasers in the offering are residents of the same state and that all purchases take place within the state. Making offerings in person at state fairs, chamber of commerce meetings, and other local venues, and making photocopies of people's driver's licenses before they buy, may end up being more cumbersome than registering with a funding portal under Regulation Crowdfunding.

Social Media Crowdfunding (Title III Crowdfunding)

The use of crowdfunding platforms to raise money for companies and business projects goes by a number of names, including equity crowdfunding, crowdfunded investing, and social media crowdfunding.

U.S. securities laws (discussed in Chapter 12) closely regulate offerings of securities by privately owned companies. Because those laws traditionally prohibited private offerings made by "general solicitation" or "general advertising" (public offerings of securities registered with the SEC can always be made via "general solicitation" and "general advertising"), the laws had to be changed to expressly permit crowdfunded offerings of securities.

The federal JOBS Act of 2012 came about because of two things: a major recession and an entrepreneurial effort by three dedicated individuals.

The 2008 financial collapse gave way to the Great Recession, which began to turn around only in 2012. After past recessions, small businesses got the country back on track, but this time around they couldn't do so because all the typical ways small businesses had traditionally gained access to capital had dried up. Banks weren't lending, credit card companies slashed credit limits and hiked interest rates, and private equity and venture capital firms were investing money in fewer than 2 percent of companies that approached them. Many people and organizations still had cash after the 2008 collapse, but that money wasn't flowing to the entrepreneurs who could use it to start businesses and to small businesses that could create jobs.

But then three entrepreneurs—Sherwood Neiss, Jason W. Best, and Zak Cassady-Dorion—got creative. Recognizing the potential of crowdfunding to provide capital not available from traditional sources, the three developed their Start-up Exemption Regulatory Framework (www.start-upexemption.com) and lobbied Congress extensively for what eventually emerged from the legislative process as Title III of the JOBS Act of 2012.

The Start-up Exemption Regulatory Framework contained the following basic elements:

- A funding window of up to $1 million for entrepreneurs and small businesses (defined as businesses with average annual gross revenue of less than $5 million during each of the last three years or since incorporation)

- Investment from nonaccredited investors capped at $10,000 or 10 percent of their prior year's adjusted gross income

- Elimination of the investor-sophistication requirement in SEC Rule 506 (discussed in Chapter 12 of this book) to reflect the fact that average investors are a lot smarter today than they were in 1933

- Elimination of the five-hundred-investor limit for companies that use crowdfunded investments (this refers to a requirement in the federal Securities and Exchange Act of 1934 that companies with more than five-hundred owners must register with the SEC as "public companies" and file annual and quarterly reports)

- Preemption of state securities laws called blue-sky laws that contain contrary requirements

- Allowance for "general solicitation" and "general advertising" on registered funding platforms where individuals, companies, and investors can meet virtually and where ideas can be vetted by the community as a sort of peer review

- Standardization of the filing process using generic term sheets and subscription agreements based on venture capital industry practices

Neiss, Best, and Cassady-Dorion have gone on to become the founders and principals of Crowdfund Capital Advisors (CCA) (www.crowdfundcapitaladvisors.com), a crowdfunding think tank that, as this book went to press, was poised to become one of the first SEC-approved funding platforms under Title III.

A number of companies are positioning themselves to play a significant role in Title III crowdfunding. Leading the pack (as of December 2015) was SeedInvest.com, an equity-based crowdfunding platform that connects accredited investors to leading start-ups seeking funding.

Other potential crowdfunded offering platforms (or funding portals), most of which are in the very early stages of development, include:

- EquityNet.com (billed as the "original equity crowdfunding platform," EquityNet boasts a patented software system that streamlines the business planning process)

- GrowVC.com (with offices in New York, London, and Hong Kong, it is positioning itself to be a player in international crowdfunded offerings)

- Crowdfunder.com (based in Los Angeles, bills itself as "the leading equity crowfunding platform" as this book goes to press)

- iFunding.com (specializes in crowdfunding of real estate offerings, investments and syndications)

- IPOVillage.com (helped launch Crowdfunding-Website-Reviews.com, one of the Internet's top sites for getting information on crowdfunding platform websites)

- TruCrowd.com (focuses on serving nonaccredited investors)

- Sprigster.com (focuses on providing crowdfunded financing for franchised businesses)

- SyndicateRoom.com (the United Kingdom's first crowdfunded offering platform that focuses on the investors and investor returns requires that issuing companies first have a lead investor, or group of lead investors, on board providing a minimum of 25 percent of the funding round out of pocket)

Lest anyone still think that crowdfunding is a passing fancy, there are already established in the United States alone are:

- The National Crowdfunding Association (www.nlcfa.org)

- The Crowdfunding Professional Association (www.cfpa.org)

- The Crowdfunding Accreditation for Platform Standards program to promote the adoption of best practices for the operation of crowdfunding platforms globally (www.crowdsourcing.org/caps)

A Brief Overview of Crowdfunding Under Title III of the JOBS Act and Regulation Crowdfunding

Regulation Crowdfunding contains almost seven hundred pages of rules and regulations for companies that want to raise capital via crowdfunding. Here's an overview of how crowdfunding will work under this regulation.

Rules for Issuers

A company looking to raise money through crowdfunding (called an "issuer" in the securities laws) is limited to raising $1 million through crowdfunded offerings over a rolling twelve-month period. This limit includes an issuer's predecessors and affiliates of the issuer (such as any other company run by the same founders as the issuer). Certain companies cannot use crowdfunding, including:

- Companies that have committed certain securities law violations

- Investment companies such as hedge funds

- Publicly traded companies

- Companies outside the United States (although their U.S.-based subsidiaries can use crowdfunding)

- Crowdfunded issuers who fail to file their annual reports with the SEC on Form C-AR

Issuers cannot offer their securities to the public directly but only through a funding portal registered with the SEC. The funding portal must be a website or similar electronic medium, and the issuer is limited to only one funding portal per offering.

Before launching a crowdfunded offering, the issuer must file electronically with the SEC and post on the funding portal an "offering statement" on the SEC's new Form C (Appendix 1, described in Chapter 5), containing much the same information as has always been required of companies in private offerings. During the offering, the issuer is required to file progress updates five business days after the offering has reached 50 percent and 100 percent of the targeted amount, as well as a final Form C-U to disclose the total amount of securities issued as part of the offering.

These offering documents may be viewed by the general public—anyone who visits the site—but investments and communications with issuers may be made only by people who open accounts with the funding portal.

As part of its offering documents, the issuer must include financial statements covering the shorter of the two most recently completed fiscal years or the period since the issuer's inception, the nature of which will depend on the amount the issuer is trying to raise:

- If the offering amount is $100,000 or less, disclosure of the amount of total income, taxable income, total tax as reflected in the issuer's federal income tax returns certified by the principal executive officer to reflect accurately the information in the issuer's federal income tax returns (in lieu of filing a copy of the tax returns), and financial statements certified by the principal executive officer to be true and complete in all material respects; if, however, financial statements of the issuer are available that have either been reviewed or audited by a public accountant that is independent of the issuer, the issuer must provide those financial statements instead and need not include the information reported on the federal income tax returns or the certification of the principal executive officer.

- If the offering amount is more than $100,000 but less than $500,000, the financial statements must be reviewed by an independent certified public accountant (CPA), using the Statements on Standards for Accounting and Review Services issued by the Accounting and Review Services Committee of the American Institute of CPAS (AICPA); if, however, financial statements of the issuer are available that have been audited by a public accountant that is independent of the issuer, the issuer must provide those financial statements instead and need not include the reviewed financial statements.

- If the offering amount is more than $500,000 but not more than $1 million of securities in reliance on Regulation Crowdfunding for the first time: financial statements must be reviewed by a public accountant that is independent of the issuer; if, however, financial statements of the issuer are available that have been audited by a public accountant that is independent of the issuer, the issuer must provide those financial statements instead and need not include the reviewed financial statements.

- If the offering amount is more than $500,000 and the issuer has previously sold securities in reliance on Regulation Crowdfunding, the financial statements must be audited by an independent CPA using generally accepted U.S. auditing standards (GAAS) or any other standard adopted by the Public Company Accounting Oversight Board (pcaob.org). Any unaudited financial statements submitted as part of a Regulation Crowdfunding offering must be labeled as such. Issuers seeking to raise up to $100,000 are not required to submit copies of their actual tax returns, due to the risk of disclosing private or personally identifiable information about the company's founders and early investors.

During the offering, the issuer cannot advertise the terms of the offering except for a short public notice (similar in form and content to the "tombstone ads" used by underwriters in public offerings) directing readers to the funding portal where the offering is conducted. These notices may, however, be disseminated broadly through general solicitation in all media channels, online and off-line, and the issuer is allowed to communicate directly with investors using communications media (such as chat rooms) furnished by the funding portal.

An offering must be posted for at least twenty-one days, but after that the offering can last as long as an issuer likes, provided the offering documents are kept up to date. If the issuer raises the targeted amount before the offering ends, the issuer can terminate the offering early (but not until twenty-one days after the offering commences) as long as it gives investors five business days' notice of the new closing date, it allows investors to cancel their investments up to forty-eight hours before the new closing dates, it notifies investors whether or not the issuer will accept investments during the final forty-eight hours, and the issuer continues to exceed the target on the new closing date.

If the issuer fails to raise the targeted minimum amount of capital before the offering expires, any investments made during the offering are returned to the investors. If the issuer raises the targeted minimum amount of capital, the offering closes—investors' funds are released to the issuer, and the issuer delivers securities to the investors.

After an offering is completed, the issuer must file annual reports with the SEC on Form C-AR; failure to do so on time disqualifies the issuer from future crowdfunded offerings.

Issuers, including their directors and officers, are liable to investors for "untrue or materially misleading statements" in their offering documents unless they can prove they did not know, and in the exercise of reasonable care could not have known, of the untruth or omission.

Rules for Investors

An individual investor is limited in the amount he or she can invest in crowdfunded offerings each year. If the investor's net worth or annual income (whichever is greater) is $100,000 or less, the investor cannot purchase more than $2,000 or 5 percent of the net worth or annual income (whichever is greater) in crowdfunded securities.

If the investor's net worth or annual income (whichever is greater) is more than $100,000, the investor may purchase up to 10 percent of the net worth or annual income (whichever is lesser).

Purchases of other types of securities are not included when calculating these limits.

An investor may cancel an investment up to forty-eight hours before the offering closes but is barred from doing so after that time.

Investors are entitled to progress reports while the offering is pending and to certain statements when an offering closes. Investors may communicate directly with issuers and other investors during the offering process but only through the communications channels maintained by the funding portal. These communications can be viewed publicly only by participants in the offering.

After an offering closes, crowdfunded securities cannot be resold by anyone for a period of one year except to the issuer, as part of a registered public offering of the issuer's securities (an IPO), or for estate planning or divorce purposes. After the one-year period, crowdfunded securities can be freely sold—if, of course, the investor can find a buyer for them.

Rules for Funding Portals

All crowdfunded offerings must take place through an intermediary, called a funding portal, which must be a website or other electronic medium.

Unless it is operated by broker-dealers who are already registered with the SEC, a funding portal must be registered with the SEC, be a member of FINRA, and maintain

THE CROWDFUNDING HANDBOOK

in place a $100,000 fidelity bond (the FINRA rules for crowdfunding portals can be found at www.finra.org/industry/rule-filings/sr-finra-2015-040).

A funding portal is required to review all offering documents submitted to it by issuers and may deny access to the portal if it believes there is the potential for fraud or the issuer is not eligible for crowdfunding under Regulation Crowdfunding. It is also required to make a reasonable effort to vet investors to make sure they haven't exceeded their investment limits in crowdfunded securities.

In operating its business, a funding portal must operate by numerous rules, including:

- It cannot offer investment advice or recommendations, or solicit purchases, sales, or offers (although it can advertise its services generally).

- It cannot be compensated based on the amount of sales it achieves or charge a contingency fee.

- It cannot hold, manage, possess, or otherwise handle investor funds or securities (it must establish accounts with banks and securities depositories to hold these).

- It can limit companies from accessing its portal using objective criteria (for example, a portal can limit offerings to just one industry or a certain type of security) but cannot deny access based on "the advisability of investing in the issuer" (that is, the portal cannot pick favorites).

- It can highlight offerings using objective criteria, but cannot highlight offerings based on "the advisability of investing in the issuer" and cannot be compensated for highlighting an offering.

- It can provide search functions to sort by objective criteria.

- It can provide communication channels by which investors can communicate with one another and with issuers but cannot participate in discussions except as a moderator.

- It can advise issuers about the structure or content of the issuer's offering, including assisting the issuer in preparing the offering documents.

- It can compensate a third party for referring people to the funding portal as long as no personally identifiable information is given.

- It can cancel an offering if the portal believes there is a potential for fraud.

The funding portal must preserve records of all offerings and communications for five years.

A funding portal, including its directors and officers, has the same liability as an issuer if fraud occurs, although it has a defense if it can prove that it used reasonable care in reviewing an issuer's offering documents and established a reasonable policy for avoiding misstatements and untruths in crowdfunded offerings.

Part 2

LAUNCHING A SUCCESSFUL TITLE III CROWDFUNDED OFFERING, STEP BY STEP

CHAPTER 3

Is Crowdfunding Right for Your Company?

Generally, if you want to engage in traditional project crowdfunding (raising money for a specific project as opposed to raising money for a company), there isn't much preparation involved. All you have to do is:

- Select the right crowdfunding portal (one that specializes in the type of project you want to launch)

- Develop a short description of the project, how much money you need, why you deserve it, and the minimum amount you want to raise within a specific timeframe

- Post the description online

- Wait for the money to roll in

There is no requirement that you have expertise or experience in the type of project (although as a practical matter it is difficult to obtain financing online without that) or even that you have a clear vision or prototype of the project once it's developed. All you need is an idea, or even just a dream, and if you catch the imagination of enough people online, you can get crowdfunded.

However, that will not be the case with crowdfunding under Title III of the JOBS Act.

Crowdfunding Is Not for Everyone

Although theoretically any type of company, at any stage of development, can seek crowdfunding under Title III, as a practical matter only select companies will be able to do so effectively.

If you are thinking about launching a crowdfunding campaign under Title III, you will need to ask yourself three specific questions:

1. Is my company the right type of company to receive investments through crowdfunding?

2. Does my company meet the requirements of the JOBS Act and Regulation Crowdfunding?

3. Am I willing to put up with dozens, if not hundreds, of demanding, immature, possibly crazy individual investors with unrealistic expectations if our Title III crowdfunded offering is successful?

Let's take a closer look at each of these questions so you can figure out if Title III crowdfunding is right for you.

Is Your Company Right for Crowdfunding?

The good news is that Title III crowdfunding opens the private equity markets to companies that traditionally have had trouble finding early-stage investors in the past. For example:

- Companies organized as LLCs or other pass-through legal entities

- Companies engaged in retail, service, or other industries that don't involve high technology

- Companies that are looking to franchise their concepts

- Companies whose business models are not scalable, such that each dollar of investment produces only a limited amount of revenue or profit

The bad news is that only a relatively small number of companies will be able to qualify for crowdfunded offerings of their securities under Regulation Crowdfunding. There are two primary reasons for this.

First, the cost of putting together the offering statement, financial statements, and other documents required by the SEC and the funding portals that will manage the offerings will probably be beyond the reach of most start-ups or concept companies that haven't yet put together a solid business plan.

Second, because of the tremendous liability Regulation Crowdfunding imposes on funding portals (discussed in Chapter 11), most of these portals will be extremely nervous about dealing with a company that they suspect doesn't have its act together yet. As an accountant friend of the author put it, "No one will want to be the first portal that gets sued or prosecuted by the SEC because they were negligent in picking the right issuers or reviewing their offering materials." As an issuer, you can expect that most funding portals will be looking at your company and your written documents with an electron microscope, looking for even the tiniest flaws that may expose them to liability.

That said, if your management team is disciplined and willing to put in long hours on legal and accounting paperwork, there is no reason why even a concept company (one with little more than an idea, although a well-articulated one with a high likelihood of success if proper funding is obtained) cannot obtaining crowdfunded capital under Title III.

Before you consider seeking Title III crowdfunded money, your company needs to put together a solid business plan. Hundreds of books have been written on the subject of business plans, a few of which are listed in the "Suggestions for Further Reading" section near the end of this book, but putting together a solid business plan boils down to answering twelve specific questions:

1. What is the product or service we are looking to develop?

2. Who are the customers for our product or service, and what needs and wants do they have that our product or service will answer?

3. Why will customers buy our product or service (in other words, how will our product or service appeal to the fears and passions of the targeted markets)?

4. How will we get our message across to our targeted markets and get the product or service into people's hands (in other words, what advertising and promotion tools will be used to market and distribute our product or service)?

5. Who are our competitors, both direct (people and companies doing the exact same thing) and indirect (people and companies doing a different type of thing that solves the same customer problems our product and service does or that renders our product and service obsolete)?

6. Why is our product or service better than any competing product or service on the market or soon to be on the market?

7. Do we have the right people on our management team to develop our product or service and get it into the market in a reasonable amount of time?

8. Are the people on our management team and advisory board (an informal collection of business mentors) likely to impress potential investors with their credentials and expertise?

9. What are the resources (money, office space, equipment, people, professional services, time) we will need to launch this product or service, and how much will we have to spend on each resource during the first one to two years of our operations?

10. When will this company break even (generate enough revenue from sales to cover basic operating expenses on an ongoing basis) and thereby become self-sustaining?

11. If our company is successful, what will our exit strategy be (launch an IPO or sell out to a large public corporation interested in acquiring our product or service)?

12. What are the legal and economic risks involved in this business, can we insure against them, and if so, how much will that insurance cost?

Okay, that's probably about fifteen or sixteen questions, and other, more-specific subquestions fall under each of the ones above, but you get the general idea. If you and your company don't have compelling answers to each of these questions and cannot articulate them in a written business plan, your company is not ready for Title III crowdfunding. It's that simple.

Qualifying Under the JOBS Act and Regulation Crowdfunding

To qualify for crowdfunding under Regulation Crowdfunding, the issuing company must be incorporated or organized under the laws of a U.S. state or territory. Unincorporated businesses cannot qualify for Title III crowdfunding.

The vast majority of Title III issuers will be C corporations and LLCs. The advantages and disadvantages of each are discussed in Chapter 4.

Public companies do not qualify for Title III crowdfunding under Regulation Crowdfunding, nor do companies based in foreign countries (although foreign companies can invest in U.S.-based crowdfunded offerings).

Companies that have engaged in any of the "bad acts" described in Rule 506(d) of Regulation D (discussed in Chapter 13) and companies whose principals have engaged in any bad acts are disqualified from Title III crowdfunding, as are issuers who concluded successful Title III crowdfunded offerings in the past but failed to file the required annual reports and other documents required to be delivered to crowdfunded investors on an ongoing basis (these are discussed in Chapter 7).

Investment companies (such as mutual funds and hedge funds) do not qualify for Title III crowdfunding, as otherwise there is a risk Wall Street firms would form crowdfunded pools of crowdfunded companies, or create holding companies that would invest in dozens if not hundreds of crowdfunded companies. This is unfortunate in some respects, as enabling investors to pool their investments in a single entity that would coordinate communications between a crowdfunded company and its investors would probably be a beneficial thing and would eliminate many of the "time vampire" issues of investor communications that are discussed in Chapter 8. But as this prohibition is contained in Title III of the JOBS Act itself (not Regulation Crowdfunding), there is probably nothing the SEC can do to correct that as this book goes to press.

Blank-check or shell companies formed for unspecified purposes or to acquire other companies cannot make offerings under Title III. Any company seeking crowdfunding under Title III must have an actual business plan, not a speculative one or one couched in alternative terms (for example, "if we raise $100,000 we will do X, but if we raise $250,000 we will do Y instead"). However, it is possible that Title III crowdfunded offerings may be tiered based on the amount of money raised and the planned use of proceeds at different levels of investment (for example, "if we raise $100,000 we will do X, but if we raise $250,000 we will be able to do Y and Z as well").

Foreign companies cannot take advantage of Title III crowdfunded offerings. Regulation Crowdfunding is not clear on this point, but that may include U.S.-based subsidiaries of overseas companies.

Finally, public companies cannot make Title III crowdfunded offerings. If they could, there would be no need for SEC registration of public offerings, would there?

Handling Your Crowd of Investors If the Offering Is Successful

As will be seen in Chapter 8, this biggest challenge in Title III crowdfunded offerings of securities and the biggest potential obstacle to the development of a viable crowdfunded securities market have nothing to do with the offering process itself but rather what happens after a successful crowdfunded offering is completed.

Once your company successfully completes a Title III crowdfunded offering, it can't just pocket the money and say "See ya!" to the dozens or perhaps hundreds of individuals and companies that invested in the offering.

Once you sell a piece or percentage of your company to an investor (as opposed to someone loaning your company money, as discussed in Chapter 4), they are your business partners. If they were issued voting securities (voting common or preferred stock for a corporation, voting membership interests for an LLC), they have the right to receive notice of investor meetings and vote on any matter for which investor approval is required by state law where the company is incorporated or organized.

Even if a company's crowdfunded investors are issued nonvoting securities (nonvoting common or preferred stock for a corporation, nonvoting membership interests for an LLC), Regulation Crowdfunding requires they be given annual reports and other financial statements, and state corporation and LLC law often requires they be given advance notice of certain major decisions affecting the company. If you fail to give them the required notice, that failure may invalidate the decision, even though the holders of your voting securities voted overwhelmingly in favor of the measure you proposed to them.

Even if your crowdfunded investors have no rights at all under your state corporation or LLC law, there is nothing to prevent them from calling your office day and night asking silly questions, making unrealistic or inappropriate demands on your company, or offering unsolicited (and sometimes stupid) advice. That is the price of having any outside investor in your company, of course, but that price is a lot higher in a crowdfunded offering of securities, for two reasons:

1. There are an awful lot more of them.

2. They are less sophisticated than investors in traditional accredited-investor private offerings of securities and therefore more likely to act unpredictably, irresponsibly, or unprofessionally.

Investors can be time vampires, requiring an inordinate amount of your management time that is much better spent developing and launching your company's products and services. Most public companies have several employees devoted exclusively to shareholder communications or investor relations. As a start-up or early-stage company, you cannot afford to dedicate employees to those tasks.

Yet if you ignore your investors, even if Regulation Crowdfunding technically allows you to do so, you do that at your peril. It's no secret that the Internet can sometimes be a very volatile, nasty, and dangerous place, where little problems and hiccups can be blown quickly and exponentially out of proportion by a negative, viral campaign on social media launched by one angry, self-appointed vigilante or a handful of them.

Probably the worst thing that can happen to a company that has successfully raised money via Title III crowdfunding is to see its crowdfunded investors turn into a disgruntled lynch mob that says nasty things about the company and its management online.

If you do decide to launch a Title III crowdfunding campaign for your start-up or early-stage company, you will have to decide if you are willing to put procedures in place to manage and communicate with your crowd after the offering is over. If you are not, then Title III crowdfunding is not for you. Stick with accredited investors or traditional friends-and-family offerings. Your elderly Aunt Irma who loaned you $5,000 isn't likely to go viral on Yelp.com because she wasn't invited to your company picnic.

CHAPTER 4

Preparing Your Company for a Crowdfunded Offering

Having decided that your company is a good candidate for a Title III crowdfunded offering, you will need to do several things before you begin drafting your offering statement, contacting funding portals, and taking the other steps necessary to launch the offering that we will discuss in Chapter 5.

Choose the Right Legal Entity

Regulation Crowdfunding requires that an issuer of crowdfunded securities be "incorporated or organized." Unincorporated businesses such as sole proprietorships and partnerships do not qualify for crowdfunding.

That leaves only three types of legal entities that legally qualify for Title III crowdfunding:

1. Regular or C corporations

2. Subchapter S corporations

3. Limited liability companies

Regular or C Corporations

A corporation is a taxable entity; when you form a corporation it is as if you have had a baby and the baby pays taxes from the day it's born. It's called a C corporation because it is taxed under Subchapter C of the Internal Revenue Code of 1986.

What's Good About a C Corporation? In two words: limited liability. Generally, the owners of a C corporation (called shareholders or stockholders) are liable only for the amounts they contribute (or agree to contribute) as capital to the corporation but will still be liable for their own negligence or stupidity.

EXAMPLE 1: A and B are shareholders of ABC Corporation. A runs over someone with his car while on the corporation's business. The injured party may sue the corporation and win a judgment up to the amount of the corporation's assets (because that's all it has). The injured party may sue A in his individual capacity and take A's house away. But the injured party cannot sue B in any way unless it can be shown that B contributed actively in some way to the injury (for example, B served A too much liquor, which caused A to be intoxicated at the wheel).

EXAMPLE 2: A and B are shareholders of ABC Corporation. ABC Corporation enters into a contract with a supplier to buy ten thousand widgets and then discovers that it doesn't have enough money to pay for the widgets. ABC Corporation breaches the contract, and the supplier sues. The supplier may sue the corporation and win a judgment up to the amount of the corporation's assets, but the supplier cannot sue A or B, even if A or B actually signed the contract as an officer or employee of ABC Corporation.

What's Bad About a C Corporation? C corporations are expensive to form. Legal expenses and filing fees are usually between $1,000 and $1,500 to form a corporation in most states. They are also expensive to keep alive: if a corporation fails to pay taxes for X consecutive years or fails to file a report (and pay a fee) every Y years with the secretary ofsState's office, the attorney general comes along and dissolves the corporation (and your limited liability along with it). To add insult to injury, you are not informed that this has been done, so you continue blissfully doing business, thinking you have a corporation when you really don't.

If you don't use the corporation and treat it with respect, you lose the corporation. People suing you for something your corporation did will always try to argue they didn't know they were dealing with a corporation—if you conducted business in your own name, wrote checks from your own checking account, and accepted money in your own name that should have gone to the corporation, you can't argue it was really the corporation that should be sued and not you personally. Lawyers call this piercing the corporate veil.

C corporations involve lots of paperwork. When you have a corporation, you don't do anything; the corporation does everything. This means that for a corporation to do anything, the shareholders (that's you) have to prepare written documents (called resolutions or minutes) authorizing the directors of the corporation (again, that's you) to do the thing, and the directors have to prepare written documents authorizing the officers of the corporation (again, that's you) to do the thing. Resolutions are a pain in the neck, but if you don't do them you will be tempting the courts to say you didn't treat your corporation with the proper respect so creditors are allowed to get at your personal assets.

Dealing with taxes is somewhat complicated when you have a C corporation. Because corporations are taxable entities, they file their own returns (IRS Form 1120, due March 15 of each year for a calendar year corporation) and pay taxes separately from the owners (albeit at a lower rate than you do, in most cases). This means that any income a corporation earns is taxed twice.

EXAMPLE: XYZ Corporation has two stockholders, A and B, and makes $100 in net income for a particular year. The corporation pays 15 percent to Uncle Sam as federal income tax and books the remaining $85 as net after-tax earnings. XYZ Corporation then resolves (remember those minutes?) to pay A and B the $85 in the form of a dividend, and distributes $42.50 to each of A and B. A and B each has to report that $42.50 as income on Form 1040 for the year and pay taxes on that $42.50 at his or her individual rate. The result? If A and B are in the top tax bracket, that $100 in corporate income has dwindled to about $26 in each of A's and B's hands after federal income taxes. Add state and local taxes to this calculation, and the tax bite becomes much larger.

The C Corporation as a Crowdfunding Vehicle. If you are planning to raise capital in an accredited-investors-only offering under SEC Rule 506(c) and Title II of the JOBS Act, you are almost certainly going to have to organize your company as a C corporation. Why? There are two basic reasons:

1. Professional investors and angel investors normally like to receive preferred stock in the companies they invest in, and S corporations, as we can see below, cannot issue preferred stock. While LLCs can legally issue preferred membership interests, the mechanics are quite cumbersome and awkward to draft in legal language.

2. When sophisticated or professional investors see the LLC designation after a company name, they tend to think "small-time, mom-and-pop, will never grow big." This is a false view, as there is nothing in the law to prevent an LLC from growing big or even eventually going public. The bias against LLCs, however irrational, is strongly felt within the investment community. Accordingly, a new business that plans to seek venture capital or private equity funding (angel money) within the first one to two years of its existence should be set up as a corporation, preferably in a state like Delaware that offers a number of advantages to venture-capital-backed companies.

C corporations are also an ideal vehicle for a Title III crowdfunded offering because of the limited liability they offer and the opportunity to create a special class of securities for your crowdfunded investors. Also, as a matter of optics, many people in the investing community take corporations more seriously than they do LLCs.

Subchapter S Corporations

An S corporation is the same as a regular or C corporation with one important difference: it is not taxed by the federal government. This means that the S corporation is taxed just like a general partnership: profits, losses, and other tax benefits flow through to the corporation's shareholders and are taxed on their individual Form 1040 tax returns, but with the powerful advantage that stockholders in an S corporation have limited liability, unlike partners in a general partnership, who are personally liable for everything that happens in the partnership business.

However, some state and local governments (including New York City) do not recognize S corporations. This means that S corporations with offices in such states or municipalities are taxed twice at the state or local level.

What's Good About an S Corporation? Like a C corporation, there is limited liability: shareholders are not personally liable for debts and obligations of the corporation. Moreover, the corporation is not taxed by the federal government, although it does file its own tax return (Form 1120-S, due on March 15 each year; virtually all S corporations are required to use the calendar year for accounting purposes).

Taxation is also favorable. Because the S corporation does not pay taxes, profits, losses, and other tax benefits flow through to the corporation's shareholders, who report these on their personal Form 1040 federal income tax returns.

What's Bad About an S Corporation? Because S corporations are taxed like partnerships, S corporations have what is called a phantom income problem. This means that, unlike C corporation shareholders, who are taxed only on amounts the corporation distributes or pays out to them, S corporation shareholders must also pay taxes on their pro rata (proportionate) share of the corporation's profits and losses that were not distributed to them.

EXAMPLE: XYZ Corporation, a subchapter S corporation, had $100,000 in taxable income this year. The corporation has two shareholders, A and B. A owns 60 percent of the corporation's shares, and B owns 40 percent. The corporation did not distribute any cash or dividends to either shareholder. At the end of the year, A must report $60,000 as income on his federal income tax return (60 percent of $100,000), and B must report $40,000 (40 percent of $100,000) as income on his federal income tax return.

Subchapter S corporations were originally designed only for small businesses; they were never intended to go big or launch an IPO. Accordingly, S corporations have lots of icky little rules to comply with if they don't want to be taxed as a regular or C corporation. (Note: if the IRS takes away your S corporation status you don't—repeat, don't—lose your limited liability; the worst thing that happens is that you're taxed as a regular or C corporation). For example:

- Only natural human beings can be stockholders in an S corporation (no corporations, LLCs, or trusts, with only one or two limited exceptions).

- S corporations can't have more than one hundred stockholders (that alone puts Title III crowdfunding out of reach for S corporations).

- S corporations can have only one class of common stock (no preferred stock, which alone puts Title II accredited-investor-only financing out of reach for S corporations).

- The shareholders of an S corporation must be U.S. citizens or green card holders (permanent resident aliens of the United States).

The S Corporation as a Crowdfunding Vehicle. Generally, it's a bad idea. Most accredited investors involved in a Title II private placement under Rule 506(c) want to receive preferred stock or some other form of senior security, which S corporations cannot issue as they are limited to a single class of security.

The one-hundred-investor limit and the prohibition on foreign and corporate shareholders will also put Title III crowdfunding out of reach for S corporations.

If your business is currently organized as an S corporation, you should discuss with your accountant or tax adviser the possibility of opting out of an S corporation and becoming a C corporation before launching any sort of crowdfunded offering. Keep in mind, however, that if you do convert to C corporation status and the crowdfunded offering goes nowhere, you will not be able to elect to be taxed again as an S corporation for three consecutive tax years.

Limited Liability Companies (LLCs)

Since the early 1990s, the LLC has become the legal entity of choice for many small businesses and early-stage technology start-ups.

What is an LLC? Well, it's basically an S corporation without all the icky little rules that make S corporations unattractive for a lot of folks.

What's Good About an LLC? Owners of an LLC (called members) have limited liability. If A and B are members of an LLC and B runs someone over with her car while on LLC business, B may lose her house, but A will not lose his house unless A actively contributed to the injury.

Like partnerships, LLCs are simple to operate. There is no need to prepare resolutions or minutes to authorize people to do things (although banks and some other folks may still require you to do resolutions because they haven't gotten the idea yet)—they just do them. If the idea of doing legal paperwork makes you want to gag, the LLC is the legal entity for you.

The costs of starting up an LLC are likely to be much less than forming a C corporation or an S corporation—$400 to $600 in most states.

LLCs are taxed like partnerships, so there is no double taxation of an LLC's income. Everything flows through to the owners of the LLC, who report their shares of the LLC's income on their personal federal income tax returns, the same as shareholders in an S corporation. However, as was the case with S corporations, owners of an LLC must pay taxes on phantom income the LLC earns that is not distributed to them in the form of cash.

If you are doing a lot of overseas business, the LLC format may give you an edge on your competition. Most foreign business organizations (such as the German GmbH and the Italian S.r.l.) are a lot closer in structure to an LLC than they are to a partnership or corporation; with an LLC, you can give your managers the same titles as their European or Asian counterparts (Europeans especially cannot understand that in America one can be a "director" of a corporation and have absolutely no power to bind the corporation; in Europe, business organizations are managed by their "directors," not by officers or mere employees).

What's Bad About an LLC? Really not a lot. While not actually flawless, LLCs are the closest thing to a perfect business organization the law has come up with to date. Limited liability, favorable tax treatment, and easy to operate: who could ask for more?

There are a few negatives, however.

It may be difficult for existing businesses to convert to LLC status: corporations and their shareholders incur double taxation upon liquidation, while general and limited partnerships formed to acquire or hold title to real estate (as many are) may incur transfer taxes and other fees on converting to an LLC.

If your business is high tech or will seek outside capital within the first twelve to eighteen months of operations, be aware that many investors (wrongly) associate LLCs with small business, mom-and-pop, no growth potential. While this perception is unfair, it is widespread, and you may want to consider becoming a C corporation instead (preferably in a high-visibility state like Delaware).

LLCs are not recommended for businesses that will have physical locations in New York State. When New York adopted its LLC statute in 1994, it included a burdensome publication requirement that drives up the costs of forming a New York LLC. LLCs in New York are required to publish a legal notice in two newspapers—one daily and one weekly—in each county in New York where the LLC maintains an office of business. In most upstate counties, the cost of doing this publication is in the $200 to $300 range. In New York City, however, the cost can be upward of $2,000 to $3,000. Also, LLCs located in New York City are subject to that city's unincorporated business tax. Overall, it may be less expensive to form a corporation or S corporation in New York State than an LLC.

A growing number of states are imposing special taxes or minimum taxes on LLCs and other unincorporated business organizations. For example:

- California and Rhode Island have a minimum $800 income tax on LLC profits, payable even if the LLC had no profits.

- Connecticut requires domestic and foreign LLCs to pay a business entity tax of $250 every two years whether or not they make money.

The LLC as a Crowdfunding Vehicle. One of the main goals of the JOBS Act was to expand the private equity market to companies that could not obtain financial support under the previous rules. The vast majority of issuers seeking traditional venture capital were high-tech ventures organized as corporations.

But in theory there is no reason why an LLC couldn't raise capital under either Title II or Title III of the JOBS Act. In recent years, some attorneys have pioneered the creation of corporate mimic LLCs for their clients. These LLCs continue to be taxed as if they were partnerships and are otherwise subject to the LLC statutes, which generally are more flexible and less restrictive than the corporation laws, but they are structured to look exactly like corporations. For example:

- The corporate mimic LLC would be structured with "units of membership interest" (think shares of stock), which could be voting or nonvoting.

- The LLC could be authorized to issue "preferred" units of membership interest with terms and provisions identical to those of preferred stock in a corporation.

- The LLC would be managed by a board of managers (think board of directors).

- The board of managers could delegate some of its responsibilities to officers with specific job titles and duties, just as in a corporation.

- The LLC's organizational document, called an operating agreement, could provide that the LLC could incorporate any time the board of managers felt it was appropriate by merely swapping each unit of membership interest for one share of stock of the same class in the new corporation.

If you are organized as an LLC, or desire the flexibility and informality of the LLC way of life, speak to your attorney about setting up a corporate mimic LLC that walks, talks, and swims like a corporation but isn't really (or legally) one.

The Bottom Line on Legal Entities

If you and your advisers cannot decide on the best form of legal entity to engage in a Title II accredited-investor-only offering or a Title III crowdfunded offering, form your company as a C corporation. That structure gives you the most flexibility in putting together the offering and limiting the rights of your investor crowd once the offering is completed. It is also what most sophisticated investors expect, and you will spend less time explaining the finer points of "Series B preferred equity units of membership interest" in an LLC.

If your company is currently organized as an S corporation, convert to a C corporation prior to launching the offering, as it will be virtually impossible for your company to maintain its S corporation status unless you restrict your crowd to fewer than one hundred individual investors who are U.S. citizens or green card holders. Even then, you may have to give these folks voting shares of common stock in your corporation, which will not only dilute your ownership of the corporation but also your ability to manage the corporation's business without outside interference from the crowd.

Still Have Questions?

For a more thorough discussion of each of these entities and the advantages and disadvantages of each, consult the detailed outline titled "Demystifying the Business Organization" available as a free download from the author's website at www.cliffennico. com. This document will answer almost all of the legal and tax questions you should be asking when forming a legal entity for your business.

Decide Where to Incorporate, or Consider Reincorporating Somewhere Else

Generally, corporations and LLCs are best advised to incorporate in the state where their physical offices are located or where the business activities will actually be conducted. There is usually no point in incorporating in another state. If your business is located in state X and you incorporate in state Y, your income will still be subject to state X taxes, so the state Y corporation or LLC will have to register as a foreign corporation or foreign LLC in state X and so end up being taxed by two states instead of one.

A corporation or LLC that wishes to take advantage of Title III crowdfunding may wish to reconsider that decision, however. Bringing on board dozens if not hundreds of crowdfunded investors changes the way corporations are governed, for better or worse, and it helps to be incorporated or organized in a state that has the most conducive rules for crowdfunded offerings of securities.

Here are some of the legal issues you will need to think of when selecting the right state of incorporation prior to launching a crowdfunded offering.

Franchise Taxes on Authorized Shares

When forming a corporation in virtually any state, you will be required to pay a tax (commonly called a franchise tax—on the permission, or franchise, of doing business with limited liability) when filing your articles of incorporation with the state.

This tax is based on the number of authorized shares of stock you designate in your articles of incorporation. So, for example, in a particular state the tax could be one cent per share for the first ten thousand shares, one-half of one cent for the next ninety thousand shares, one-quarter of one cent for the next four hundred thousand shares, and one-tenth of one cent thereafter. There is almost always a minimum franchise tax that must be paid, and sometimes (in nicer states) a maximum franchise tax as well.

This is traditionally one of the main reasons entrepreneurs like to incorporate their businesses in Delaware. Like virtually all states, Delaware has a franchise tax, but it allows corporations to calculate the tax in two different ways and pay only the lower amount of tax. The two methods are known as the authorized shares method and the assumed par value capital method. Almost always, the assumed par value capital method results in a much lower tax than the authorized shares method.

Using the authorized shares method, a corporation would pay $35 up to the first three thousand shares, then $62.50 for the next two thousand shares, then $112.50 for the next five thousand shares, then $62.50 for each additional ten thousand shares, up to a maximum of $165,000.

To use the assumed par value capital method, you begin by determining your corporation's total gross assets (basically the corporation's total assets as reported on its Form 1120 federal income tax return) for the fiscal year. The calculation is fairly involved and is easier to illustrate than it is to explain in words.

So here's an example: Let's say a Delaware corporation with one million shares of stock with a par value of $1, and two hundred fifty thousand shares of stock with a par value of $5, has gross assets of $1 million and issued shares totaling four hundred eighty-five thousand. Here's how you would calculate the corporation's Delaware franchise tax:

1. Divide the corporation's total gross assets by its total **issued** shares carried to six decimal places. The result is the corporation's assumed par. So: $1,000,000 assets ÷ 485,000 issued shares = $2.061856 assumed par.

2. Multiply the assumed par by the number of **authorized** shares having a par value of less than the assumed par. So: $2.061856 assumed par x 1,000,000 shares = $2,061,856.

3. Multiply the number of authorized shares with a par value greater than the assumed par by their respective par value. So: 250,000 shares x $5 par value = $1,250,000.

4. Add the results of 2 and 3 above. The result is the corporation's assumed par value capital. Example: $2,061,856 + $1,250,000 = $3,311,956 assumed par value capital.

5. Figure the franchise tax due by dividing the assumed par value capital, rounded up to the next million if it is over $1,000,000, by 1,000,000 and then multiply by $250. So: 4 x $250 = $1,000.

Corporations that plan to engage in Title III crowdfunded offerings will need to have lots of authorized shares: at least one million and possibly as many as ten million. Choosing the state with the lowest franchise tax for a large number of authorized shares will be critical to many start-up companies, especially those on extremely limited budgets.

One way to avoid the whole franchise tax issue, believe it or not, is to form a corporate mimic LLC and authorize it to issue voting and nonvoting units of membership interest. An interesting loophole in the law is that in virtually all states, franchise taxes are limited only to shares of stock in corporations.

The idea that LLCs could be set up to mimic the capital structure of corporations using units of membership interest did not occur to state legislatures when they drafted their LLC statutes in the 1990s. They probably assumed that LLCs would be used only by small businesses managed by their owners and accordingly would operate as partnerships in which owners have percentage interests in the LLC's profits and losses rather than shares. If that was the case, they certainly underestimated the creativity and shrewdness of your average corporate attorney.

As a result of this discrepancy between the two statutes, in virtually every state I'm aware of:

- A corporation with one million authorized shares of common stock would have to pay a hefty franchise tax upon incorporation.

- An LLC with one million authorized units of membership interest would not.

That loophole may well be closed in future years (especially after state tax authorities get hold of this book). Until that happens, however, many companies seeking to avail themselves of Title III crowdfunding that do not want to (or cannot afford to) reincorporate in another state with a lower franchise tax may want to consider forming an LLC, at least temporarily, to eliminate their franchise tax exposure.

If the crowdfunded offering is successful, the LLC will then have plenty of money to convert into a C corporation and pay the franchise tax at that time.

Shareholder Rights

Next, look at the rights granted to shareholders in your state corporation statute. Generally, you want to be able to limit your crowdfunded investors' rights as much as possible without jeopardizing the success of the offering. You want (and need) their money, but you do not want their unsolicited advice, and you certainly do not want them to have the right to tell you how to run your company. Yet if these rights are granted by your state corporation law, you must honor them in your dealings with investors.

LLC statutes in virtually all states are much more flexible—the rights of LLC owners (called members) are generally not set out in the statute but rather in an operating agreement (similar to a partnership agreement) that you would prepare as one of your crowdfunded offering documents. You or your legal counsel would set out the rights your investors would have when becoming members of your LLC and any limits on those rights. As part of the offering terms, investors would be required to agree to be bound by the terms and conditions of the LLC operating agreement.

Here are some basic rights state corporation laws grant to shareholders of corporations (both C and S). A summary of how these rights are granted in each state appears as Appendix 3.

Voting Rights. Virtually all state corporation laws grant shareholders the right to vote at meetings of shareholders and participate in the management of the corporation's business unless these rights are denied in the articles of incorporation. Most corporations have two classes of common stock, one of which (sometimes called Class A) carries with it the right to vote, while the other one (sometimes called Class B) does not. The rights of each class of shares would be spelled out in the corporation's articles of incorporation. The company founders and key executives would own the voting shares, while investors would own the nonvoting shares. For an example of what the articles of incorporation for a corporation with voting and nonvoting shares looks like, see Appendix 1.

Inspection Rights. Virtually all state corporation laws grant shareholders the right to inspect and review the books and records of the corporation at reasonable times and on advance notice to the corporation.

Antidilution Rights. There are two types of antidilution rights shareholders can have:

1. *Price based antidilution protection*: the right to acquire additional shares (without paying for them) in the event the company makes a subsequent offering of securities at a lower valuation than the offering the shareholder subscribed to; the number of shares would be enough so the shareholder would maintain its original percentage ownership of the corporation's shares.

2. *Structural antidilution protection*: the right to acquire additional shares (again without paying for them) in the event of a stock split, stock dividend, or other event that increases the number of the corporation's issued and outstanding shares other than a public or private offering of those shares.

Virtually all state corporation laws deny these rights to holders of a corporation's common stock. These rights are almost certain to be included, however, in offerings of preferred stock, by agreement between the corporation and the investors. As will be seen later in this chapter, it wouldn't make much sense to launch a crowdfunded offering of preferred stock, although an accredited-investor-only offering under Title II of the JOBS Act could easily be structured that way.

Preemptive Rights. A shareholder with a preemptive right has the right to acquire additional shares (and pay for them, at the same price per share offered to subsequent investors) in the event the company makes a subsequent offering of securities at a higher valuation than the offering the shareholder subscribed to; the number of shares would be enough so the shareholder would maintain its original percentage ownership of the corporation's shares.

Right of Nonvoting Shareholders to Receive Notice of Shareholder Meetings. Even if shareholders in a corporation are denied the right to vote, they still may have rights under the state corporation statute. For example, do they have the right to receive notice of meetings of the voting shareholders, even though they have no legal ability to influence the decisions made at those meetings? In many states, the answer is yes, especially if the matter being voted on is a major change, such as a merger or acquisition, the sale of all or substantially all of the corporation's assets, the amendment of the corporation's articles of incorporation, or the corporation's dissolution or liquidation (including a filing in bankruptcy). The failure to give notice to your nonvoting shareholders within the time frame required by the statute (usually ten days before the meeting is held) could void any decision made at that meeting.

Shareholder Rights to Compel Dissolution of the Company. A handful of states allow owners of a significant minority percentage of a corporation's shares (usually 10 or 20 percent) to petition a court to dissolve the corporation, or force the majority shareholders to buy out their interest at fair market value, if they can demonstrate they were "oppressed" by the majority shareholders. The definition of "oppressed" in these states is left up to the courts to decide.

What Type of Security Will You Be Offering?

There are three types of securities you would consider for a crowdfunded offering: notes (or promissory notes), common stock, or preferred stock.

Notes or Promissory Notes

These are debt instruments. The investor in a note agrees to make a loan to the corporation or LLC at a set rate of interest. The loan is repaid with interest over a period of months or years, in monthly or quarterly installments. The investor's return on the investment is limited to the amount of interest set forth in the note.

Convertible notes may be exchanged for shares of common or preferred stock in the corporation at the option of the investor and may also be convertible on demand of the corporation immediately prior to an IPO or a merger or acquisition transaction.

Notes may also be issued with warrants attached—these are like options to acquire shares of the corporation's common or preferred stock in the future and are in addition to the note. An investor exercising a warrant to acquire shares in the issuing company still has the right to receive interest on the note until it is paid in full.

Common Stock and Preferred Stock

These are equity instruments, representing ownership of a percentage of the corporation's total issued and outstanding shares. Investors in common stock are entitled to all the rights granted to common stockholders in the state corporation statute and the corporation's articles of incorporation, while investors in preferred stock receive the rights granted to them in a purchase agreement with the corporation that is usually the subject of some negotiation.

Unlike common stockholders, preferred stockholders are entitled to a liquidation preference. If the corporation is dissolved or otherwise goes out of business, preferred stockholders get their money out before the common stockholders get a penny. Preferred stock may be voting or nonvoting, convertible into common stock or not, as the corporation's board of directors determines, and may afford the investor the right to receive preferred distributions of cash, known as cumulative dividends, before dividends are paid to the common stockholders.

LLC Membership Interests

If you are planning to launch a crowdfunded offering of equity securities in an LLC, you will be issuing membership interests or units of membership interest in the LLC to investors. Like shares of a corporation's stock, units of membership interest in an LLC can be voting or nonvoting and can grant investors whatever rights are spelled out in the LLC's operating agreement. You can even grant investors preferred membership interests containing many of the same terms and conditions as would apply to preferred stock in a corporation.

Which Security Is Best for a Crowdfunded Offering?

Most early-stage companies want to avoid debt like the plague, especially if the debt is being held by dozens or possibly hundreds of individual lenders. It is unlikely that a company will want to offer notes in a Title III crowdfunded offering, but one of the most common private placement structures under SEC Rule 506 is the offering of convertible promissory notes, and an offering of debt securities in an accredited-investor-only offering under Title II may make sense for a more seasoned company.

Similarly, it would make little sense for a company to issue preferred stock in a Title III crowdfunded offering because the sheer number of investors having the right to a liquidation preference upon the dissolution or liquidation of the company may discourage anyone from investing in the corporation's common stock in subsequent offerings because they would fear being wiped out in that event. Because most accredited investors will want preferred stock in your company, you may want to consider convertible preferred stock as the vehicle for a Title II accredited-investors-only offering, or indeed any other offering under the SEC's Rule 506.

Accordingly, it is anticipated that the vast majority of Title III crowdfunded offerings will involve common equity securities: voting or nonvoting common stock in a corporation, or membership interests in an LLC.

Amend Your Articles of Incorporation to Create a Separate Class of Shares for Your Crowdfunded Offering

Most early-stage companies launch multiple offerings of securities over time—a friends-and-family or crowdfunded offering to begin with, followed by subsequent offerings of notes, preferred stock, or common stock to angel investors and other accredited investors, followed by one or more so-called mezzanine offerings to venture capital firms, followed (it is hoped) by an initial public offering.

As will be seen in Chapter 9, Title III and Regulation Crowdfunding make it particularly easy for companies to launch multiple offerings. Many companies, for example, may want to launch an "upstairs-downstairs" offering—a Title II offering of preferred stock to accredited investors, together with a Title III crowdfunded offering of common stock to nonaccredited investors.

Create Multiple Classes of Stock

It is therefore important to prepare and file articles of incorporation with several different classes of stock, allowing for maximum flexibility in structuring future offerings. Because this is seldom done when a corporation is first incorporated, it is customary for the corporation to "amend and restate" its articles of incorporation to spell out the rights, privileges, and limitations for each class of its common and preferred stock.

Create a Class of Convertible Preferred Stock. If your company is considering a private placement to accredited investors under Title II of the JOBS Act, you will need to create at least one class of preferred stock. Investors like preferred stock because if hedges their bets on a start-up company: if the company crashes and burns, preferred stockholders get their money before common stockholders get a penny. Also, preferred stock can be structured so the investors get cumulative dividends—a guaranteed return on their investments that accrues over time (albeit without interest) if the company fails to pay dividends on time.

Accredited investors will want your preferred stock to be convertible into common stock at the investor's option. That way, if the company takes off and becomes wildly successful, the investor can convert preferred into common stock and participate in the rapid growth of the company.

Keep in mind that you must be a C corporation in order to have one or more classes of preferred stock; S corporations are prohibited by law from having more than one class of stock.

Create Voting and Nonvoting Classes of Common Stock. Now let's look at your company's common stock—the security you are most likely to offer to your crowdfunded investors in a Title III offering.

Generally, it's a bad idea to give crowdfunded investors voting common stock. Holders of voting common stock are granted extensive rights under state corporation laws, including the right to vote on matters affecting the company's business and operations, the right to participate in the company's management, (sometimes) the right to appoint members of the company's board of directors, and in general the right to make themselves into time vampires if they so choose. You want to keep those rights in as few (and trusted) hands as possible: yourself, the other company founders, the key members of your management team, and perhaps one or two angel investors who provide the seed capital that gets the company off the ground.

Simply put, everyone else should get nonvoting common stock: not just your crowdfunded investors but employees, consultants, advisers, and other people who are not essential to the success of your company or its business plan. Now, I realize that may sound a bit nondemocratic to some readers and not consistent with the spirit of crowdfunding, which is to open start-up investment opportunities to the masses. But as someone who has advised hundreds of start-up companies in my career, I can tell you that having too many powerful investors too early in a company's life cycle is more likely than not to crush a company's prospects. Investors can be (and frequently are) demanding. They ask lots of questions (facilitated by the ease of using email, instant messaging, and texting), they expect prompt response from management, and if they don't like what's happening, they can turn into hostile and unruly whistle-blowers who post unfavorable, unfair, possibly incorrect, and overly critical information about your company on social media.

Those problems won't go away even with nonvoting common stock and are discussed in Chapter 8 on shareholder communications. But giving investors voting stock creates the possibility of a hostile voting bloc that will attempt to take over your company, or at least act collectively as a roadblock to important business decisions that must be made as quickly and efficiently as possible.

Even if your voting shareholders are as quiet as mice and complacent as lambs, you must give them notice and explain to them in detail what's going on before making important decisions.

While it may seem unfair, undemocratic, or downright Neanderthal to offer crowdfunded investors nonvoting common stock, I think you will find most of them understand that for an investment of $2,000 or less they cannot, and should not, have the right to tell management what to do. If they really feel your company is headed in the wrong direction, they should take that $2,000 and start companies of their own rather than invest in yours. Those who don't understand that should be investing in your competition.

Consider Making Your Nonvoting Common Stock Redeemable. Virtually all state corporation laws give corporations the right to make one or more classes of their stock redeemable, thereby allowing the corporation to repurchase those shares for cash under certain circumstances. Frequently, corporations will make one or more of their classes of preferred stock redeemable so they can remove that class at the demand of subsequent investors (or investment bankers as part of an initial public offering) or otherwise due to market conditions.

Historically, corporations have not chosen to make classes of their common stock redeemable, although state corporation laws do not prohibit them from doing so. The reason has more to do with marketing than the securities laws: many investors will in theory be reluctant to buy shares in a company if those shares can be repurchased out from under their noses days, weeks, or months after the investment is made—especially if the shares are nonvoting common stock that don't give them the right to complain about that decision.

Title III crowdfunding may, however, lead more corporations to conclude that having redeemable common stock—which would enable them to buy out overly difficult or needy shareholders and otherwise help them cull the herd whenever necessary—outweighs the possible negative impact on the company's ability to market the offering.

You should discuss with your attorney the relative advantages and disadvantages of redeemable nonvoting common stock. If you do decide to offer redeemable shares as part of your Title III crowdfunded offering, make sure:

- The repurchase price is at least 120 percent of the price per share you are asking for in the offering (this gives the investor a guaranteed return if the shares are repurchased)

- You stipulate that you are not allowed to redeem any shares in the offering for a period of at least one year after the closing date of the offering

These provisions will make the idea of redemption more palatable to your crowd-funded investors and make it easier for you to make a successful offering.

Appendix 3 to this book is a sample amended and restated articles of incorporation for a Delaware corporation having classes of convertible preferred stock, voting common stock, and nonvoting common stock (which is not redeemable).

Can LLCs Have Multiple Classes of "Stock"? LLCs can be structured the same way as corporations, with common and preferred, voting and nonvoting units of membership interest. The rights, privileges, and limitations of each class of units are normally spelled out in the operating agreement of the LLC rather than by amending the LLC's articles of organization.

Appendix 4 to this book is a sample provision for an LLC operating agreement creating two classes of membership interest—voting and nonvoting—with the option to issue nonvoting units as either common units having the same rights as the voting units (except for voting) or preferred units having the same rights, privileges, and limitations as preferred stock in a corporation.

Set Your Offering Amount and Determine the Dilution for Existing Investors

Now is the time to make two key determinations:

1. How much money do you plan to raise in the offering?

2. How much of your company do you want to give up?

Offering Amount

Before you determine this, it is a good idea to put together a use-of-proceeds chart or Excel spreadsheet with the help of your accountant listing exactly what you will do with the proceeds of the offering if it is successful. Under the Title III regulations for crowdfunded offerings, you will be required to spell this out in some detail, and one of the most common entrepreneurial mistakes is to underestimate how much capital will be needed to fulfill specific purposes.

The more capital you wish to raise, the more investors will have to participate. The Title III crowdfunding regulations require that you set the amount of capital you wish to raise at the beginning of the offering; fail to hit that target and you have to give all the investors their money back. The more money you ask for, the less likely you will be able to hit your funding target.

Accordingly, it will be difficult for start-up companies to raise more than a couple of hundred thousand dollars in a Title III crowdfunded offering. Concept companies probably should not ask for more than $50,000. More established private companies will be able to raise more significant sums under Title III, but after a certain point it will be much more cost-effective to raise money via a traditional Rule 506 private placement, or an accredited-investors-only offering under Title II.

Dilution: How Much Equity Do You Want to Give Up?

When issuing debt securities such as notes, you do not give up any equity in your company.

Because equity securities involve owning a percentage of your company's shares, by issuing new common or preferred stock (or membership interests in an LLC) to anyone, you end up owning a lower percentage of your company than you did previously. To use the simplest possible example, if you and your founders own 100 percent of your company today and you sell common stock for 20 percent of your company to crowdfunded investors, you and your founders will end up owning 80 percent of the company when the offering closes. You and your cofounders continue to have the same number of shares as previously, but because your company has issued additional shares, your shares constitute a lower percentage of your company's total issued and outstanding shares after the offering is completed.

(I apologize if I appear to be condescending or talking down to the reader, who presumably has at least some college-level mathematics experience, but you would be amazed at how many otherwise sophisticated first-time entrepreneurs fail to grasp this very basic and simple concept.)

You cannot issue more than 100 percent of a company's shares, so each new issue of equity securities dilutes the percentage owned by the founders and the previous investors. How much dilution are you and the other founders willing to tolerate each time you launch an offering of securities, crowdfunded or otherwise?

As an attorney who has represented start-ups for more than thirty years, I can tell you that these can be extremely difficult conversations for entrepreneurs.

Larger corporations make this decision by hiring experts to perform a valuation of what the company is worth. Once the valuation has been determined, the company determines how much money it needs and how much of the current valuation that amount constitutes. For example, if a corporation is worth $500,000 and needs to raise $100,000, it would issue stock constituting 20 percent of the total issued and outstanding equity in the company after the investment is completed.

For a start-up company that is still trying to develop or perfect its products or services (or concept companies that are little more than an idea), valuation is pretty much impossible. Any valuation you put on your company is mostly guesswork because the company has no revenue and no tangible assets.

Here are some basic rules of thumb:

- Don't even attempt to project revenues or profits—focus instead on the things you need to do to make your product or service a reality and get it into the marketplace, and on how much each of those things will cost.

- Always ask for more (120 percent to 150 percent) of what you think you will need—there are always hidden costs you fail to foresee, and it's helpful to have the money readily available when you realize that's the case (just keep in mind that you will have to explain to your funding portal and the SEC what you will do with any excess proceeds of your offering).

- Do not give up more than 10 percent of your company in your initial offering, especially a crowdfunded one.

The last point is by far the most important one. If your company has an exciting product with huge market potential, you are likely to get some investors in your crowdfunded offering no matter how many risks you disclose in your offering statement. Under no circumstances do you want a crowd (or mob) of people owning a significant percentage of your company, especially if they have the right to vote on matters affecting the company's business. There are three reasons for this:

1. The more equity investors own of your company, the more power they have to influence your decision making (and may have legal rights under your state corporation laws).

2. Future investors will not like your having a significant percentage of minority owners to deal with.

3. The more equity you give away early on, the less you will have for yourself and the other founders later.

Unlike the title characters in the famous Mel Brooks movie (and Broadway show) *The Producers*, you can't sell more than 100 percent of your stock. I have personally seen companies give away so much of their equity during the first two years of operations that the founders ended up owning less than 10 percent of their companies when the big venture capitalist firms started knocking on their doors wanting a 40 or 50 percent equity stake.

Prepare a Term Sheet for the Offering

Once you have determined the rights you want your investors to have, the amount of money you need, and the percentage of your company you wish to give up, it is time to put together a term sheet and begin looking for funding portals to manage and handle your Title III crowdfunded offering.

As opposed to a traditional private offering, in a Title III crowdfunded offering you must make two sales pitches: first, you must sell the funding portal; second, once accepted by a portal, you must sell prospective investors. The term sheet is the document that will help you sell the funding portal.

A term sheet is not a legal document and is therefore not binding on your company as a contract or legal obligation. It does not commit your company to follow through on the offering; it merely indicates your interest in launching an offering of securities on those terms. Your term sheet should be as detailed as possible, but be sure to leave room for some negotiation, as funding portals, accredited investors, and others will surely comment on your terms and try to change them more to their advantage.

In structuring your offering, you should look closely at the terms and conditions of other offerings involving similar companies in your industry offering comparable products and services. Unfortunately, as will be seen in Chapter 11, funding portals are extremely limited by the Title III regulations in their ability to advise and coach issuers on market conditions and ways to improve their offerings' likelihood of success.

Appendices 6, 7, and 8 are, respectively, sample term sheets for:

- An offering of convertible promissory notes

- An offering of convertible preferred stock in a corporation

- An offering of nonvoting membership interests in an LLC

Get Your Management Team and Initial Investors On Board

State corporation laws require any offering of securities to be authorized by resolution of the corporation's board of directors and (often) its shareholders. Similarly, state LLC laws require any offering of membership interests or units to be authorized by the LLC's members.

This must be done at a special meeting called for the express purpose of approving the offering and must be documented (minutes must be taken). Advance notice of the meeting must be given to all shareholders or LLC members as required by the statute. Failure to conduct this meeting may void the offering as being not properly authorized under state law.

Once your Title III crowdfunded offering has received all required internal approvals, you are ready to launch.

CHAPTER 5

Launching Your Crowdfunded Offering

I f your company has offered securities in the past, you will probably be able to launch a Title III crowdfunded offering with little assistance from outsiders. Start-up companies, first-time issuers, and concept companies will have a tougher time. Regulation Crowdfunding contains dozens of rules issuers have to comply with when offering securities under Title III, and it is relatively easy to make mistakes if you don't have at least some professional help.

Finding the Help You Need

Companies making Title III crowdfunded offerings for the first time will need help from at least three, and possibly four, professionals:

- A good accountant

- A good lawyer who is experienced in private offerings of securities and familiar with the Title III and Regulation Crowdfunding rules for crowd-funded offerings

- A business mentor or adviser who can coach the company founders throughout the offering process

- (Perhaps) a social media marketing expert who is familiar with crowd-funded marketing campaigns under Kickstarter, Indiegogo, RocketHub, and other project crowdfunding platforms

The accountant will be necessary to put together the financial statements, cash-flow projections, and other financial information in the offering documents. The lawyer will be responsible primarily for drafting the disclosure documents required by Regulation

Crowdfunding but also for coaching the company founders on what they cannot do or say during the offering process.

As Title III crowdfunding becomes a reality, there will be an explosion in the number of people offering advice to entrepreneurs on structuring and managing their crowdfunded offerings (including, perhaps, the person whose book you are reading). Like all business mentors, many of these will know what they're talking about and many won't. The ideal mentor for a start-up company contemplating a Title III offering is someone who:

- "Gets" social media and the triggers that make successful social media marketing campaigns work

- Understands the industry your company is in and the factors that make for success in that industry

- Has successfully managed Title III crowdfunded offerings for at least one or two other companies

- Has the honesty, integrity, and reputation for fairly dealing with clients who you and your cofounders trust

Of course, at the time this book was being written, virtually no one met all those criteria because no Title III crowdfunded offerings had taken place yet.

Do you need to work with a social media marketing expert when launching a Title III crowdfunded offering? I'm frankly of two minds on this. On the one hand, success in marketing a Title III offering will depend on your ability to leverage your social networks effectively. If you do not live on social media every day, you probably do not know what works and what doesn't on each of the most popular social media platforms, and any help in this area will likely improve your batting average with prospective investors, especially those younger people (and they seem to be legion) who trust their Facebook friends' recommendations more than anyone else's.

On the other hand, many social media marketing consultants may not be familiar with Title III and the many detailed rules and regulations for crowdfunded offerings of securities. Reaching out to people you don't know may work on Kickstarter and help you raise money for an invention or a charitable fund-raising campaign, but it almost certainly will shut down your Title III offering if the SEC finds out you're doing it.

If you have to choose between a brilliant marketing expert who doesn't understand Title III and a halfway decent lawyer who does, choose the latter, at least until you know what you are doing.

Preparing Your Disclosure Documents

Before you begin approaching funding portals to launch your offering, you will need to put together a term sheet—a nonbinding summary, often in bullet form, of the principal terms and conditions of the offering you propose to make. Appendices 6, 7, and 8 are sample term sheets for offerings of different types of securities (debt securities, common/preferred stock in a corporation, and LLC membership interests, respectively).

Most funding portals will not accept your offering on the basis of a term sheet, however. They will want to see the actual documents you will be using to solicit investors through the portal. These documents fall into two categories:

1. The disclosures you are required to make to investors under Regulation Crowdfunding, in an offering statement using the SEC's new Form C (from now on we will call these Form C disclosures)

2. Any other materials—such as PowerPoint slide shows, video presentations, detailed business plans, online product reviews, newspaper/magazine articles and blog postings, and advertisements and marketing materials you plan to use when selling products and services to customers—you think investors should see in order to fall in love with your company, its mission, its products, its services, and its good-looking-enough-for-Hollywood management team, as long as they don't violate Regulation Crowdfunding (from now on we will call these the supplemental materials)

Becoming Familiar with Form C

Before you begin working on your crowdfunded offering, it's a good idea to become familiar with the SEC's Form C. A copy of the current text, as issued by the SEC on October 30, 2015, is included as Appendix 1 at the end of this book.

The SEC requires issuers to use an XML-based fillable form to input Form C and discourages the submission of paper filings. Information not required to be provided in text boxes in the XML-based fillable form would be filed as attachments to Form C.

Form C is used for all of an issuer's filings with the SEC related to the offering made in reliance on Regulation Crowdfunding. The issuer checks one of the following boxes on the cover of Form C to indicate the purpose of the Form C filing:

- "Form C: Offering Statement" for issuers filing the initial disclosures required for an offering

- "Form C-A: Amendment" for issuers seeking to amend a previously filed Form C for an offering

- "Form C-U: Progress Update" for issuers filing a progress update

- "Form C-AR: Annual Report" for issuers filing the annual report

- "Form C-TR: Termination of Reporting" for issuers terminating their reporting obligations

The SEC's data-handling system—Electronic Data Gathering, Analysis, and Retrieval (EDGAR)—would automatically provide each filing with an appropriate tag depending on which box the issuer checked so investors could distinguish among the different filings. An issuer who did not already have EDGAR filing codes and to which the SEC had not previously assigned a user identification number, called a Central Index Key (CIK) code, would need to obtain the codes by filing electronically a Form ID at www.filermanagement.edgarfiling.sec.gov.

An issuer is permitted to submit exhibits to Form C in Portable Document Format (PDF) as official filings.

Because the prospect of filling out an SEC form can be quite daunting, especially for a first-time issuer, the SEC gives issuers the option of submitting some of the required information in a question-and-answer format. Issuers opting to use this format would prepare their disclosures by answering the questions provided and filing that disclosure as an exhibit to the Form C filed electronically in XML format. The text of the question-and-answer version of Form C, as issued by the SEC on October 30, 2015, is included as Appendix 2 at the end of this book.

The Form C Disclosures

The SEC requires issuers to provide certain information to investors through the funding portals and to the SEC directly via an electronic filing of SEC Form C on EDGAR. While some of the Form C disclosures will be included in the itemized fields of Form C, other information will be included as attachments to Form C.

The Form C disclosures for each issuer are:

- The name, legal status (whether corporation or LLC), state of organization, date of organization, physical address, and Uniform Resource Locator (URL), or website address

- The names of the directors and officers, the positions and offices held by those people, how long they have served in those positions, and the business experience of those people over the past three years

- The name of each person who is (as of the most recent practicable date but not earlier than 120 days prior to the date the offering statement is filed) a beneficial owner of 20 percent or more of the issuer's outstanding voting equity securities

- A description of the business of the issuer and anticipated plan of business (merely a short description of the business and its plan going forward, not a detailed business plan, although this may and probably should be included in the supplemental materials)

- The current number of employees of the issuer

- A discussion of the material risk factors that make an investment in the issuer speculative (see Appendix 9 for a sample risk-factors disclosure for an issuer creating a mobile smartphone app)

- The target offering amount and the deadline, or closing date, to reach the target amount

- A statement with respect to whether the issuer will accept investment in excess of the target amount and the maximum amount it will accept (if the issuer accepts investments above the stated target, it must state the method it will use to allocate oversubscriptions), and a description of how the issuer will use any excess funds

- A description of the purpose and intended use of the offering proceeds or, if an issuer is uncertain how the proceeds will be used, a statement of the probable uses and the factors impacting the selection of each use (these descriptions must be fairly detailed and include what proceeds will be used to compensate the funding portal, salaries to the company founders and others, repurchase shares issued to previous investors, and so forth—a mere statement that proceeds will be used for "working capital" or "general corporate purposes" will not suffice)

- A statement of how long the issuer expects the proceeds to last

- A description of the process to complete the transaction or to cancel an investment commitment as prescribed by Regulation Crowdfunding

- The price of the securities or the method for determining the price (if the issuer has not set a price at the start of the campaign—not recommended—it must provide a final price prior to any sale of securities)

- A description of the owner and capital structure of the issuer

- The terms of the securities being offered as well as each other class of security of the issuer

- Any rights held by the company founders or other principal shareholders

- How the securities being offered are valued and how the securities may be valued in the future

- The risks to investors relating to minority ownership and the risks associated with corporate actions like the additional issuance of shares, issuer repurchases, and the sale of the issuer or issuer assets to related parties

- A description of any restrictions on transfer of the securities (for example, any buy-sell provision that might appear in the issuer's shareholders' agreement or LLC operating agreement)

- The name, SEC file number, and Central Registration Depository (CRD) number of the funding portal that will conduct the offering

- The amount of compensation paid to the funding portal for conducting the offering and the amount of any referral or other fees associated with the offering (which can be disclosed either as a dollar amount or percentage of the offering amount or as a good faith estimate if the exact amount is not available at the time of the filing)

- Any other direct or indirect interest in the issuer held by the funding portal, or any arrangement for the funding portal to acquire such an interest

- A description of the material terms of any indebtedness of the issuer (if the issuer has debt, it will need to disclose all material terms, including the principal amount, interest rate, maturity date, and any other terms an investor would deem material)

- A description of any exempt offering under Regulation D, Regulation A, or Section 4(a)(2) of the 1933 Securities Act conducted within the past three years (the description should include the date of the offering, the offering exemption relied on, the type of securities offered, the amount of securities sold, and the use of proceeds)

- A description of any completed or proposed transaction by the issuer or any affiliated company for value exceeding 5 percent of the amount being raised in the Title III offering since the beginning of the issuer's last fiscal year, including the current offering, when a control person, promoter, or "member of the family" (defined as a child, stepchild, grandchild, parent, stepparent, grandparent, spouse or spousal equivalent, sibling, mother-in-law, father-in-law, son-in-law, daughter-in-law, brother-in-law, or sister-in-law, including adoptive relationships of any such control person or promoter) had a direct or indirect material interest

- A description of the financial condition of the issuer (which must include, to the extent material, a discussion of liquidity, capital resources, and historical results of operations)

- The tax returns, reviewed financial statements, or audited financial statements of the issuer, depending on the level of the offering and other offerings within the previous twelve months

- A description of any events that would have triggered disqualification under the "bad actor" disqualification rules in the SEC's Rule 506(d) had they occurred after the effective date of Regulation Crowdfunding

- A statement that the issuer will file annual reports on EDGAR within 120 days after the end of each fiscal year

- The location on the issuer's website where investors will be able to find the issuer's annual report and the date by which such report will be available on the issuer's website

- Whether the issuer or any of its predecessors previously has failed to comply with the ongoing reporting requirements of Regulation Crowdfunding

- Any material information necessary in order to make the statements made, in light of the circumstances under which they were made, not misleading

- Updates on the progress of meeting the target offering amount

For the full text of the Form C disclosures, the reader should consult the actual text of Form C, which appears as Appendix 1, or the question-and-answer version of Form C, which appears as Appendix 2.

By far the most important Form C disclosure—which should appear in as many places as possible not only in the Form C disclosure but also in your supplemental materials, in your Regulation Crowdfunding offering announcement (described in

Chapter 6), and in every communication you make to investors during the offering period, and in capital letters—is the simple statement, "INVESTMENT IN THESE SECURITIES IS HIGHLY RISKY, AND THERE IS A CHANCE YOU MAY LOSE YOUR ENTIRE INVESTMENT." As will be seen in Chapter 8, including that statement in as many investor communications as possible goes a long way to avoid trouble with disgruntled investors down the road.

The SEC does not specify the format in which the Supplementary Materials must be presented, leaving some flexibility for issuers to present some information in written offering documents, some in videos, and other information by graphic means.

While the SEC does not review, comment on, or in any way approve the Form C disclosures, it would be foolish to assume that the SEC will not read information that is on EDGAR. When preparing your Form C disclosures and supplemental materials, you should assume that if and when they suspect problems, the SEC staff and the state regulatory authorities (who under Title III have the primary responsibility for preventing fraud in Title III offerings) will thoroughly review the Form C disclosures for potentially misleading statements and also review the supplemental materials on the funding portal's platform.

The Form C disclosures may include screen shots and other visual aids, such as tables and charts, but cannot be submitted in the form of a PowerPoint presentation.

In order to file the Form C disclosures on EDGAR, your company will need to have EDGAR filing codes and a CIK code. If an issuer does not already have these codes, it can obtain them from the SEC. Since virtually all funding portals will already have these codes and will be experienced in filing documents on EDGAR, it may be best to have the funding portal file your company's Form C disclosures on EDGAR. Just don't be surprised if the portal charges an additional fee for that service.

Your Supplemental Materials

Only the Form C disclosures are required to be filed with the SEC. Regulation Crowdfunding does not, however, limit your offering documents to the Form C disclosures. Issuers in crowdfunded offerings are not only allowed but encouraged to post a wealth of information about themselves and the offering on the funding portal that is listing the offering, by way of supplemental materials that go beyond the Form C disclosures. This is a departure from prior law, in which investors were allowed to see only the statutory prospectus for an offering.

Your supplemental materials may include, among other things:

- PowerPoint presentations about your company and its products and services

- Audio and video presentations by the company founders

- Screen shots of the company's website

- Sample marketing materials your company will use to promote its products and services once funding has been successfully raised

- A detailed written plan of the sort venture capitalists, angel investors, and other traditional players in the venture capital market are accustomed to seeing (I would venture to say that posting such a plan on the funding portal is essential if you are looking to raise money from accredited investors)

Regulation Crowdfunding does not limit the form or content of your supplemental materials in any way. You are, however, liable for any misstatements or omissions in the supplemental materials.

The one rigid, inflexible rule in Regulation Crowdfunding is that the supplemental materials must be posted only on the funding portal while your Title III crowdfunded offering is in progress. You cannot post them on your website or social media pages during the offering period, and you cannot send them directly to investors as part of a direct pitch. As will be seen in Chapter 6, you are permitted to send members of your social media network only an announcement of the offering that points them to the funding portal.

While the SEC and state securities regulators are unlikely to plow through your supplemental materials looking for problems, the funding portal may well do so in order to protect itself against legal liability for any false or misleading claims you may make there. Also, keep in mind that if the SEC, in reviewing your Form C disclosures, suspects there may be compliance problems with your offering, it is not prevented from looking at your supplemental materials, and it will almost certainly do so.

Your Financial Statements

Issuers of securities under Regulation Crowdfunding are required to provide financial statements prepared in accordance with U.S. generally accepted accounting principles (GAAP) covering the two most recently completed fiscal years (or since inception if the company is less than two years old). The financial statements cannot be more than eighteen months old. If more than 120 days have passed since the end of the issuer's most recently ended fiscal year, the issuer will have to produce financial statements for that most recent year but until that point can use financial statements from the preceding year.

The extent to which an issuer's financial statements will need to be reviewed by an independent accountant or accounting firm will depend on (1) the amount of money you are seeking to raise and (2) the amount of securities your company has already sold under Regulation Crowdfunding during the preceding twelve months. Here are the rules:

- If your current crowdfunded offering plus previous Regulation Crowdfunding offerings were for $100,000 or less, the financial statements must be certified by your company's "principal executive officer" or founder and accompanied by the company's tax returns (if any). Basically, the founder(s) will need to include a sworn statement that everything in the financial statements is "true, correct, and complete in all material respects" (Regulation Crowdfunding is not clear, but I doubt the SEC will allow company founders to qualify that statement by saying the financial statements are true and correct "to the best of their knowledge and belief").

- If your current crowdfunded offering plus previous Regulation Crowdfunding offerings were for more than $100,000 but less than $500,000 in total, the financial statements must be reviewed by an independent CPA.

- If your current crowdfunded offering plus previous Regulation Crowdfunding offerings were for $500,000 or more, your financial statements must be audited by a CPA unless this is your first crowdfunded offering and you are raising less than $1 million, in which case only reviewed financial statements are required.

Reviewed Financial Statements. Reviewed financial statements provide the investor with comfort that based on the accountant's review, the accountant is not aware of any material modifications that should be made to the financial statements in order for the statements to be in conformity with GAAP. A review engagement involves the CPA performing procedures (primarily analytical procedures and inquiries) that will provide a reasonable basis for obtaining limited assurance that there are no material modifications that should be made to the financial statements in order for them to be in conformity with GAAP.

In a review, the CPA designs and performs analytical procedures, inquiries, and other procedures, as appropriate, based on the accountant's understanding of the industry, knowledge of the client, and awareness of the risk that he or she may unknowingly fail to modify the accountant's review report on financial statements that are materially misstated. A review does not contemplate obtaining an understanding of the entity's internal control, assessing fraud risk, testing accounting records, or other procedures ordinarily performed in an audit.

The CPA then issues a report stating that the review was performed in accordance with Statements on Standards for Accounting and Review Services; that management is responsible for the preparation and fair presentation of the financial statements in accordance with the applicable financial reporting framework and for designing, implementing, and maintaining internal control relevant to the preparation and fair presentation of the financial statements; that a review includes primarily applying analytical procedures to management's financial data and making inquiries of management; that a review is substantially less in scope than an audit; and that the CPA is not aware of any material modifications that should be made to the financial statements in order for them to be in conformity with the applicable financial reporting framework.

Audited Financial Statements. Audited financial statements provide the user with the auditor's opinion that the financial statements are presented fairly, in all material respects, in conformity with GAAP. In an audit, the auditor is required to use GAAS to obtain an understanding of the entity's internal controls and assess fraud risk. The auditor is also required to corroborate the amounts and disclosures included in the financial statements by obtaining audit evidence through inquiry, physical inspection, observation, third-party confirmations, examination, analytical procedures, and other procedures.

The auditor issues a report that states the audit was conducted in accordance with GAAS and the financial statements are the responsibility of management, and provides an opinion that the financial statements present fairly, in all material respects, the financial position of the company and the results of operations in conformity with GAAP, or the auditor issues a qualified opinion if the financial statements are not in conformity with GAAP. The auditor may also issue a disclaimer of opinion or an adverse opinion if appropriate.

As initially proposed, Regulation Crowdfunding required all issuers raising $500,000 or more to provide audited financial statements to prospective investors. This requirement was hotly debated during the comment period leading up to the adoption of Regulation Crowdfunding in October 2015, with most commentators insisting that the high cost of an audited financial statement would effectively prohibit early-stage companies from launching crowdfunded offerings under Title III. The SEC backed down on this requirement in the final version of Regulation Crowdfunding, but only for first-time issuers raising between $500,000 and $1 million. After that, audited financial statements are required.

The SEC defended its position on audited financial statements on the grounds that financial statements prepared in accordance with GAAP generally are "self-scaling to the size and complexity of the issuer." Or, to put it in plain English, start-ups and concept companies that need $500,000 or more in upfront money to launch their business plans are much more likely to fail and thus pose a bigger threat to investors than start-ups and concept companies that need only $50,000 to get up and running. If a start-up or concept company needs $500,000 or more to launch its business plan, then its CPA better be willing to back that up in writing, even if it means putting his or her license at risk. Needless to say, few CPAs will be willing to take that risk for anyone but their largest clients unless they cover their rear ends ten times over to avoid liability if the company fails.

The requirement of reviewed and audited financial statements may well mean that, as a practical matter, only companies with significant track records and a product or service that is well on its way to being marketed will qualify to raise more than $100,000 using Title III crowdfunded offerings.

Finding the Right Funding Portal for Your Offering

Prior to January 26, 2016, the earliest date on which funding portals were allowed to register with the SEC, there were no Title III crowdfunding portals operating anywhere in the United States because the final version of Regulation Crowdfunding authorizing the existence of funding portals wasn't released until October 30, 2015.

By the time you read this, there still may not be any Title III crowdfunding portals in existence. Before a company can operate as a funding portal under Title III, it must:

- Register as a funding portal with the SEC

- Register with FINRA

- (Possibly) have its principals take examinations in order to qualify under SEC and FINRA requirements

- Hire and train the many people that will be necessary to comply with Regulation Crowdfunding's many requirements for funding portals

As we will see in Chapter 11, funding portals will require tons of cash to get off the ground and will be extremely labor-intensive to operate. It's a fair bet that funding portals will need to charge high fees for their services in order to cover their high start-up and operating costs. While it is anticipated that most of these fees will be charged in the form of commissions (that is, a percentage of the amount successfully raised in each crowdfunded offering), the SEC does not prohibit funding portals from charging flat upfront fees for their services. This, in fact, is how most funding portals will probably charge for handling offerings of $100,000 or less. Also, it is almost certain that funding portals will charged fixed breakage fees for crowdfunded offerings that fail to raise the minimum amount of capital on or before the scheduled closing date.

Your company will not be able to make a Title III crowdfunded offering of its securities except through a funding portal. How do you find the right portal for your specific offering? Generally, you want to work with the funding portal that is likeliest to get a successful result for your crowdfunded offering. Here are the questions to ask:

Does the Portal Handle My Type of Company?

Most funding portals will be focused on technology-related companies, for three reasons:

1. That's what the funding portal's founders know and understand (keep in mind always that funding portal executives are entrepreneurs just like yourself. Most will be coming from venture capital backgrounds and accordingly will be more familiar with tech companies than other issuers).

2. Tech companies generally have higher valuations and therefore higher offering amounts (leading to greater commissions for the funding portal) than other issuers.

3. Most serious investors (angels and venture capitalists) will be focused on tech companies and other scalable businesses to the exclusion of everyone else.

However, one of the great selling points of Title III crowdfunding is that it opens up the securities markets to retail, service, distribution, franchise, and other companies that have not historically had an easy time attracting investors. It is not inconceivable that specialized funding portals may emerge to focus on these nontraditional issuers.

Is the Portal Handling Other Issuers in the Same Industry (Is It Vertical)?

Generally, you want to work with a funding portal that understands your industry and is handling offerings for other companies in your industry, for two reasons:

1. They are in a better position to vet your offering and point out areas where your offering documents may need improvement.

2. They are more likely to attract investors who are interested in your specific industry.

The downside, of course, is that you may find your offering being listed shoulder to shoulder with an offering by one of your competitors. That is great for investors, of course, as it permits side-by-side comparison of different offerings by similar companies, but is highly stressful for the participating issuers, who may find themselves in a beauty contest to attract the best investors. In such a situation, competing issuers will be under pressure to outdo the others in their offering terms and conditions (because your offerings are publicly available for view online, they can see yours and you can see theirs), with a greater risk of fraud or misstatement if one or the other competitors promotes its offering too aggressively.

It can be a difficult decision to make: is your company better off being the only one in its industry listed with a particular portal (and therefore more likely to stand out) or being one of many similar companies handled by a portal known for its expertise in that industry (and therefore more likely to attract the best and most knowledgeable investors in that industry)?

Does the Funding Portal Have Lots of Investors On Board?

Not only issuers but investors are required to list with funding portals. The difference is that while investors may register with more than one portal, issuers are limited to one portal for their crowdfunded offering.

While funding portals will be prohibited from providing you with personally identifiable information about their investors—for fear you will try to contact them directly and circumvent the portal's role as intermediary—they probably will offer aggregate information about the number of investors that have registered with them, the percentage of accredited investors, and other statistical information that may help you make a more informed portal selection decision.

Is the Portal Marketing Itself Aggressively?

Remember that funding portals are start-up companies just like yours, competing with other portals for business, and that just like your company, they have to market themselves to attract issuers and investors to the portal. Maybe—just maybe—some funding portals themselves use Title III crowdfunding to raise capital for their business operations (which raises the question of who would be acting as their funding portal?)

Regulation Crowdfunding specifically allows portals to advertise themselves and to seek brand recognition from broker-dealers, investment banks, and other players who may recommend investors to the portal. Your company should be looking for funding portals that are marketing themselves aggressively and securing the capital they need to grow their operations. As in all industries, aggressive competition among funding portals will lead eventually to a handful of companies dominating the industry. Your company should be listed with a winner in that competition, not an also ran.

Will the Portal Coach My Company Through the Process?

Regulation Crowdfunding allows funding portals to advise an issuer about the structure or content of the offering, to a limited extent. For example, a portal can:

- Provide predrafted templates or form documents to the issuer

- Provide advice on the types of securities the issuer can offer and the terms of those securities

- Provide advice on compliance with crowdfunding regulations (including advice on correcting mistakes in the Form C disclosures)

Obviously, the line between telling an issuer what it did wrong in its offering documents and coaching an issuer on the right way to do its offering documents can be a very thin one, and funding portals will have to train their employees dealing with issuers carefully to make sure no one crosses a line that might invalidate an offering or (worse) put the funding portal's SEC or FINRA registration in jeopardy.

Just as obviously, your company will probably have to pay a bit extra for any hand-holding services a funding portal believes it is safe to provide.

What a funding portal cannot do, under any circumstances, is play favorites or discriminate between your company and other issuers. This would include giving you advice that would give you a leg up over any issuers competing for the same investors.

Should I Use a Matchmaker?

Because under Regulation Crowdfunding issuers are required to work with only one portal when launching a Title III crowdfunded offering, the selection of that portal will become mission critical to the offering's success. To avoid mistakes in portal selection, it may be worth getting professional help in making that decision. It is almost certain that some individuals and companies will set themselves up as matchmakers who will help link issuers and funding portals online.

Regulation Crowdfunding allows you to use a matchmaker to find the right portal, as long as you disclose the amount of its compensation in the Form C disclosures. Unless the matchmaker is a registered broker-dealer, it cannot accept a percentage of your successful offering as compensation: it must charge a flat fee, hourly rate, or other compensation that is not tied to the amount or success of your offering.

Setting the Offering Schedule and the Minimum/Maximum Amounts

The last question you need to ask before launching a Title III crowdfunded offering is: when do we really need the money?

Setting the Offering Closing Date

You must first set a closing date for your crowdfunded offering. Crowdfunded offerings are not open ended; they must close at a specific date and time set forth in the Form C disclosures. Regulation Crowdfunding requires that crowdfunded offerings last a minimum of 21 days. Even if it takes only two or three days to raise your minimum offering amount, you cannot grab the cash until 21 days have passed. This is a cooling-off period required by the SEC to give investors more time to study your company and possibly withdraw their investments if they get cold feet or a better opportunity comes along, and give you time to fine-tune and update your offering documents to reflect the latest changes,.

You can set as long a period as you like for your crowdfunded offerings, although periods of 90 to 180 days will be commonplace, and periods of more than a year probably will be discouraged. You may be able to extend the closing date of your offering if you find yourself close to achieving your minimum offering amount, but you will have to give the portal at least five business days before the scheduled closing date to process and post the extended closing date, and the portal will be required to give existing investors five days in which to reconfirm their investments. If an investor fails to reconfirm an investment within the five-day period, the investment is canceled and the investor gets the money back.

An extended closing date may give your investors additional time to get cold feet and pull the plug on their investments, as they will be able (as they always were) to withdraw their investments up to forty-eight hours before the extended closing date.

Also, the funding portal is almost certain to charge your company an additional fee for keeping the offering documents posted for an extended period of time.

All in all, if your offering has generated lots of investments within the scheduled offering period, it may be advisable to take the money and run.

Setting a Minimum Offering Amount

Regulation Crowdfunding allows you to set a single target amount for your crowdfunded offering, but most issuers will opt for the so-called min/max offering, with a minimum offering amount they will accept and (sometimes) a maximum offering amount. Even without a maximum offering amount, it is recommended that you set a minimum offering amount to hedge your bets in case your target amount proves unrealistic.

So, for example, you can stipulate in your Form C disclosures that you are seeking to raise $500,000, but with a minimum offering amount of $200,000. If at least $200,000 is raised by the scheduled closing date, the offering is successful and will close even though you didn't raise the full $500,000.

Keep in mind, though, that crowdfunded offerings are all or nothing: if the minimum offering amount you set has not been raised by the scheduled closing date, the offering has failed and your funding portal will be required to return any investments that have been made to the investors.

Setting a Maximum Offering Amount

You also have the option under Regulation Crowdfunding to set a maximum offering amount for your crowdfunded offering, such that the offering automatically closes if the maximum is reached prior to the scheduled closing date. If your crowdfunded offering is wildly successful, and you raise the full amount of capital you need in twenty-one days or less, why would you want to shut off the spigots? The only requirement in Regulation Crowdfunding is that you state in your Form C disclosures what you will do with any excess proceeds of your offering.

Also, by setting a maximum offering amount, if your offering is oversubscribed, you will be forced to decide which investors you will accept and which you will reject (or accept only a percentage of each investor's subscription to keep everyone happy), and describe in your Form C disclosures how you will handle the oversubscription.

CHAPTER 6

Managing and Marketing Your Crowdfunded Offering

You have prepared the offering documents for your Title III crowdfunded offering and found the perfect funding portal to handle the offering. You have posted your offering documents to the portal, and either you or the portal has filed the Form C disclosures with the SEC. The portal has listed your offering on its website.

Congratulations! You have now reached the starting gate.

To get to the finish line, you now have to raise the money within your scheduled offering period.

While your funding portal has helped you get to the starting gate (indeed, you could not have gotten there without it), there are only a limited number of things the portal can legally do to help you get to the finish line. At the end of the day, a successful crowdfunded offering depends entirely on you—the strength and sex appeal of your business plan, the extent and depth of your social networks, and your ability to persuade prospective investors that you and your cofounders have a winner on your hands.

Or, as the publisher of my first business book told me, "Cliff, it's our job as the publisher to get your books into the bookstores. As the author, it's your job to get them out of there."

Here's how you get there, and what to do if you should stumble along the way.

Your Offering Announcement: Where It Should Go, Where It Can't Go

The success of any crowdfunded offering depends on your company's ability (and its founders' ability) to leverage its networks—on social media and otherwise—to find investors willing to shell out their hard-earned money in exchange for a piece of your company.

Regulation Crowdfunding requires you to file your offering documents—the Form C disclosures and supplemental materials discussed in Chapter 5—with the SEC and your funding portal. But you cannot—*cannot*—send these materials to your website, your social media pages, or anyone else. They exist only on the funding portal, and that is the only place online where people should be able to find them.

What you can send to your social networks—once and once only—is a notice, in the form prescribed by Regulation Crowdfunding, directing investors to the funding portal that is handling your offering.

Under Regulation Crowdfunding, the notice may contain no more than the following:

- A statement that the issuer is conducting an offering, the name of the funding portal conducting the offering, and a link to the portal's website.

- The terms of the offering, including the amount of securities being offered, the nature of the securities, the price of the securities, and the closing date of the offering period.

- Factual information about the legal identity and the business location of the issuer, limited to the name of the issuer, the address, the phone number, the website URL of the issuer, an email address for a representative of the issuer, and a brief description of the issuer's business.

The notice would be similar in appearance to tombstone ads for initial public offerings permitted by the SEC's Rule 134, except that the Regulation Crowdfunding notice must direct potential investors to the funding portal. One of the guiding rules of Regulation Crowdfunding is that all communications between an issuer and investors during the offering period must take place not directly but only through the funding portal to ensure that all investors receive the same information at the same time and that all communications are available for public scrutiny in one place only.

Regulation Crowdfunding does not place restrictions on how the issuer distributes these notices. An issuer could place these notices on its own website, on various social media websites, or in newspaper and magazine ads (theoretically, the notice could be given over radio and television as well, but the cost is likely prohibitive to most issuers), and the notice would direct those interested to the funding portal page, where they could access the Form C disclosures and supplemental materials necessary to make informed investment decisions. Posts on Facebook, tweets on Twitter, LinkedIn updates, and the like that do not follow these limitations would violate Regulation Crowdfunding and legally disqualify your crowdfunded offering.

The prohibition on advertising the terms of the offering and related requirements apply to people acting on behalf of the issuer. For example, those acting on behalf of the issuer are required to identify their affiliation with the issuer in all communications on the funding portal's platform. Note also that if an issuer is offering securities under another SEC exemption at the same time as it is offering securities under Regulation Crowdfunding, the other offering might have to limit its advertising activities in order to avoid being integrated with the crowdfunded offering.

Advertising and Promoting Your Offering on the Funding Portal

Regulation Crowdfunding requires funding portals to maintain communications channels enabling issuers and investors to communicate directly with each other; such channels include chat rooms, discussion threads, frequently-asked-questions pages, webcasts, podcasts, and webinars. Issuers are not only allowed but encouraged to communicate about the terms of the offering through these channels, as such communications will be publicly available for view by all potential investors.

Regulation Crowdfunding requires that any communication from the issuing company, its founders, or other management team members be clearly identified as such. Also, any communications made on the portal by someone who has received compensation or a gift from the issuing company, its founders, or other management team members must state clearly the compensation or gift received by the person making the communication (for example, in paid reviews or testimonials by celebrities who receive gifts in exchange for their endorsement).

The downside, of course, is that funding portal channels may be used by people—such as competitors—who masquerade as investors in an effort to solicit confidential information about your company or post negative comments designed to frighten investors away from your offering. Regulation Crowdfunding allows communications on funding portals only by investors who have opened accounts with the portal, and presumably the portal will conduct the necessary due diligence to ensure that those claiming to be investors are indeed who they say they are. Still, despite a portal's best efforts, a few bogus email accounts are likely to find their way over the threshold.

The only remedy offered for such activities is to do the same thing you would do if the posting appeared elsewhere on the Internet: find out who the posting is from and then out them publicly on the funding portal. Issuers should also notify the funding portal of any such activities in the hopes it may take action to ban offenders from the portal.

Advertising and Promoting Your Offering Elsewhere

In two words, you can't.

Other than posting or sending the Regulation Crowdfunding notice to folks, you cannot advertise or promote your offering other than through the funding portal.

Each member of your management team will need to be made aware of this requirement, as each no doubt will send emails, post on his social media pages, and generally do everything he can to get word out about your offering to the maximum number of potential investors.

What you and your management team need to understand is that even a single communication in violation or Regulation Crowdfunding may disqualify the entire offering and force you to withdraw it from the funding portal, at great cost and potential embarrassment in the marketplace.

Can the Funding Portal Help You Advertise Your Offering?

In a word, no. A cryptic statement in Regulation Crowdfunding says that a funding portal is permitted to "highlight issuers or offerings based on objective criteria that would identify a large selection of issuers." The criteria used, however, cannot implicitly endorse one issuer or offering over others, and the criteria must be consistently applied to all issuers and offerings. Some of the objective criteria noted by the SEC are the type of securities being offered, the geographic location of the issuer, and the number or amount of investment commitments made.

Similarly, a funding portal is permitted to provide search functions or other tools that allow investors and potential investors to search and categorize the offerings on the portal based on objective criteria. In addition, Regulation Crowdfunding allows a funding portal to (1) categorize its offerings into general subject areas so a potential investor can find an offering, and (2) give potential investors the ability to create automated email notifications about offerings on the portal.

A funding portal is prohibited from endorsing specific offerings or receiving special or additional compensation for identifying or highlighting an issuer or offering on the platform. So, for example, promotions such as Kickstarter's "Deals We Love!" highlights on its home page would violate Regulation Crowdfunding.

Updating or Changing Your Offering Documents Midoffering

Time does not stand still once an issuer's offering documents are filed with the funding portal and the SEC. Change happens, and an issuer will want to keep its offering materials as up to date as possible to reflect changes such as:

- The addition of new members to the management team

- The withdrawal of any member of the management team

- News articles and media coverage about the company that appear during the offering period

- Changes in the company's product and service offerings

- News that may negatively impact the company's success, such as a competitor's introduction of a similar or identical product, or a regulatory change making the company's service less desirable

Issuers are not only allowed but encouraged to update their offering documents. The supplemental materials (described in Chapter 5) may be updated at any time by posting them to the funding portal (and, perhaps, paying an additional fee—this will be up to each individual portal).

If the change affects the Form C disclosures (described in Chapter 5), then either the issuer or the portal must also file on EDGAR, the SEC's data-handling system, a formal Amendment to Offering Statement, using Form C-U, as soon as possible after learning of the change.

What If You Made a Mistake in Your Offering Documents?

Despite your best efforts to get everything right when filing your initial offering documents, you may find out later that something in the offering documents is wrong when you or a member of your management team discovers the error or when someone responding to your offering on the funding portal points it out to you.

When it comes to offering document mistakes, there are three levels of concern.

Insignificant Deviations

Under Regulation Crowdfunding, "insignificant deviations" do not affect a crowdfunded offering's exemption under Title III. In order for a mistake to qualify as an insignificant deviation, an issuer must show that:

- The failure to comply with a term, condition, or requirement of Regulation Crowdfunding was "insignificant with respect to the offering as a whole"

- The issuer made a reasonable and good faith effort to comply with all terms, conditions, and requirements of Regulation Crowdfunding

- The issuer did not know of the failure to comply, where the failure to comply with a term, condition, or requirement was the result of the failure of the funding portal to comply with the requirements of Regulation

Crowdfunding, or such failure by the funding portal occurred solely in offerings other than the issuer's offering

The SEC acknowledges that whether a deviation from the requirements would be "significant to the offering as a whole" will depend on the facts and circumstances of the offering and the deviation.

Given the serious penalties that could attach to a mistake in crowdfunded offering documents (including loss of the Title III exemption, liability to investors in a class-action lawsuit, action by state and federal regulators, and possibly personal liability for the offending company's founders and management team members), an issuer should never assume that a mistake is an insignificant deviation from the Regulation Crowdfunding rules. If the issuer can correct the mistake in time, it should.

Material Mistakes

A material mistake—any error that could potentially mislead an investor into making the wrong investment decision—should be corrected as soon as possible on the funding portal, and an announcement should be made on the portal's communications channels. If the mistake affected the issuer's Form C disclosures, a formal Amendment to Offering Statement, using Form C-U, should also be filed on EDGAR.

When a material change to an issuer's offering documents is announced, the following actions must take place:

- The funding portal must send notice to committed investors that their investments will be canceled unless reconfirmed within five business days.

- Investments that are not reconfirmed by their investors must be canceled.

- Upon canceling an investor's investment, the portal must send notice of cancellation to the investor, together with the reason for cancellation and a statement of the investor's refund amount.

- If the material change occurs within five business days of the offering's scheduled closing date, the offering period must be extended for five business days to give investors sufficient time to reconfirm their investments.

Serious Mistakes

If the mistake is so serious as to render the offering documents meaningless, seriously misleading, or in material violation of Regulation Crowdfunding, the issuer will need to consult with the funding portal and decide if the offering should be withdrawn. Regulation Crowdfunding permits the issuer to withdraw an offering at any time and for any reason prior to the scheduled offering date. The issuer cannot, however, accept any money from investors (even if the offering has reached the minimum offering amount), and the portal must return all investor funds to investors.

Either the issuer or the portal would file Form C-TR on EDGAR announcing the withdrawal of the offering. It is also advised that the issuer and portal agree on a statement to be made to investors explaining the reason for the offering's withdrawal so the issuer is not precluded from making a subsequent crowdfunded offering with improved and compliant offering documents.

Closing Your Offering Early, or Quitting While You're Ahead

Regulation Crowdfunding allows issuers to terminate their offerings before the scheduled closing date and take whatever money has been invested up to that point, as long as:

- At least twenty-one days have elapsed since the offering commenced

- Investors are given five business days' notice of the new closing date

- Investors are allowed to cancel their investments up to forty-eight hours prior to the new closing date

- The issuer notifies investors whether or not it will continue to accept investments during the final forty-eight hours

- At the time of the new deadline, the issuer has exceeded its target offering amount or minimum offering amount

Filing Progress Reports with the SEC: Form C-U

While an offering is pending, issuers (or the portals acting on their behalf) must file the following documents on EDGAR:

- Any changes to the Form C Disclosures on Form C-A

- A progress update on Form C-U within five business days after reaching 50 percent of the target offering amount

- Another progress update within five business days after reaching 100 percent of the target offering amount

- A final Form C-U to disclose the total amount of securities sold in the offering and the total amount of investment, among other things

Issuers may rely on a funding portal to make publicly available on the offering platform frequent updates about the issuer's progress toward meeting the target offering amount, but an issuer relying on the portal's progress reports must still file a Form C-U at the end of the offering to disclose the total amount of securities sold in the offering.

CHAPTER 7

After Your Successful Crowdfunded Offering Is Completed

If your offering fails to reach its target amount (or the minimum offering amount you specified in your offering documents) by the scheduled closing date, the ball game's over. The funding portal takes down your listing, those who invested in your offering get their money back, and you and your management team go back to square one.

If your offering reaches its target amount within the specified offering period, congratulations! I predict you and your cofounders will be enjoying a very wild (and well deserved) celebration indeed. Just make sure you don't use any of your investors' money to fund the party (they really, really don't like that).

And don't celebrate for too long. You and your management team have lots more work to do.

Getting Your Money from the Funding Portal

While an offering is pending, Regulation Crowdfunding requires a funding portal to direct investors to transmit funds to a "qualified third party" (usually a bank, brokerage firm, or other financial institution) that has agreed in writing to hold the funds for the benefit of, and to promptly transmit or return the funds to, whoever the funding portal directs.

Upon completion of a crowdfunded offering, the funding portal is required to direct the qualified third party to transmit funds to the issuer on the later of the following dates:

- The date on which the total invested funds exceeds the target offering amount (or the minimum offering amount described in the issuer's Form C disclosures) and the five-business-day cancellation period has elapsed for all investors

- Twenty-one days after the offering commenced

The funding portal is also required to deliver:

- To each investor: a confirmation of her transaction at the time her funds are released to the issuer

- To the issuer: a list of the names, addresses, and other contact information for each investor who participated in the offering, along with the number of securities purchased by that investor and the total amount of his investment

Issuing Your Securities to Investors

Now you and your management team have work to do. Because funding portals under Regulation Crowdfunding are prohibited from handling securities or money, you will have to deliver your securities to each investor in your crowdfunded offering or provide some other evidence of their interest in your company.

Debt securities such as promissory notes almost always exist in physical form. You should have a separate note for each investor and send the original note to each investor, keeping only photocopies for your company records.

Equity securities are different. Under the corporation laws of virtually every state, securities can be either "certificated" or "uncertificated."

Certificated Securities

Certificated means that the investor receives an actual certificate—a piece of paper made from dead trees—as evidence of his or her shares in your company.

Under the corporation laws of virtually all states, a corporation must have stock certificates for each class of its capital stock (common and preferred) that state on their faces:

- The name of the issuing corporation and that it is organized under the law of the state of X

- The name of the person to whom the certificate was issued

- The number and class of shares the certificate represents

In addition, the designations, relative rights, preferences, and limitations applicable to the class of stock represented by the certificate must be summarized on the front or back of each certificate. Alternatively, each certificate may state conspicuously on its front or back that the corporation will furnish the shareholder this information on request in writing and without charge.

When you incorporated your company, your lawyer probably sent you a corporate minute book—a three-ring binder with room for your corporate resolutions and other important corporate papers. That minute book had a section called "Certificates" with preprinted certificates for you to fill in when you issue them to somebody.

I have formed literally hundreds of corporations in my career, and I can tell you two things about those certificates:

1. There aren't nearly enough of them to accommodate a crowdfunded offering of securities.

2. The information required to be placed on the front and back of each certificate with the designations, relative rights, preferences, and limitations of the class of stock represented by the certificate isn't there.

You and your management team will have to type that information on each certificate—every bleeding one—by hand. If you run out of certificates, or didn't have enough in the first place, you will have to order more. This process will take at least a week to two weeks, so be sure to order the extra certificates before you begin your crowdfunded offering.

LLCs are not required to have certificated membership certificates, although the LLC laws in virtually every state permit LLCs to issue them. The information required in a membership certificate is basically the same as that in the corporation statute, with one or two minor exceptions that your attorney can explain to you.

I always recommend that my LLC clients issue membership certificates to their investors: they look nice, investors feel they got something for their money, and if your company crashes and burns, they might have some residual value as collectibles on eBay.

Uncertificated Securities

Uncertificated means there is no physical security—the number of shares is recorded on the issuer's books and records and exists only as an electronic data entry.

The corporation laws of most states require corporations to send holders of uncertificated shares a written statement of the information required on stock certificates for certificated shares. While it is tempting to treat all crowdfunded securities as uncertificated and just send the required statement by email (or even less personally, to rely on the confirmation statement from the funding portal as containing the required information), I'm in favor of issuing actual certificates to your investors, for the reasons stated above.

Complying with State Blue-Sky Laws

Title III of the JOBS Act expressly preempts state securities laws requiring registration or filing of documents in connection with crowdfunded offerings. That does not mean, however, that your company is off the hook when complying with these laws.

Title III does not restrict the states' ability to take enforcement action with respect to fraud or deceit by issuers or funding portals. Especially for smaller offerings of $100,000 or less, which will certainly be deemed too small for the SEC to care about, it is more likely than not that your company will be sued by a state regulator if it commits fraud or otherwise makes material misstatements in Title III crowdfunded offering documents.

States are also allowed under Title III to impose fees for Title III crowdfunded offerings if (1) the issuer is located in that state and/or (2) more than half of the participating investors in the offering reside or have a place of business in the state. You will need to check with your lawyer to see if any state rules require you to pay a fee, especially if both your company and most of your crowdfunded investors are located in the same state.

Creating a Stock Transfer Ledger

There is one other section of your corporate minute book you need to look at: the "Stock Transfer Record" or "Stock Transfer Ledger," which usually appears at the end of the book.

As anyone who has ever written or self-published a newsletter can tell you, the hardest part of the job is keeping track of your mailing list.

It's the same with investors: you need to keep track of every outstanding share in your company at all times. If you ever decide to solicit large investments from venture capitalists or accredited investors under Title II or Regulation D, launch a mezzanine offering with institutional investors, or (from my lips to God's ears) decide to make an initial public offering of your shares, your underwriters or venture capital investors will want to see this information on demand.

This means keeping track of the name, address, telephone number, and email address of each investor and updating that information every time the investor:

- Changes her address or email address

- Adds a cell phone or other telephone number as a secondary number

- Dies, so that his shares are transferred to someone else (hopefully just one) as part of probating his will

- Sells her shares to someone else after the one-year holding period required by Regulation Crowdfunding

- Gets divorced, so that some of his shares are transferred to his ex-spouse by court order

- Files for bankruptcy, so that her shares are transferred to a creditor by court order

- Updates his will and transfers the shares to a trust benefiting his descendants in perpetuity (called a dynasty trust; this is becoming an increasingly popular tool in estate planning)

- Has any other change that may prevent you from getting hold of her when you really need to do so

Traditionally, companies kept track of this information in the "Stock Transfer Record" at the end of their corporate minute book. Today, an Excel spreadsheet is probably a more efficient way to keep track of this information, or, for email communications especially, an account with Constant Contact or another website that facilitates email newsletters.

If you do use a spreadsheet, I recommend that you print it out periodically, make two copies, put the original in your corporate minute book, and send the copies to your accountant and your lawyer. This is information you absolutely, positively cannot afford to lose.

I always advise that companies maintain their own shareholder lists. If this is a task you really don't feel comfortable doing yourself, I'm sure some funding portals will offer this as an additional service to their issuers—for a hefty fee, of course.

Updating Your Capitalization Table

The last thing you should do before you start spending your crowdfunded cash is update your capitalization table (cap table), a chart that shows:

- Each class of your company's securities

- The number of issued and outstanding shares of each class

- The number of options and warrants you have granted to people to acquire shares of each class in the future

- The percentage ownership of each class

- A brief summary of the principal terms and conditions of each class of securities

If you don't already have a cap table for your company, now is the time to create one, as this will be one of the first things venture capitalists and other professional investors will ask for when considering your company for a follow-up offering.

Here is an example of what a cap table looks like (the example is from an offering of nonvoting Class B membership interests in an LLC, but it can be easily adapted to a corporation or other legal entity):

_____, LLC

OFFERING PROCEEDS AND CAPITALIZATION TABLE

OFFERING PROCEEDS		
	Minimum Offering	Offering Amount
Gross offering proceeds	$_____	$_____
Less: Legal and closing costs*	($_____)	($_____)
Net Proceeds	$_____	$_____

*Management's estimate of offering legal and advisory costs.

The offering price is $_____ per Class B Common membership unit (the "Original Purchase Price") for an aggregate of_____ Class B Common membership units

CAPITALIZATION TABLE		
	Minimum Offering	Offering Amount
Class A Voting Units held by Founder A	_____	_____
Class A Voting Units held by Founder B	_____	_____

	Minimum Offering	Offering Amount
Class B Nonvoting Preferred Units issued [date]	_____	_____
Class B Nonvoting Common Units issued [date]	_____	_____
Total all class units outstanding	_____	_____
Class B Nonvoting Common Units offered [date]	_____	_____
Total all issued and outstanding units (all classes)	_____	_____
Options/warrants outstanding for Class B Voting Common Units	_____	_____
Total units outstanding (all classes on a fully diluted basis)	_____	_____

_____, LLC ("the Company") is a Limited Liability Company formed in the State of _____ on [date of formation] and was subsequently capitalized with _____ Class A Voting Membership Units owned 50% each by Founder A and Founder B.

On _____, 20 ___, the Company issued _____Class B Nonvoting Preferred Units to a relative of Founder A. On _____, 20___ the Company issued _____ Class B Nonvoting Preferred Units to friends and family of Founder A and Founder B. Class B Nonvoting Preferred Units are an investment in capital only which collectively earn a preferred distribution equal to ___% of the Company's cash flow available for distribution, paid quarterly. Class B Nonvoting Preferred Units can also be converted into Class B Common Equity Units or redeemed for the original investment at the choice of the investor. Holders of Class B Nonvoting Preferred Units are not entitled to a share of the losses or profits of the Company but are an investment in capital (distributions of the Company's available cash flow) only.

On _____, 20___the company issued warrants to acquire ___Class B Common Equity Units to Mr. _____, the Company's Chief Technology Officer. The warrants have a ___-year life and are subject to terms as more fully described in the warrant agreement. The warrants were issued in connection with Mr._____'s role as Chief Technology Officer. Mr. _____ is party to a ___-year noncompetition, nondisclosure, and confidentiality agreement, on file and the Company's headquarters.

Filing Your Annual Reports and Holding Your Annual Shareholders Meeting

Your company will be required to file an annual report with the SEC on Form C-AR (basically an update of the information submitted on your initial Form C) within 120 days after the end of your company's fiscal year. You will also be required to post a copy of each annual report on your company website. Failure to file the annual report on time will, among other things, disqualify your company from future offerings under Regulation Crowdfunding, which requires that any ongoing annual report that was due during the two years immediately preceding the currently contemplated offering must be filed before an issuer can make an offering under Regulation Crowdfunding.

Your company will be required to file the annual report until the earliest of the following events occurs:

- Your company is required to file periodic reports under the Securities and Exchange Act of 1934.

- Your company has filed at least one annual report and has fewer than three hundred holders of record.

- Your company has filed at least three annual reports and has total assets that do not exceed $10 million.

- Your company or another party purchases or repurchases all the securities issued pursuant to Regulation Crowdfunding, including any payment in full of debt securities or any complete redemption of redeemable securities.

- Your company liquidates or dissolves in accordance with state law.

Virtually every state corporation law requires companies to hold an annual meeting of shareholders and special meetings of shareholders to approve particular matters. For most start-up companies, these are relatively informal affairs, which may take the form of conference calls or casual meetings over lunch.

No more.

If your crowdfunded investors have voting rights (not recommended), you will have to involve them in these meetings. Depending on your state's corporation laws, you will be required to give notice of each meeting to all your investors at least ten days prior to the meeting date and confirm that they received the notice. You must also allow your investors to be physically present during the meeting, either in person or by telephone conference call (in a handful of extremely forward-thinking states, meetings can take place via webinar or other electronic means).

Even if your crowdfunded investors do not have voting rights (highly recommended), you may be required by your state corporation law to give them advance notice of shareholder meetings if particular items are on the agenda (such as mergers, acquisitions, or amendments of your company's charter documents affecting their rights as shareholders). You may also be prohibited from dealing with your nonvoting shareholders in a harsh and oppressive manner in some states. Talk to your attorney to learn more about your state's specific rules for dealing with nonvoting shareholders.

Making Sure Your Company Doesn't Get Too Big

Generally, a company that has more than two thousand total investors or more than five hundred investors who are not accredited investors is required to register its securities and file periodic reports with the SEC under the Securities and Exchange Act of 1934, just like a public company is required to do. Regulation Crowdfunding exempts a crowdfunded issuer from this requirement as long as it:

- Files its annual reports promptly and on time

- Has $25 million in total assets or less

- Appoints an SEC-registered transfer agent for its securities

An issuer that exceeds these thresholds will be granted a two-year transition period before it will be required to start filing periodic reports under the 1934 act, provided it timely files all its ongoing reports pursuant to Regulation Crowdfunding during the two-year period.

Part 3

COMMUNICATING WITH YOUR CROWD

CHAPTER 8

Keeping Your Crowd Under Control

Once your crowdfunding offering is complete, you have dozens, if not hundreds, of new business partners. Yes, you read that correctly. I said partners—not shareholders, not investors, not LLC members.

The reason is simple: the people who invest in your company are, for all legal and practical purposes, partners. They may not have the right to vote on management decisions (denying them this right is recommended—see Chapter 4), but they have the right to speak, they have the right to be heard (or at least tolerated in a professional manner), they have the right to complain, and they have the right to file a class-action lawsuit or launch a takeover of the company if they are really, really unhappy with the way things are going.

In some states (listed in Appendix 5), disgruntled investors also have the right to petition state courts to dissolve and liquidate your company if they feel things aren't going anywhere fast.

Coping with Your New Partners

When you have investors, you have responsibilities. Today's crowd can easily turn into an unruly mob tomorrow, as anyone who's ever been flamed on social media knows only too well. Communications with your new investors is critical to avoiding misunderstandings, rumormongering, and outright revolt in your crowdfunded community.

Even if your investor community is quiet and complacent, keep in mind that Regulation Crowdfunding requires them to hold your shares only for a period of one year (see Chapter 10). You don't want a mass exodus of investors at the end of that year; word of that gets around quickly and will tarnish your company's reputation in a hurry.

Developing a Shareholder Communication Program

Now is the time—as soon as the investors' money hits your company bank account—to develop a program of communicating regularly with your shareholders.

Communicate Regularly and Often. When it comes to investors, silence is not golden. The less often your investors hear from you, the more nervous they become. Frequent and regular communication with your investors will prevent or solve 90 percent of the problems you will ever have with these folks.

Your company should do three things right away:

1. Open an account with Constant Contact or another email communications service and create a list with the email addresses of all your investors, founders, management team members, advisers, and principal customers.

2. Select one of your employees (preferably one who writes well) to create a monthly email newsletter that, after review and approval by the company founders, you will send to everyone on the email list.

3. Create a separate email address where investors can send their comments, suggestions, and other communications, and have one of your key employees check that address at least twice a day (including weekends—many investors are "part timers" who will send messages only on weekends).

Your Company E-Newsletter. What should you say in each e-newsletter? Basically, each newsletter should be a progress report dedicated to answering the investor question, "How's it going?" At the very least, send copies of all updates to your Form C disclosures to every one of your investors via email as soon as the updates have been filed on EDGAR.

When you receive favorable media attention, forward copies to all your investors with a short cover note.

In your e-newsletter, "accentuate the positive," reporting everything good that happens to you company, but do not "eliminate the negative"; when you have suffered a reversal of fortune, notify your investors immediately and let them know your plans for turning things around. It is not good for your investors to find out bad stuff about your company before you tell them about it. While some investors will still grumble about the bad news, most will forgive you because they will perceive that you are still on top of your game.

Here is the most important rule regarding e-newsletters: Say something, even if you have nothing to say.

It will come as no surprise to you that most people don't read e-newsletters. How many of the dozens of e-newsletters cluttering your inbox do you actually open and read top to bottom? Probably very few. Most of the time, you just skim the heading and maybe the first couple of sentences.

A friend of mine—a very successful author and consultant—sends out an e-newsletter once a week to hundreds of subscribers, including your humble author. One day a few months ago, I was scanning my inbox and deleting all the junk mail (including, I'm sad to say, this person's e-newsletter most of the time) when I saw his latest one, with the word "crowdfunding" in the heading. At that time I had just begun writing this book and was hungry for any information about what was then a virgin topic. So, for the first time in I can't tell you how many months, I actually opened his e-newsletter and started reading it.

The first three paragraphs were terrific and actually helped me organize one of the chapters of this book. After the first three paragraphs, which were below the fold on my computer screen, the text suddenly changed into a bunch of gibberish that looked to be written in Latin.

I emailed the author and told him there was something wrong with his e-newsletter feed. About an hour later, he called me on my cell phone. Here is what he told me:

"Good to hear from you, Cliff. Listen, I just got your email about my newsletter. Thanks for your comment, but I'm afraid I have a dirty little secret. I put that pseudo-Latin gibberish in all my e-newsletters after the first couple of paragraphs. In my experience, people read only the first couple of sentences in any newsletter, but they feel cheated if the message is too short. So rather than write a long-winded essay that no one will read, I just spend my time each week crafting the two paragraphs and then plug in the gibberish. Would you believe that in the years I've been doing that e-newsletter, you are the first person to bring this to my attention?"

Do you understand why this guy called me on the phone rather than send me an email?

Now, I'm not recommending that any reader plug gibberish into an email delivered to investors. It's just an illustration of how to write one: spend most of your time on the first couple of paragraphs, and spend less and less time on the information that follows. Don't spend so much time making each newsletter so perfect that you fail to get it out regularly to your community.

One of the advantages of having a crowd of investors is that you have access to their knowledge, experience, and personal networks. Don't hesitate to ask for advice or feedback when sending your e-newsletters. That makes your investors feel that they are part of the team and that you want to know their opinions (even if you don't). You may also find, to your pleasant surprise, that there's someone in your crowd who can really help your company get to the next level. You will want to know about such people and develop special relationships with them. Just make sure they aren't after your job.

Don't forget to post a link to each e-newsletter on your company website(s) and all your social media pages. After all, that's how you found these people in the first place, and where you are likely to find more.

Also, don't forget to give readers the opportunity to opt out of the e-newsletter submissions as required by federal and state antispam laws.

Responding to Your Investors. The person charged with reading emails sent to your investor hotline (the special email address you created just for the investors) should be trained to respond quickly—and briefly—to each email you receive from an investor.

Most email inquiries will deal with fairly routine matters. Don't be surprised if some messages ask about job opportunities at your company, with an attached resume from a relative of the investor who just graduated from Nowhere U. with a degree in Victorian English literature. While you would almost certainly ignore such an email from a member of the general public, you are not always free to do so if it's from an investor.

If an investor email surfaces a problem, however, that must be dealt with immediately. Your investor-relations employee (that's what they call them in big companies) needs to be told to report such messages to you and the other company founders immediately so a prompt response can be prepared and sent to all investors.

Dealing with Time Vampires, Mata Haris, and Know-It-Alls

It happens to all start-up and early-stage companies: one or two of your investors are emailing you every day asking silly questions, volunteering useless information, and otherwise making a royal pain of themselves and taking up valuable management time.

We have a special name for such people in our industry: time vampires.

Most time vampires are relatively harmless. They probably just don't have enough to do or want to feel like they're part of your management team even though they legally aren't. The best way to deal with such people is to give them a task or project to work on, especially one involving lots of research time that will get the investor out of your hair for a while. Who knows? The research may actually prove useful.

A more dangerous type of time vampire is the person who thinks he or she knows more about how to run the company than you do. Most of the time these people just have outsize egos that will be satisfied with a little stroking. But there are two more dangerous types of know-it-all investor:

1. Someone who has a relationship with one of your competitors and has infiltrated your company through crowdfunding to get intelligence that he passes on to your enemy (years ago these were called Mata Hari investors, named for a famous World War I spy)

2. Someone who really does know more about your industry and your marketplace than you do and has the credentials to prove it; if such an expert investor becomes too disgruntled with your company's performance, she could easily turn into an instigator who will launch and lead an investor revolt

If you suspect someone in your crowd is a Mata Hari investor, there are three basic strategies you can consider:

1. Limit the amount of sensitive, inside information you send investors as part of your regular communications.

2. Do research on the investor and, if you uncover his relationship with a competitor, out him to the community at large (just be sure you are 100 percent accurate, otherwise you will be staring down a libel lawsuit from a very hostile investor indeed).

3. Contact the investor discreetly, point out the evidence, and offer to repurchase her shares for the same price your investors paid in your crowdfunded offering (if you do this, be sure the investor agrees in writing to remain silent about your repurchase and to refrain from disparaging your company in any future communications).

When dealing with a know-it-all investor, it's best to remember the famous quote from the film *The Godfather, Part II*: "Keep your friends close, but your enemies closer." You will need to embrace the know-it-all, suck up to his ego, and make sure he has only positive things to say about your company: if properly managed, a know-it-all can become a convincing and influential champion of your company within the investor crowd.

When You Have to Change Your Business Plan

If you have put together your crowdfunded offering documents the right way (see Chapters 4 and 5), you have included the following statement in several places where it could be clearly seen by investors:

"Our business plan is based upon our assessment of market opportunities as they exist today; management reserves the right to change our plan, and possibly pursue a different direction for our company, due to changes we perceive in the marketplace, advances in technology, the legal or regulatory environment, the competitive picture, or any other factor affecting the company, its products, and services."

It's always difficult for companies to change direction, especially when it becomes necessary to turn a luxury liner around in a bathtub, but it becomes much more difficult when a company has lots of investors sitting in the Class C cabins wondering what's going on.

More sophisticated and experienced investors will understand the need to make changes, but some less experienced or naïve investors may feel you have committed a bait-and-switch crime with their money.

As in all dealings with investors, communication is key to a successful change in plans. There are three key steps:

1. Issue a special e-newsletter to your investors announcing the change in plans and the reasons for the change, and invite them to participate in a free webinar to discuss the proposed change.

2. Prepare a PowerPoint slide deck and use it to host an online webinar where investors are encouraged to comment and ask questions about the proposed change (consider doing more than one if attendance at the first webinar is low).

3. File a Form C-U (progress update) with the SEC regarding the change.

If the proposed change is extremely unpopular, to the point that you and your cofounders fear an investor revolt, you should consider offering to buy back your investors' shares on a limited-time-only, first-come-first-served basis, for the same price they paid for their shares plus a small amount of interest (basically what they would have earned on a bank certificate of deposit during the same time period). You will need to find the money to pay for their shares, and will need to involve your attorney and accountant, as corporate repurchases of shares are subject to state corporation laws and may have unpleasant federal income tax consequences for your company and the investors.

Do not even think about launching a Title III crowdfunding offering of securities to raise money to repurchase shares from investors in your previous Title III crowd-funded offering! Although I confess there would be a certain admirable chutzpah in doing so, I have to believe there is at least some limit to people's stupidity, such that your offering would be laughed off the funding portal.

When It's Time to Throw in the Towel

You have completed a successful Title III crowdfunded offering. You raised a ton of money. You spent it all trying to launch your business plan. And the business went nowhere. A follow-up offering of securities won't help. The idea was a bad one, or wasn't right for the times. Your company is dead: dead as a doornail (with apologies to Charles Dickens). You have dozens or hundreds of investors waiting for a return on their investments, and now you have to break the news that your company is worthless, your investors will have to write off their investments, and you are going back to school to learn a profitable trade.

You have a big, big problem.

There is no easy way to get out of this one. Investors in any company love to sue when things go wrong. They will not only sue your company, but they will try to pierce the corporate veil (a lovely image—it derives from the death of Polonius in Shakespeare's *Hamlet*) and sue you and your cofounders personally as well. They may even sue your lawyers, your accountants, your funding portal, and anyone else involved in your offering in an effort to prove they knew about undisclosed weaknesses in your business plan and didn't warn investors about them (what lawyers call securities fraud). It is not inconceivable that an entire class of plaintiffs' lawyers will spring up to help crowdfunded investors bring class-action lawsuits to recover their money, or at least achieve lucrative settlements.

Frankly, if Title III crowdfunding goes nowhere and fails to become a popular means of raising capital for small companies, it will be for this reason: company founders and their professional advisers not wanting to take the risk of a class-action lawsuit by disgruntled investors.

Still, most start-up companies fail in the first few years of operations, and you did warn your investors up front, in capital letters, that, "INVESTMENT IN SECURITIES OF THIS TYPE IS HIGHLY RISKY, AND THERE IS A CHANCE YOU COULD LOSE YOUR ENTIRE INVESTMENT." You did say that in your offering documents, right? If you didn't, you have not only violated Regulation Crowdfunding but set yourself up for a whole world of hurt.

Of course, if you still have your investors' money, you can always get out of trouble by announcing your company's failure, publicly taking responsibility, apologizing for the failure, and giving your investors' their money back. They won't be happy, but they aren't likely to sue over a small or inconsequential monetary loss.

In the real world, of course, you won't realize your company has failed until after your investors' money has all been spent. Here is what you need to do, with the understanding that no amount of explanation, groveling, or falling on your sword will prevent righteously angry investors from seeking redress in a court of law.

First, prepare an email announcement of your company's failure and send it to all of your investors. The announcement should contain the following information:

- The date on which your company will cease business

- An explanation, in reasonable detail, of the reasons behind your company's failure

- A statement, in plain English, that while you "regret" having to break this bad news to investors, the circumstances behind your company's failure were not known or "reasonably foreseeable" by you or your management team at the time of your Title III crowdfunded offering

- A statement that you have explored alternative means of staying in business but have found no viable way to continue your operations

- A detailed accounting of how your investors' money was spent, down to the very last penny (the investors will need to see that you did not use any of their investment money to pay personal expenses or bills that were unrelated to the company's business plan; ideally, if you can, you should also say that none of the investors' money was used for salaries or other management compensation to the company founders)

- A statement that investors will be entitled to share in any proceeds of your company's liquidation and the sale of your company's assets, if anything is left after payment of the company's debt (remember that debt always has to be paid off in full before you and your fellow shareholders get anything; if you have shares of preferred stock outstanding, those will have to be paid off in full as well)

- A statement that investors should "consult with their tax advisers" to determine if any portion of their investment can be deducted for federal income tax purposes as "worthless investments"

Can Your Investors Write Off Your Company Failure on Their Taxes? After reading that last bullet point, some of you are probably thinking, "Hey, wait a minute—you mean my investors can write off their investments in my company on their taxes? Whew—you had me worried there for a minute. Why didn't you tell me before that I can walk away from my company and not get sued by angry investors who will be only too happy to have tax deductions?"

Not so fast.

Whenever the IRS allows you to write off something on your taxes, there's always a heap of conditions.

In order for your investors to write off their investments as total losses, the shares they purchased may have to qualify as Section 1244 stock. Section 1244 of the Internal Revenue Code allows losses from the sale of shares of small, domestic corporations (sadly, LLC membership interests do not qualify for Section 1244 treatment) to be deducted as ordinary losses instead of as capital losses up to a maximum of $50,000 for individual tax returns or $100,000 for joint returns.

To qualify for Section 1244 treatment, the corporation, the stock, and the shareholders must meet certain requirements. The corporation's aggregate capital must not have exceeded $1 million when the stock was issued, and the corporation must not derive more than 50 percent of its income from passive investments. The shareholder must have paid for the stock and not received it as compensation, and only individual shareholders who purchase the stock directly from the company qualify for the special tax treatment. This is a simplified overview of section 1244 rules; because the rules are complex, companies looking to hedge their bets against failure in a crowdfunded offering are advised to consult a tax professional for assistance.

Even if your shares do not qualify for Section 1244 treatment, investors may be able to deduct their losses under Section 165 of the Internal Revenue Code, but their deductions will be capital losses, which in general are not as valuable as the ordinary losses they would receive had your shares qualified for Section 1244 treatment.

Once you have released your announcement and have dealt with the inevitable barrage of shareholder emails, it is time to consult with your attorney and wind down your company. You will need to follow the procedures in your state corporation or LLC statute for dissolving your company, winding up its affairs, selling its assets, paying off your company debts, and distributing the balance to your shareholders. You will also need to file Form C-TR on EDGAR, terminating your obligation to continue filing periodic reports with the SEC.

When the Revolution Has Begun

You wake up one bright, shiny morning, open your front door to get your newspaper, and there on your front lawn are a crowd of people waving pitchforks and torches, preparing vats of tar and feathers, and tying a hangman's noose around the branch of your favorite oak tree.

It's your crowd, and they are not happy.

Shareholder revolts rarely happen out of the blue, and you will rarely be surprised by them. When investors are unhappy, they let you know in no uncertain terms well before they consider taking legal or other action against you and your cofounders. The best time to deal with an investor revolt is well before it happens, by proper communication using the methods described in this chapter.

There are two types of shareholder revolt. In the first, they post negative comments and reviews about your company, its products, services, and management on social media and elsewhere. A member of your management team (the same person who is responsible for investor relations) should be monitoring Yelp.com and other review-oriented websites for mentions of your company (you should be doing this anyway, using tools such as Google Alerts to inform you of online posting of any kind affecting your company). The minute you see a negative or critical posting from one of your crowdfunded investors, someone on your management team should immediately contact that investor and do everything possible to set matters right.

If you sense that a handful of investors have launched a smear campaign against your company online, it may be best to deal with them as a group: invite them to a conference call or other online meeting to discuss their grievances and see if there's a way to resolve them without dramatically changing the direction of the company.

In extreme cases, you may have to amend your charter documents (the articles of incorporation if you are a corporation, the operating agreement if you are an LLC) to give your crowdfunded class of investors the right to appoint one or more members to your company's board of directors (board of managers for LLCs). By doing so you ensure that they will have a seat at the table with the right to oversee, comment on, and otherwise influence your management decisions. That may calm your crowd down, but there are disadvantages:

- Because your company now has an outside director, you will have to call formal directors' meetings complying with your state corporation or LLC laws.

- Your outside directors may insist that you purchase insurance covering them against any liability they may incur by acting as directors.

- Venture capitalists and other professional investors who may invest in your company in future years will want to appoint directors of their own and may not want to share the table with directors they perceive as less experienced in that role.

The second type of investor revolt involves legal action, which may take two forms: a class-action lawsuit or a proxy fight.

In a class-action lawsuit, your investors would pool their resources to hire an attorney to sue your company. Investors would be invited to participate in the class, and those participating in the class would share in any settlement. The class-action lawsuit would take one of two forms: a direct action (shareholders sue for violation of their rights as shareholders) or a derivative action (shareholders sue third parties on behalf of the corporation based on your management team's failure to take appropriate action in the corporation's best interests).

In a proxy fight, your investors would pick several of their members to run for office as directors of your corporation and present their dissident slate to compete with your management team for approval at your company's next annual meeting of shareholders (discussed in Chapter 7). If a majority of your company's shareholders approve the dissident slate offered by your crowd, then you and your cofounders have been voted out of office and will have to quit the company you founded (although you would continue to hold your shares in a company that's now being run by your adversaries). Of course, if you and your management team hold the majority of the corporation's shares (highly recommended), then there will be little chance of a proxy fight. If you and your cofounders have given up so much of your company that you own less than 50 percent of your company's shares, then all bets are off, as a mere handful of investors with small holdings of securities may be the swing votes that determine the future course of your company.

If it appears your shareholders are getting ready to take legal action of any kind against your company, you may have no choice but to file for bankruptcy under the federal Bankruptcy Code. By doing so, you will freeze any legal action your shareholders may be contemplating against your company and give yourself the opportunity to work out differences with your shareholders under the supervision of a bankruptcy court, in the hopes of gaining a favorable settlement that will allow you to emerge from bankruptcy.

Bankruptcy proceedings are extremely expensive and time consuming and will probably kill off any hope your company may have of generating investment in the future, as bankruptcy proceedings would have to be disclosed in any future offering of securities.

CHAPTER 9

Going Back for Seconds:
Launching Multiple Crowdfunded Offerings

Raising money for your company through crowdfunding techniques is a little bit like getting hooked on drugs, alcohol, or other addictive substances: if your experience is a good one overall, you probably won't be able to wait until the next hit.

Generally, as I've hinted throughout this book, the fewer investors your company has, the better and easier it will be to keep them happy and on board for the long haul. Managing a crowd of hundreds or thousands of investors is easy for large public companies with the staff and budget to have an investor-relations department wholly devoted to the task. It is far more difficult for a start-up company that needs to devote 100 percent of its management time to developing the products and services that will ensure the company's success, with as few distractions as possible.

While Title III crowdfunded offerings may be an excellent way (heck, perhaps the only way) for start-ups and concept companies to raise the capital necessary to start down the entrepreneurial path, your long-term goal in managing finances should be to raise money from fewer and fewer, and better and more sophisticated investors as you grow your business.

Can You Launch Other Offerings at the Same Time as Your Crowdfunded Offering?

Generally, yes. Title III does not prohibit you from having concurrent (simultaneous) offerings of your company's securities. Regulation Crowdfunding specifically states that Title III offerings are not to be "integrated" with other offerings for purposes of determining the limitations on those other offerings. So, for example, if you are raising money from accredited investors in an offering under SEC Rule 506(b), which prohibits general solicitation and advertising, the fact that you are using general solicitation methods in your Title III crowdfunding will not "taint" your Rule 506(b) offering as long as you don't make any general solicitation of the latter offering (for example, by inadvertently mentioning it in an email to your Title III investors in one of your funding portal's chat rooms). But—and it's a big but—an issuer conducting a concurrent exempt offering for which general solicitation is not permitted will need to be satisfied that purchasers in that offering were not solicited by means of the offering made in reliance on Regulation Crowdfunding. For example, the issuer may have had a preexisting substantive relationship with such purchasers. Otherwise, the solicitation conducted in connection with the crowdfunding offering may preclude reliance on Rule 506(b).

The amount your company can raise under Regulation Crowdfunding in any 12-month period is limited to $1 million. So, if your company raises $800,000 in an offering that closes on June 30, it will have to wait until July 1 of the following year if it wants to raise more than $200,000 under Regulation Crowdfunding. Similarly, if an affiliate of your company (defined as an entity "under common control with" the issuer) or a predecessor of the affiliate, has raised capital under Regulation Crowdfunding during the preceding 12 months, that offering will limit the amount your company can raise under Regulation Crowdfunding until the 12-month period has expired.

Although the SEC allows concurrent offerings of securities under different exemptions, it may be difficult as a practical matter to keep each offering within its particular "silo" of regulations. Your funding portal and advisors will need to keep a watchful eye on the progress of each offering to make sure they don't "cross paths" in such a way as to lose their specific exemptions.

Keep in mind, though, when launching private offerings of securities outside the JOBS Act, that the old restrictions on those offerings remain in effect. So, for example:

- When making an offering under SEC Rule 506(b), you cannot use general solicitation or general advertising to promote the offering and cannot have more than thirty-five investors who are not accredited investors.

- When making an offering under SEC Rule 504, you cannot use general solicitation or general advertising to promote the offering and cannot raise more than $1 million from private offerings (other than Title III crowdfunded offerings) during a twelve-month rolling period.

- You may be required to file your offering documents with state securities regulators under state blue-sky laws that haven't been specifically preempted by the JOBS Act.

The "Upstairs-Downstairs" Offering

A (potentially) very effective way for start-up technology companies to raise money under the JOBS Act may be a two-tiered offering structure that I call an "upstairs-downstairs" offering (with apologies to the much-loved British television series of that name, which had much higher ratings than our *MoneyHunt* show).

An upstairs-downstairs offering would be a simultaneous launch of two offerings:

- An offering of preferred stock (or LLC membership interests with preferred distributions) or convertible debt securities to accredited investors only under Title II of the JOBS Act and new SEC Rule 506(c)

- A Title III crowdfunded offering of nonvoting common stock (or nonvoting LLC membership interests without preferred distributions) for friends, families, customers, employees, advisers, mentors, and others whose contributions to the company deserve to be rewarded but who do not qualify as accredited investors under the federal securities laws

An upstairs-downstairs offering allows a company's founders to reward their friends, families, and other supporters in a way that doesn't jeopardize their ability to raise money from sophisticated venture capital players. Generally, venture capitalists, angel investors, and other accredited investors do not like to rub elbows with people they feel (rightly or wrongly) do not belong in the room. They want the right to get their money out first if the company crashes and burns, and they want significant influence, input, and control over the way the company is managed. In contrast, most Title III investors are looking only to share in some small way in your company's (and your) success. While some may have dreams of getting rich, few people will expect to play a significant role in your company for only a $100 or $1,000 investment (the few who do are the ones you have to watch out for, as discussed in Chapter 8).

By denying voting rights to Title III investors and giving your Rule 506(c) investors preferred shares, you have given the players what they want without really taking anything away from your Title III investors.

Another way to do an Upstairs-Downstairs offering, although one that will be possible only for larger companies, would be to combine a "mini-IPO" offering under Tier II of the new Regulation A-Plus (adopted under Title IV of the JOBS Act) with an offering under Regulation Crowdfunding.

Can You Launch Another Crowdfunded Offering Right After You Complete Your First One?

Regulation Crowdfunding expressly permits follow-up offerings of crowdfunded securities up to a maximum of $1 million over a rolling twelve-month period. Whether you should do so, of course, is a different matter.

It is axiomatic that success breeds success. A successful Title III offering may make it easier for your company to launch a second, third, or fourth offering because if you do things properly, your pool of potential investors increases geometrically with each offering (your investors tell their friends, who tell their friends, and so forth). If there has been a significant growth in your company's social media profile since the first Title III offering, it may be particularly worthwhile to launch a follow-up offering, as you will be making essentially the same pitch to a new group of people.

But that success may come with a price: the more crowdfunded offerings you launch that are successful, the bigger the number of investors you have to manage on an ongoing basis. Keeping track of a couple of dozen investors is much, much easier than managing hundreds or thousands of them. Also, the more crowdfunded investors you bring on board, the more difficult it will be to raise capital from more sophisticated accredited investors, who won't like sharing the table with lots of small investors, any one of whom could potentially wreak havoc by going rogue and posting negative information about your company online.

Before you launch a following Title III crowdfunded offering, it might be a good idea to poll your existing investors to see how they feel about the idea. Some may see your decision as an admission that your management team goofed with the first offering by not asking for enough money. More important, investors are always nervous about being diluted by subsequent offerings that reduce the percentage of a company's total shares they own (discussed in Chapter 4). They will want to know that the subsequent offering will be at a higher price per share than they paid so that they will have a smaller piece of a much larger and more valuable pie. If they see their piece of the pie shrinking without an increase in the value of the company, they won't like that, and you want to manage their adversity before you launch the follow-up offering.

Some Things to Consider When Launching a Follow-Up Offering

Here are a few things to consider when launching a follow-up offering:

- You will have to prepare entirely new Form C disclosures and supplemental materials for the following offering; these may be updated versions of your previous offering documents but will have to be filed separately with the SEC and the funding portal.

- You will have to justify the new offering by claiming new financial needs in the "use of proceeds" section of your Form C disclosures.

- You will have to disclose the prior offering and its success in your Form C disclosures.

- If you have not filed your Regulation Crowdfunding annual report (Form C-AR) on EDGAR on time, you may be barred from a following offering until that filing has been made and you have otherwise caught up with all required filings.

- Your funding portal will undoubtedly charge additional fees for hosting your following offering (although these are likely to be lower than they were in the previous offering because you and your portal have a better idea of what to expect).

Part 4

CONSIDERATIONS FOR INVESTING IN A CROWDFUNDED OFFERING OR SETTING UP A FUNDING PORTAL

CHAPTER 10

Should You Invest in a Crowdfunded Offering?

This is primarily a book for start-up or early-stage companies looking to raise capital via crowdfunding and for the people who advise them. It is not primarily a book for investors. Indeed, an entire book could be written on investing in crowdfunded securities, and someday, no doubt, will be written (probably very soon).

Nonetheless, people who run early-stage companies frequently invest in other early-stage companies or act as advisers or mentors to them. Also, if you are thinking about investing in a crowdfunded company, you probably already have some sort of relationship, personal or business, with the people who are reading the rest of this book and want to know what they are getting into.

The rules that govern crowdfunded offerings—Title III of the JOBS Act and Regulation Crowdfunding—have a lot to say about issuers and funding portals but hardly anything to say about investors, including who can or cannot invest in crowdfunded offerings. So I decided to put together what little information there is for investors into a single chapter.

Just keep three things in mind:

1. This is not a primer for investing in companies generally. There are plenty of books out there about general investing principles, and you should read at least two of them before you consider making any sort of investment in securities.

2. I am assuming that you have identified a crowdfunded company you want to invest in (or have received an offering announcement from someone you know on social media) and want to know how to go about doing it. There are so many factors in deciding which companies to invest in and which to avoid that they really deserve a book of their own.

3. The information in this chapter is just that—information—and should not be construed as investment advice of any kind.

Why Are You Investing in a Crowdfunded Company?

The vast majority of start-up companies in the United States fail within a few years of being formed. Why would anyone want to invest in such risky ventures?

Basically, there are two reasons for investing in a crowdfunded company. Either:

1. You know the company founders personally or through social media.

2. You are a high-risk investor (also known as a gambler), you think you have uncovered the next Facebook, and you want to get in on the ground floor before everyone else knows about it.

If you are in the first category—you know the company founders (or are related to them), you like them, you care about them, and you want to see them succeed—then you won't really care about much of the information in this chapter. You are making this investment out of affection, not for a return on your investment. You really do not care if you lose your entire investment; it's the thought that counts (although if the company tanks and you lose a lot of money, you may be thinking a bit differently about the founders afterward). You should not apologize to anyone for feeling this way about your investment: motives such as these have fueled much of traditional project and gift crowdfunding (discussed in Chapter 2).

If you are in the second category (the get-rich quick investor), you are exactly the person the SEC and Congress were worried about when they passed the crowdfunding regulations. The federal government cares about you, you see, and it doesn't want you doing anything crazy and losing all your money. The crowdfunding regulations are designed 100 percent with you in mind. You should feel honored.

It doesn't really matter which type of crowdfunding investor you are, as long as you know which type you are and are prepared to act accordingly.

Can You Legally Invest in a Title III Crowdfunded Offering?

While Regulation Crowdfunding contains detailed rules about who can and cannot issue crowdfunded securities, there are hardly any rules about who can and cannot be an investor. Generally, anyone who is twenty-one or older and has a pulse can invest in crowdfunded securities.

You do not even have to be a citizen or resident of the United States. While foreign companies cannot issue crowdfunded securities in the United States, they are free to invest in them, as are foreign individuals. The only exception would be an offering of securities in a subchapter S corporation; shareholders of those tax-advantaged corporate entities must be either U.S. citizens or green card holders. For that reason, as discussed in Chapter 4, it is highly unlikely subchapter S corporations will engage in crowdfunded offerings under Regulation Crowdfunding.

Even some people who don't have a pulse can be crowdfunded investors. If you wish to invest in a crowdfunded offering through your IRA, SEP-IRA, or other retirement plan, Regulation Crowdfunding does not stop you (although there may be issues about whether an investment in crowdfunded securities is a legal investment for your plan or constitutes a prohibited transaction under federal pension laws; you will need to speak to your investment adviser about that before making a crowdfunded investment that way).

Similarly, corporations, trusts, and other legal entities are not legally prohibited from investing in crowdfunded offerings (although if they buy too many shares they may turn the issuer into a holding company that cannot legally issue crowdfunded securities; this is an issue you will need to discuss with the funding portal before making a specific investment).

In short, anyone of legal age can invest legally in crowdfunded securities. The only legal restriction is that you can't buy too many of them. That restriction is discussed in Calculating Your Investment Limit Under Title III.

Are You an Accredited Investor?

The concept of an accredited investor under the federal securities laws was briefly defined in Chapter 1. Here is a bit more detail; Rule 501 of the SEC's Regulation D, adopted in the early 1980s, defined accredited investors as:

- Certain institutional investors such as banks, employee benefit plans, venture capital firms, and the like

- Insiders such as directors, executive officers, or general partners of the issuing company

- Wealthy individuals—people who have a net worth or joint net worth with a spouse in excess of $1 million or who had an individual income in excess of $200,000 or a joint income with a spouse in excess of $300,000 in each of the last two years and anticipated in the current year

- Entities—all of whose beneficial owners meet the above three criteria of accredited investors

In determining whether you have sufficient net worth to be an accredited investor, you exclude the value of your principal residence. In determining whether you have sufficient annual income to be an accredited investor, you can include your spouse's income.

The concept of accredited investor has no meaning for crowdfunded offerings of securities. You do not have to be an accredited investor to buy securities under Title III of the JOBS Act.

The concept is much more important, however, if you are thinking about making an investment in a private placement under the SEC's Rule 506(c), created by Title II of the JOBS Act (and discussed at length in Chapter 13), which by definition is limited to only accredited investors.

To see if you have what it takes to be an accredited investor, fill out the sample investor questionnaire in Appendix 10 and see where you come out. If you are close to the line, you should consider speaking to your tax adviser or a lawyer familiar with securities law, either of whom can help you refine the calculation of your net worth and annual income for the requisite time periods and decide one way or the other if you qualify.

What Is Your Tolerance for Risk?

Investing in crowdfunded securities is not for the faint of heart. Every investment portfolio should contain three types of securities:

1. *Income-only securities.* These may not be too exciting, but they provide regular income with a minimum of risk (think bank certificates of deposit and money market funds).

2. *Growth-and-income securities.* These give you both income and the opportunity for growth with a moderate amount of risk (stock in publicly traded companies, for example).

3. *Aggressive-growth securities.* These give you little current income and are highly risky. When they hit, they tend to hit big, but when they crash and burn, you lose your entire investment.

Make no mistake: any sort of crowdfunded investment is in the aggressive-growth category.

Let me put it a different way: when you buy securities in a crowdfunded offering, you are rolling the dice in Vegas. Despite your best due diligence before buying the security, you have absolutely no clue how things are likely to turn out. You are trusting 100 percent that the company founders know what they are doing and that their business plan is a solid one.

There are countless reasons small companies do not survive. Among some of the situations I have personally encountered in my practice were:

- The company's founder died in an auto accident.

- The company failed to secure the necessary patents for its invention.

- Key members of the management team left the company (sometimes to a competitor).

- A large competitor entered the field and wiped out all smaller companies.

- The market for the company's products and services wasn't as robust as the company founders thought.

- The company founder chucked it all and went to law school.

- (Ahem) an investor stole the company's idea and launched his own company with better funding.

Issuers of crowdfunded securities are required to post a notice on all their offering documents saying, "THESE SECURITIES HAVE A HIGH DEGREE OF RISK, AND YOU MAY LOSE YOUR ENTIRE INVESTMENT IN THESE SECURITIES." The offering documents will contain pages and pages of risk factors, describing everything that could possibly go wrong with the crowdfunded company and cause you to lose your entire investment.

They aren't kidding—they really, really mean it when they issue these warnings. You should not—*not*—invest in a crowdfunded company unless you are psychologically prepared to lose your entire investment if the company crashes and burns, as start-up companies frequently do.

Calculating Your Investment Limit Under Title III

Regulation Crowdfunding allows you to purchase securities in crowdfunded offerings up to certain limits. Generally:

- If your annual income or net worth (whichever is greater) is less than $100,000, you can invest up to 5 percent of your annual income or net worth (whichever is greater) in crowdfunded securities during a rolling twelve-month period up to a maximum of $5,000 (5 percent of $100,000).

- If your annual income or net worth (whichever is greater) is $100,000 or more, or if you are an accredited investor (as defined earlier in this chapter), you can invest up to 10 percent of your annual income or net worth (whichever is lesser) in crowdfunded securities during a rolling twelve-month period up to a maximum of $100,000 (10 percent of $1 million).

Table 1 illustrates a few examples:

TABLE 1. EXAMPLES OF INVESTMENT LIMITS UNDER TITLE III			
Investor Annual Income	Investor Net Worth	Calculation	Investment Limit
$30,000	$105,000	Greater of $2,000 or 5% of $30,000 ($1,500)	$2,000
$150,000	$80,000	Greater of $2,000 or 5% of $80,000 ($4,000)	$4,000
$150,000	$100,000	10% of $100,000 ($10,000)	$10,000
$200,000	$900,000	10% of $200,000 ($20,000)	$20,000
$1,200,000	$2,000,000	10% of $1,200,000 ($120,000), subject to $100,000 cap	$100,000

As with the accredited investor determination, your net worth excludes the value of your principal residence, and your annual income includes your spouse's income.

The investment limits are the SEC's way of determining a safe amount investors can put at risk by investing in crowdfunded securities. How it determined that someone with an annual income of $30,000 can afford to spend $2,000 a year on extremely risky securities is beyond my comprehension, but that's the way it is.

Can You Lie About Being Legally Able to Invest?

Title III of the JOBS Act and Regulation Crowdfunding impose hefty penalties on issuers and funding portals that run afoul of the rules, but, interestingly, they say nothing about investors who engage in bad behavior.

THE CROWDFUNDING HANDBOOK

Here's a question: as an investor, can you lie when submitting information to a funding portal before investing in a crowdfunded offering?

Let's say you have reached your investment limit for the year but a really, really terrific investment crosses your email inbox. You know the industry, you've read something about the company, the founders are all ex-Google employees, and all necessary patents have been secured. How can this possibly go wrong?

You contact the funding portal that is handling the offering, send it all your personal financial information it requests (more on that below), and answer most of its questions straightforwardly, but when it asks if you have exceeded your investment limit under Regulation Crowdfunding, you answer no.

Now, this is not a good thing you did (and I am not encouraging you to do anything of the sort), but unless the portal has information to the contrary (for example, all of your prior crowdfunded investments were handled by the same portal), there isn't really a practical way for it to find out—at least right away (if the portal is looking at your tax returns and bank statements over a long period of time, sooner or later your investment activity will be transparent to it).

What happens?

Under Regulation Crowdfunding, your lie would not void the company's crowdfunded offering. Issuers under Regulation Crowdfunding can rely on a funding portal's determination that you were a qualified investor for a crowdfunded offering. The bigger questions are:

- How much diligence does the portal have to do to determine you are not lying?

- What remedies and recourse does the portal have if it finds out you lied to it?

This, in my humble opinion, is probably the biggest loophole in Regulation Crowdfunding. While funding portals will almost certainly ban from future offerings any investor they discover has lied to them, I'm not sure the portals will have the practical ability to sue those investors in court. How would they calculate damages in such a case, since the crowdfunded offering went ahead as planned and may have been wildly successful, despite the investor's lie?

Participating in a Crowdfunded Offering

Since I haven't been able to dissuade you from investing in crowdfunded offerings in the last few pages (and hopefully have not encouraged you to lie about your investment limits when dealing with crowdfunding portals), here are the steps you need to take to make your investment the right way:

Opening Accounts with Funding Portals

Although you will be able to view information regarding crowdfunded offerings on a funding portal without having to register or otherwise log in to the portal's website, you cannot participate in a crowdfunded offering, or communicate with the issuer through the portal's communications channels, unless you have opened an investor account with the funding portal that is handling the offering. If you are planning to buy crowdfunded securities on more than one funding portal, you will have to open an account at each portal.

Although the SEC does not specify the exact information the funding portal must obtain from an investor, it is expected that opening an account will include at least providing the portal with basic identifying information, such as the investor's full name, email address, and physical mailing address.

Also, as part of the process, you would consent to the electronic delivery of materials. Besides email, electronic delivery may include such methods as posting material on the funding portal's website. A funding portal could comply with its obligation to provide materials to investors simply by posting materials on the website and would not be required to send any messages directly to investors.

You will also be asked to disclose whether you are engaging in promotional activities on behalf of the issuer, whether you are receiving compensation from anyone if you are engaging in those activities, and the amount of such compensation. Likewise, the portal must disclose to you how it is being compensated for handling the issuer's offering.

You may also be required to disclose any relationship you have or have had with the company, its founders, and its promoters.

Reviewing the Portal's Educational Materials

Funding portals are required by Title III of the JOBS Act to provide disclosures and investor educational materials at the time you open your account. These materials must be in plain English and include information about:

- The process for investing on the funding portal

- The risks associated with crowdfunded offerings of securities

- The types of securities that may be offered on the funding portal and the risks associated with each, including dilution

- Restrictions on resale of crowdfunded securities

- The type of information an issuer is required to deliver annually, including a statement that such information may cease to be provided in the future

- Investor limit amounts

- The circumstances in which an investor may cancel an investment commitment

- Limitations on the investor's right to cancel an investment commitment

- The need for an investor to consider whether crowdfunded securities are appropriate for him or her

- The possibility that at the end of the offering, there might not be any ongoing relationship between the issuer and the funding portal

Each time you express a desire to make an investment on the funding portal, it is required to send you these educational materials.

Satisfying the Portal's Investor Due Diligence

Regulation Crowdfunding requires not only that the funding portal provide you with educational materials but that it receive "positive affirmation" from you that you have reviewed and understood the materials, that you understand you can lose the entire amount of your investment, and that you are in a financial position to absorb that loss.

There is no required form for the positive affirmation document. Funding portals are permitted to create a process—whether a multiple-choice quiz, a yes/no or true/false question-and-answer document, or other format—that is suited to its particular business model and types of offerings as long as that process is reasonably designed to demonstrate your receipt and understanding of the information.

Each time you make an investment on a funding portal, you will be required to go through the positive affirmation process.

Now, here's where things get interesting.

The scope of a funding portal's obligation to verify that you are qualified to invest in crowdfunded offerings is not specified in Regulation Crowdfunding. The funding portal must have a "reasonable basis" for believing that you have not exceeded your investment limit across all funding portals on which you may be investing and is entitled to rely on your representations with respect to your annual income, your net worth, and the amount of other crowdfunded investments you may have made on other funding portals. As discussed, there is no specific penalty or liability for funding portals under Regulation Crowdfunding if an investor decides to submit a false written representation.

This means that funding portals will have a wide range of discretion as to how much information to request from you in support of your positive affirmation document.

In the absence of an express requirement on investors to perform due diligence, many funding portals unquestionably will choose not to do so, to avoid offending potential investors and ensure that they will build as large a database of investors as possible.

Some funding portals, however, may request that you show them copies of tax returns, brokerage or bank statements, or other information supporting your statements in the portal's positive affirmation document, especially if you are making an extremely large investment constituting a large percentage of your investment limit. In such a case, you will need information about the funding portal's privacy policy and what it is prepared to do to keep your sensitive financial information private and secure. You will also need to know whether, and how frequently, you will need to update the information it has on file as long as you maintain your account with the portal.

Communicating with Issuers and the Portal During the Offering Process

You will not be allowed to communicate directly with the issuer and its personnel while the crowdfunded offering is pending. All communications between you, the issuer, and its personnel (or with other investors) must be conducted on the communications channels provided by the funding portal, such as chat rooms, webinars, recoded conference calls, and the like.

Keep in mind that:

- The funding portal must permit public access to all discussions made in the communications channels.

- The funding portal must restrict posting of comments in the communications channels to those people who have opened an account with the funding portal.

- The funding portal must require that any person posting a comment in the communications channels clearly and prominently disclose with each posting whether he or she is a founder or an employee of the issuer or of someone engaging in promotional activities on behalf of the issuer, or is otherwise being compensated, whether in the past or prospectively, by anyone to promote the issuer's offering.

THE CROWDFUNDING HANDBOOK

There is no expectation of privacy here, so be careful what you say.

Funding portal personnel may not participate in these communications (unless they are registered as broker-dealers with the SEC), and the portal may establish guidelines for communications and for removing abusive or potentially fraudulent communications. For example, funding portals can decide whether their registered users must post under their real names or may do so under aliases (this is a difficult decision: requiring investors to use their real names might limit participation, but aliases could encourage inaccurate or abusive posts).

Making Your Investment

You can make your investment at any time while the offering is pending by sending notice to the funding portal and wiring or otherwise transmitting the amount of your investment to a separate bank account maintained by the funding portal for that particular offering with a bank or financial institution, where it stays until the close of the offering (when it is promptly transmitted to the issuer) or you cancel your investment (when it is promptly transmitted to you).

Funding portals are prohibited from handling funds or securities; they must direct your funds to the qualified bank that has agreed to hold the funds in escrow. Any funding portal that asks you to transfer the funds directly to it is a fraud and is operating in violation of Regulation Crowdfunding.

You cannot use a credit card to make an investment in a crowdfunded offering. While Regulation Crowdfunding does not expressly prohibit payment by credit card, federal banking regulations prohibiting the purchase of securities on credit, the complexities of credit card chargebacks, and the economics of credit card transactions have made the use of credit cards unworkable, at least for now.

As this book goes to print, investors may make their investments by bank wire transfer or debit card, from amounts on deposit in a PayPal account, or from PayPal accounts linked to bank accounts or debit cards (not credit cards).

In addition to sending money, you may also be required to sign some of the offering documents that appear on the portal. These may include:

- A subscription agreement (by which you agree formally to the terms and conditions of the offering)

- A signature page to the company's shareholders' agreement (for a corporation) or operating agreement (for an LLC) agreeing to be bound by the terms and conditions of that document, including (possibly) some restrictions on your ability to transfer shares to others without first giving the company a right of first refusal to repurchase them

- A confidentiality and nondisclosure agreement preventing you from discussing any inside information you may receive about the company, its products, services, and management

On receipt of your funds, the funding portal is required to promptly give you a written record confirming the dollar amount of the commitment, the price of the securities, the name of the issuer, and the date up to which you may cancel your investment commitment. It is not clear under Regulation Crowdfunding if the issuer will receive a copy of this information prior to the closing of the offering or if it will be permitted to thank you on the funding portal's communications channels for making your investment.

Withdrawing Your Investment Before the Scheduled Closing Date

You may withdraw your investment at any time, and for any reason, up to forty-eight hours before the offering closes. If the issuer chooses to close the offering early, as is permitted by Regulation Crowdfunding under certain circumstances once the minimum offering amount has been raised (see Chapter 6), you still have forty-eight hours before the revised closing date.

If the issuer makes a material change in the offering, you will be given notice of the change and five business days to reconfirm your investment by email to the funding portal. If you fail to reconfirm your investment within that five-day period, your investment will be deemed withdrawn, and you will get your money back promptly from the bank or financial institution acting as escrow agent.

When You Get Your Money Back Unexpectedly

You may receive your investment back from the funding portal unexpectedly because of certain conditions, including:

- The scheduled closing date has come and gone, and the issuer has failed to raise the target offering amount (or the minimum offering amount if there was one).

- The issuer made a material change to the offering, and you did not reconfirm your investment within five business days after receiving notice of the change.

- The issuer withdrew the offering because of a change in its business plan or because it discovered serious mistakes in its offering documents.

- The funding portal discovered false or misleading statements in the issuer's offering documents and pulled the plug on the offering.

In the latter two scenarios, you should receive some sort of explanation, either from the issuer or the funding portal.

Bringing in Other Investors

During the offering process, the issuer will encourage you (possibly ad nauseam) to forward its offering announcement to your friends and social media contacts and encourage them to view the issuer's offering materials on the funding portal. The issuer is looking to reach as many people as possible, and one of the benefits of a crowd-funded offering is the ability to tap into not only the issuer's own social networks but those of its early investors as well.

You are certainly free to do so if you wish (although if you truly believe you have uncovered the next Facebook, why would you shout about it to the entire world?).

There is only one important rule: you cannot accept any form of compensation or finder's fee from the issuer or from the people you bring in. If you do, the entire offering may be disqualified under the JOBS Act, and any compensation you receive from third parties will need to be disclosed publicly on the funding portal.

Selling Your Crowdfunded Securities

Under the JOBS Act, you must hold on to your crowdfunded securities for one year. Prior to that time, you can sell your securities only to:

- The issuer (that is, it repurchases its shares)

- An accredited investor

- As part of the company's IPO with the SEC

- A member of your family (your child, stepchild, grandchild, parent, step-parent, grandparent, spouse or spousal equivalent, sibling, mother-in-law, father-in-law, son-in-law, daughter-in-law, brother-in-law, or sister-in-law, including adoptive relationships) or to a trust, for bona fide estate-planning purposes

- Your ex-spouse as part of a divorce decree or separation agreement

The one-year resale restriction applies to any purchaser during the year beginning when the securities were first issued, not just the initial purchaser, so if you acquired the securities from another investor during the one-year period, you are required (among other things) to have a "reasonable belief" that any subsequent purchaser during the one-year period is an accredited investor.

At the end of the one-year holding period, you may sell your crowdfunded securities to anyone you like, without restriction, under Regulation Crowdfunding. There are only two small problems:

- There may not be a market for such securities, meaning you will have to negotiate the terms of sale one-on-one with your purchaser, providing all of the company's current information available online and on EDGAR.

- State securities laws may prohibit you from reselling the securities under certain circumstances (these aspects of state blue-sky laws were not pre-empted by the JOBS Act).

Generally, at least until some enterprising people create a new securities market expressly for crowdfunded securities (don't hold your breath, as it would take years to register a new stock market with the SEC, the National Association of Securities Dealers, and other regulators), your crowdfunded securities will be highly illiquid, and you must expect to hold on to them for the long term.

Getting Involved in Your Crowdfunded Company

One of the nice things about investing in a small company is that you are not just a number—you are family.

If you buy one hundred shares of stock in Microsoft Corporation, you don't get a telephone call from Bill Gates thanking you for your investment. When you invest in a small company, your investment counts. Not only do you get a telephone call from the company's CEO thanking you for your investment, you may get periodic calls for help in building the business. In some cases there may be too much communication with the issuer's management team.

As an investor, you are entitled to information about the company from time to time. You probably will receive monthly e-newsletters from the company highlighting its progress and quarterly emails with copies of the progress reports crowdfunded companies are required to file with the SEC every three months. When there's bad news, a reputable company will inform you about the problem before you read about it elsewhere.

You are also entitled to ask questions via email of the company's management from time to time and offer comments and suggestions if you think you have something to contribute. You should strive not to become a time vampire, however. If you find yourself sending emails to the crowdfunded company more than once or twice a month, that's probably too much. Remember that this investment is supposed to be "play money"—your retirement doesn't depend on the success or failure of this company. If you are losing sleep over your crowdfunded investment, you probably never should have made it in the first place. As Bob Dylan once sang, "It's all over now, baby blue."

If you have particular expertise in the company's market, business, or industry, or are well connected within that industry, don't be surprised if company management reaches out to you after you invest and offers you a more involved role in the company. If you are such a person, you may want to volunteer yourself as a mentor or adviser to the company—nothing in the JOBS Act or Regulation Crowdfunding prohibits you from doing so.

Most start-up companies have informal boards of advisers consisting of their mentors, professional advisers, and industry or marketplace players. The author himself serves on several advisory boards established by his law clients. There are four things you need to know about serving on advisory boards:

1. You will be required to participate in quarterly conference calls to discuss issues facing the company; to be an effective advisory board member, you will need to commit the time to be available for those calls.

2. You will not be paid for your services.

3. You are not a part of the company's management team, and any advice you give the company is completely nonbinding.

4. Advisory board members are customarily expected to assist management in its future fund-raising efforts.

The good news is that as a member of a company's advisory board you have no legal liability if the company is sued.

If you truly are a player, you may be invited to join the company's board of directors or become employed by the company in a senior management capacity. You will need to consult with your attorney before doing so. Officers and directors of a privately owned company are exposed to a lot of legal risk under state corporation statutes and federal securities laws. When such a company experiences trouble, shareholders frequently sue the company's officers and directors for fraud, breach of fiduciary duty, misappropriation of corporate funds, and other nasty things, whether or not there is any legal basis for the claim.

The good news is that most small companies will indemnify you and hold you harmless in the event you are sued because of your role as an officer or director of the company. The bad news is that if the company is broke, its indemnity will be worthless, and you will have to defend the lawsuit at your own expense.

Before joining the management team of a small company, you should ask if it provides its directors and officers with liability coverage known as D&O insurance. This is similar to the malpractice or "errors and omissions" coverage a doctor, lawyer, or other professional would maintain. If the company is unable to provide such coverage, do not join the management team unless you have deep enough pockets to defend yourself if the company is sued.

Note to issuers: you should consider using some of the proceeds of your crowdfunded offering to buy a D&O insurance policy. This will make it much easier for your company to attract industry leaders, experts, and other highly desirable players to serve as officers or outside directors of your company.

When Can You Write Off Your Worthless Investment in a Crowdfunded Company on Your Taxes?

If your investment in a crowdfunded offering turns out to be a total loss, you may—may—be able to write it off as a worthless investment. But, as always with tax deductions, there are rules and exceptions.

In order to write off an investment, there has to be a total loss. As long as the issuer is in business or is going through bankruptcy proceedings, there is always hope (however slim) that things may turn around. Until the company is 100 percent dead and gone, with no hope of resurrection (even as a zombie), you cannot write off any portion of your investment.

When you are finally able to write off your investment, you and your accountant will need to determine whether you can write it off as an ordinary loss or a capital loss.

In order to write off your investment as a total loss, the shares you purchased may have to qualify as Section 1244 stock. Section 1244 of the Internal Revenue Code allows losses from the sale of shares of small, domestic corporations (LLC membership interests do not qualify for Section 1244 treatment) to be deducted as ordinary losses instead of as capital losses up to a maximum of $50,000 for individual tax returns or $100,000 for joint returns.

To qualify for Section 1244 treatment, the corporation, the stock, and you must meet certain requirements. The corporation's aggregate capital must not have exceeded $1 million when the stock was issued, and the corporation must not derive more than 50 percent of its income from passive investments. You must have paid for the stock and not received it as compensation, and only individual shareholders who purchase the stock directly from the company qualify for the special tax treatment.

This is a simplified overview of section 1244 rules; because the rules are complex, investors in crowdfunded offerings are advised to consult a tax professional for assistance.

Even if your crowdfunded investment does not qualify for Section 1244 treatment, you may be able to deduct your loss under Section 165 of the Internal Revenue Code, but your deduction will be a capital loss, which in general is not as valuable as the ordinary loss you would receive had your investment qualified for Section 1244 treatment, because of the difference in tax rates between ordinary income and capital gains under the federal tax laws.

CHAPTER 11

Should You Set Up a Funding Portal?

Throughout this book we have looked at the role funding portals will play in the crowdfunding process and the responsibilities they have for ensuring that crowd-funded offerings of securities go smoothly and legally. In fact, both the JOBS Act and Regulation Crowdfunding put the burden squarely on funding portals to make sure the crowdfunding systems work—most of Regulation Crowdfunding's nearly seven hundred pages are devoted to rules and regulations governing funding portals.

A few enterprising readers may be thinking to themselves, "Hey, the money in crowdfunding is with the funding portals! I should be thinking about starting up a funding portal!" This chapter will discuss funding portals, the advantages and disadvantages of getting involved in the funding portal business, and the right way to set up a funding portal operation.

It May Be Too Late for the Early Money

As this book goes into print, about a dozen companies are positioning themselves to open funding portals under the JOBS Act. By the time you read this book, at least some of those portals will have registered with the SEC and FINRA and will have opened their doors for business.

In addition, the JOBS Act and Regulation Crowdfunding not only allow but appear to encourage investment banking firms, brokerage houses, and other registered broker-dealers to get into the funding portal game, and it may be expected that at least some of these firms will consider opening crowdfunding divisions in coming months. Any such firms would, of course, be extremely powerful competitors in an early-stage market because of their extensive experience in the securities industry and because of the huge amounts of capital they already have available for building a successful portal business.

It may therefore already be too late to get into the funding portal game in a big way and become a key player.

Picking a Crowdfunding Niche

There may, however, be opportunities to develop funding portals that focus on specific industries or verticals, specific types of companies, and specific types of offerings. Regulation Crowdfunding expressly permits such specialization as long as it is based on objective criteria that are designed to result in a broad selection of offerings, are applied consistently, and are clearly displayed on the portal website. Examples of such specialized portals are:

- Energy-related companies

- Start-up fast-food franchises

- LLC securities

- Issuers located in a particular state or region

- Offerings of less than $50,000

Focusing on a niche may well reduce the costs of setting up a funding portal and get you into the market more quickly than offering a broad range of crowdfunding services. In looking for the right niche, however, it is important to ask:

- Is the niche big enough to generate substantial revenue in the first few years of operations?

- Is the niche small enough to be unattractive to the large investment banks, brokerage firms, and early-stage portals that may come to dominate the industry?

- Do issuers in the particular niche have enough money to pay decent commissions and the add-on fees the portal will need to stay afloat?

- Are there enough investors interested in the niche to justify an exclusive portal?

• • •

Setting Up a Funding Portal

There are five basic steps in setting up a funding portal:

1. The founders must form a corporation for the funding portal (due to the high degree of liability imposed on funding portals, an LLC would not provide enough protection to the portal's shareholders).

2. The portal is then required to register with the SEC as either a funding portal or a broker, using the SEC's new Form Funding Portal (the text of which can be found at SEC Release No. 33-9974, www.sec.gov/rules/final/2015/33-9974.pdf, beginning on page 21).

3. The portal is then required to register with FINRA and pay a fee of $2,700 (the text of the FINRA application form is at www.finra.org/industry/rule-filings/sr-finra-2015-040).

4. The portal must obtain a $100,000 fidelity bond.

5. The portal must hire the staff necessary to provide all the services and perform all the obligations imposed on funding portals by Regulation Crowdfunding.

It will likely take at least a year, and possibly longer, to complete all these steps.

The cost of setting up a funding portal is likely to be prohibitive for many start-up companies. Operating a funding portal is also likely to be extremely labor intensive: reviewing offering documents from dozens or perhaps hundreds of issuers, furnishing them with advice on putting together their offerings, dealing with dozens or perhaps hundreds of investors, and keeping track of dozens of crowdfunded offerings at the same time, without making mistakes that could subject the portal to liability—performing these functions will require many, many warm bodies sitting at computer terminals.

Many funding portals are likely to try to minimize these costs by outsourcing their internal operations to a location in India or another country in the developing world—a highly ironic outcome, to say the least, for a statute designed to create jobs in the United States.

Before launching a portal, each of the its founding executives must understand that they cannot:

- Have a financial interest in any issuer

- Participate in offerings either as an issuer or investor

- Engage in any activity that might constitute a conflict of interest with an issuer, investor, or any other third party (for example, by referring the portal's business to another company in which the executive has a financial interest)

The Portal's Obligations to Vet Issuers

The JOBS Act and Regulation Crowdfunding impose somewhat inconsistent obligations on funding portals in their dealings with issuers.

When reviewing an issuer's offering documents, funding portals must have a "reasonable basis for believing" that the issuer (1) has met the disclosure and other requirements of Regulation Crowdfunding and (2) has the means to keep accurate records of investors once an offering is completed. Regulation Crowdfunding provides that funding portals may rely on representations to that effect by the issuer, absent any indication that the representation is not true.

On the other hand, Regulation Crowdfunding states that funding portals must be able to "adequately and effectively assess the risk of fraud from the issuer or its offering." Funding portals are also required to investigate whether any of an issuer's directors, officers, or other key executives have committed "bad acts" sufficient to disqualify the issuer's offering under Regulation Crowdfunding. If it cannot do so (for example, because an issuer's directors are foreign nationals whose country of origin does not allow for third parties to review criminal or regulatory enforcement background information), the funding portal must deny access to its platform.

If a funding portal becomes aware that any crowdfunded offering "presents the potential for fraud or otherwise raises concerns regarding investor protection," it must deny the issuer access to the portal. If a funding portal becomes aware that there is the potential for fraud after an offering has commenced, or that one or more of the issuer's principals is disqualified as a bad actor, it must cancel the offering and return any investors' money.

Can an issuer sue a funding portal if the portal mistakenly rejects its offering or denies it access to the portal? That is an interesting question, the answer to which will hinge on how the issuer would calculate damages for not having access to that particular portal.

Given these heavy obligations, to what extent must a funding portal conduct due diligence on issuers before accepting their offerings? Regulation Crowdfunding isn't clear, and each funding portal will need to determine how closely and aggressively to review offering documents.

While Regulation Crowdfunding allows a funding portal to rely on an "issuer representation" that all rules have been complied with, I don't think many portals will feel comfortable that their obligation to prevent fraud can be satisfied by having the issuer click "I agree" to accept terms and conditions that it has never read—and I strongly doubt that legal counsel representing a portal will sanction such an informal approach.

On the other hand, the need to generate a high volume of issuer offerings during the early years of a portal's operation may lead it to go easy on issuers in an effort to gain a competitive advantage.

The Portal's Obligations to Investors

As discussed in Chapter 10, funding portals are required to develop educational materials for each offering it handles and to deliver them to each investor who opens an account and expresses a desire to participate in a particular offering. It must also develop a means of confirming that the investor understands the information in the educational materials and agrees to play by the rules. This send-out-materials-and-obtain-confirmation procedure must be repeated each time an investor indicates an interest in a particular offering.

Funding portals are not, however, required to investigate or do background checks on investors to make sure they legally can participate in crowdfunded offerings. While a funding portal can check its records to see if the total amount of an investor's commitments exceeds her investment limit, there is no practical way for a portal to confirm if she has exceeded her limit by reason of investments with other portals. Accordingly, Regulation Crowdfunding provides that a funding portal may rely on an investor's representations concerning the investment limits that apply to the investor and the amount of the investor's investments in crowdfunded securities through other portals.

That said, funding portals will be best advised to make each investor focus hard and long on his other crowdfunded investments when completing the affirmation documents for each offering by asking as many focused, specific questions as possible and requiring the investor to respond to each one. That way, there will be little likelihood an investor can claim he wasn't sure what the portal was getting at if he is later found not to have been qualified to invest in a crowdfunded offering.

Can a funding portal bar access to an investor who is found to have lied in his statements to the portal? Perhaps. If the investor is a heavy hitter who participates in lots of offerings and has an otherwise decent track record, I have a suspicion most funding portals will find a way to deal with the problem discreetly.

What is clear from Regulation Crowdfunding is that a funding portal may not reject an investor because it feels a particular investment isn't suitable for the investor.

Funding portals must provide to investors all information about an offering by one of three methods: via email, via a link to the portal's website, or via notice on the portal website as to where such information can be found. Investors must be allowed to save, store, or download the information.

When an investor commits to an offering, the founding portal must accept the investment on the issuer's behalf but must direct funds to the qualified bank that has agreed to hold them in escrow for that offering. Funding portals are expressly prohibited from holding investor funds or issuer securities. The portal must also ensure that an investor fills out and signs any and all subscription documents the issuer has required for the offering, and issue a "notice of investment commitment" to both the issuer and the investor. If an investor cancels an investment commitment up to forty-eight hours before the offering closes, the portal must refund the investor's money promptly.

When an offering closes, the portal must issue a confirmation statement to the investor detailing the amount of the investment, the number of securities purchased, and other information required by Regulation Crowdfunding.

The Portal's Obligations to the SEC

Funding portals are not required to file documents periodically with the SEC the way issuers are. Funding portals are, however, required to maintain extensive books and records, subject to examination by the SEC at any time. These records include:

- Records related to an investor who purchases or attempts to purchase securities through the portal

- Records related to issuers who offer and sell or attempt to offer and sell securities through the funding portal and the people who "control" such issuers (for example, people who own a majority of the issuer's shares, or an affiliated company that is owned by the same company that owns the issuer);

- Records of all communications occurring on or through the portal

- Records relating to promoters

- Records required to demonstrate compliance with Regulation Crowdfunding

- Notices provided by funding portals

- Written agreements entered into by the funding portal

- Daily, monthly, and quarterly summaries of transactions effected through the portal, including successful issuers, amounts distributed, and transaction volume (number of transactions, number of securities involved, total amounts raised by and distributed to issuers, and total dollar amounts raised across all issuers on the portal)

- A log reflecting the progress of each issuer toward achieving its target offering amounts

- The organizational documents of the funding portal

Funding portals are required to preserve all records for five years. During the first two years, records are required to be kept in an easily accessible place.

While the SEC does not require funding portals to register as broker-dealers, funding portals are not exempt from the compliance requirements that apply to registered brokers. These compliance requirements include the SEC's anti-money-laundering regulations, customer-privacy protections, and the provisions relating to examination and inspection of books and records and facilities by the SEC and FINRA.

The Portal's Obligations to Market and Grow Its Business

Funding portals are allowed to advertise their own existence, and (with some limitations) to pay third parties for referring issuers and investors to the portal. For example:

- A portal can pay a third party for referring potential investors to the portal so long as the third party does not provide the portal with any personally identifiable information about any of the potential investors (information that can be used to distinguish or trace an individual's identity), as long as the payment is not based on the number of investments made by those investors on the portal.

- A portal can enter into agreements with registered broker-dealers by which they can pay each other for services.

Funding portals cannot, however, charge issuers for special placement for their offerings on the portal, or for recommendations or endorsements of specific offerings. Funding portals also cannot solicit offers or sales to buy securities offered on the portal.

THE CROWDFUNDING HANDBOOK

The Portal's Obligations in Managing Offerings

A funding portal is a platform only, a "program or application accessible via the Internet or other similar electronic medium" as defined in Regulation Crowdfunding, designed to facilitate interactions between issuers and investors but without itself getting involved in the offering process. In many ways, funding portals are intended to be set up the same way as eBay is: buyers and sellers interact with each other without any intervention from eBay (except, of course, for the collection of fees from buyers and sellers).

Funding portals are obligated to ensure public access to all offering documents posted to the portal and to all communications taking place on the portal, including search functions to enable issuers and investors to find each other.

Funding portals are obligated to set up communications channels by which issuers and investors communicate with each other, such as chat rooms, discussion threads, webinars, and telephone conference calls. Funding portals may not, however, participate in any discussions other than to establish guidelines, to moderate, and to remove postings that violate the rules or their own communications guidelines.

What happens if the portal website goes down and issuers and investors cannot communicate for a period of time? Regulation Crowdfunding does not provide specific liability for such a situation, and presumably funding portals will do everything possible to limit their liability for such outages in their published terms and conditions.

A more significant question, however, is what happens if an offering closes during a portal outage, such that investors are prevented from making last-minute investments during the outage period? To avoid liability to the issuer in such a situation, I suspect most funding portals will develop a policy of automatically extending the offering period for the same amount of time that the portal site was down or five business days, whichever is longer. Such a policy would not be prohibited by Regulation Crowdfunding as long as the portal follows the rules for extending an offering (giving investors notice of the extended period and five business days within which to reconfirm their investments). Of course, issuers won't be too happy if investors fail to reconfirm their investments during the five-business-day period and the funding portal is required to give them back their money because of something that wasn't the issuer's fault.

During the offering period, funding portals are also obligated to:

- Maintain accounts with banks or other financial institutions to hold investors' money until an offering closes

- Accept investment commitments on behalf of issuers and ensure that investors fill out and sign all subscription documents required for the offering

- Release funds to the issuer when the offering closes (or the minimum offering amount has been reached)

- Deliver confirmations of investment to the issuer and each investor when the offering closes

The Portal's Liability for Mistakes

Issuers, including their directors and officers, are liable under the JOBS Act to investors for "untrue or materially misleading statements" in their offering documents. Funding portals, their directors and officers, and lower-level employees who are "involved in the offering" are also liable to investors for "untrue or materially misleading statements" in an issuer's offering documents, unless they or the issuer can prove they did not know, and in the exercise of reasonable care could not have known, of the untruth or omission.

The good news is that a funding portal's liability is limited to the amount paid by each investor affected by the mistake, plus interest. The bad news is that investors can sue the funding portal even after they have sold their investments. Funding portals are, however, permitted to exercise discretion in limiting the offerings and issuers they allow on their platforms, which may give them some ability to limit their liability to investors under Regulation Crowdfunding.

Funding portals will also have liability to the SEC for, among other things, failing to maintain all required books and records relating to the offerings it handles, and for a funding portal's own breach of the requirements of the JOBS Act and Regulation Crowdfunding (for example, by advertising a particular offering or highlighting one offering over another in violation of the rules). Funding portals that violate specific provisions of the JOBS Act and Regulation Crowdfunding will be subject to the same civil and criminal penalties as are imposed for violations of the Securities Exchange Act of 1934.

How a Funding Portal Makes Money

As this book is going into print prior to January 26, 2016 (the date funding portals are first allowed to register with the SEC), no funding portals have been approved by the SEC. It is therefore difficult to predict the revenue model most funding portals will adopt over time.

Funding portals are prohibited from taking a "carried interest" (a piece of the action) in the crowdfunded offerings they manage. But there is nothing in the JOBS Act

THE CROWDFUNDING HANDBOOK

or Regulation Crowdfunding preventing funding portals from charging issuers and investors a commission or other fee for their services at both ends of the transaction.

Accordingly, it may be anticipated that most early funding portals will charge issuers a flat fee or commission for handling their offerings, which may be tiered based on the amount of the offering, the timing of the offering, and/or the amount of offering documentation the funding portal will be expected to process for a particular issuer.

In addition, funding portals are almost certain to charge extra for such add-on services as helping issuers prepare their offering documents or managing their shareholder lists and capitalization tables after an offering is completed.

While funding portals are prohibited from endorsing or promoting specific offerings in their communications with the outside world, the rules are a bit fuzzy when it comes to allowing issuers to add bells and whistles to their online presence so as to stand out from other offerings on the portal. Regulation Crowdfunding allows funding portals to "highlight and display" offerings on the portal based on "objective criteria that would identify a large selection of issuers." Some of the objective criteria noted by the SEC are the type of securities being offered, the geographic location of the issuer, and the number or amount of investment commitments made. Funding portals are prohibited, however, from receiving special or additional compensation for identifying or highlighting an issuer or offering on the portal.

To the extent permitted by the rules, funding portals will almost certainly charge add-on fees for such bells and whistles as an issuer may request and are consistent with Regulation Crowdfunding, similar to the way eBay charges its sellers for using different colors, visuals, or graphics when listing items for sale on the site.

Given the high start-up and operating costs of running a funding portal business, the many responsibilities funding portals have under the JOBS Act, and the high degree of liability to which they are subject, portal fees may be expected to be quite high, at least during the early years of the portal's operations, in amounts comparable to what an investment bank or brokerage firm would charge for handling a similar offering.

Funding portals may also charge fees to investors, although at least initially most funding portals will probably keep these as low as possible in order to maximize investor interest and participation.

Using Crowdfunding to Raise Money for a Funding Portal

A start-up funding portal is an entrepreneurial company just like any other. As long as it meets the qualifications for crowdfunded issuers under the JOBS Act and Regulation Crowdfunding, there is nothing to legally prevent a funding portal from using crowdfunding techniques the same as any other issuer to raise start-up capital.

Of course, a funding portal using crowdfunding techniques will need to find another funding portal to manage its offering, and other funding portals will be unlikely to want to help you if they see your operation as a potential competitor. In soliciting crowdfunding assistance from a funding portal, you will need to convince its management that (1) you are operating in a specialized niche that poses no threat to them and (2) once you are up and running you will be in a position to refer business to it or otherwise assist it in developing its business plan.

As to how you will do that successfully, I haven't a clue. Good luck!

Part 5

BACKGROUND ESSENTIALS

Crowdfunding History, Law, and Regulations

CHAPTER 12

Federal Regulation of Private Offerings of Securities Prior to the JOBS Act

Prior to the twentieth century, offerings of securities in the United States were not regulated by government at any level. The prevailing laissez-faire philosophy of the time dictated that government should interfere with commercial activities only when absolutely necessary to protect the public interest. Investors were held strictly accountable for their own mistakes, negligence, and bad investment choices under the maxim of *caveat emptor*, or "buyer beware."

Early 1900s: The States Get the Ball Rolling with Blue-Sky Laws

That changed in the early twentieth century, largely as the result of several panics (today we call them recessions) in which many investors lost their shirts by putting money into thinly capitalized start-up companies launched by promoters who in many cases were little better than thieves.

During the Progressive Era of the early 1900s, a number of states, including New York, enacted securities laws designed to protect investors against these unscrupulous promoters. These were called blue-sky laws in a 1917 U.S. Supreme Court opinion, which described the purpose of these laws as preventing "speculative schemes that have no more basis than so many feet of 'blue sky.'"

Blue-sky laws vary from state to state but have traditionally focused on the registration of broker-dealers and securities offerings. With respect to the registration of private offerings, most states impose some sort of merit review (state regulators tear apart the offering documents, offer comments, and suggestions, and generally make a nuisance of themselves). States also typically have in place antifraud provisions that make actionable false statements made in connection with securities offerings. These antifraud provisions apply regardless of whether registration is required.

Absent an exemption, blue-sky statutes typically require registration in each state where the offering occurs. Registration, therefore, may be required in multiple states. Researching each individual law and completing the registration process can add delay and cost to an offering and discourage capital raising.

State blue-sky laws still play an important role in the regulation of private offerings. Under the U.S. Constitution, the states and the federal government have the concurrent power to regulate offerings of securities. That means the federal government and the states can pass laws affecting private offerings. Unless the federal government expressly preempts or prohibits the states from passing laws in a particular area, the states are free to pass laws of their own as long as they are at least as restrictive as federal law and do not allow behavior that is prohibited by federal law.

So, for example, if federal law says you can't have more than thirty-five nonaccredited investors in a private offering of securities, State X is free to pass a law saying, "Yes, but for this type of offering you can't have more than ten nonaccredited investors who are residents of this State without filing an offering statement with the State X Department of Securities." A number of states have such rules, and companies planning offerings of securities need to be aware of the limitations that apply in the states where their investors reside.

While Title III of the JOBS Act expressly prohibits (or preempts) states from passing laws to regulate Title III crowdfunded offerings, there is no such blanket preemption for Title II accredited investor offerings, which may still require notice filings in some states. Also, as discussed in Chapter 2, a number of states have amended their intrastate offering rules (for offerings of securities that take place entirely within state borders) to allow for limited crowdfunding of these offerings. Therefore, companies looking to make Title II crowdfunded offerings (offerings to accredited investors only) or intrastate offerings (offerings of securities that take place entirely within state borders) may still have to comply with blue-sky laws in the states where they are physically located or where their investors live.

1933: The Federal Government Wades into the Securities Markets

Fast-forward to the early 1930s, after the 1929 stock market crash, followed by the Great Depression, followed by President Franklin D. Roosevelt and his New Deal.

One of the most important pieces of New Deal legislation Congress passed during this period was the Securities Act of 1933, the first federal statute regulating the offerings of securities.

The Securities Act imposed rules for offerings of several types of securities: stocks, bonds, notes, debentures, certificates of interest, participations in profit-sharing agreements, preorganization certificates, preorganization subscriptions, voting trust certificates, and investment contracts. A piece of paper may be a security, even if not denominated as a share of stock or a note, if it is deemed to fit within one of a group of other less clear-cut categories such as "investment contract."

In a 1946 opinion, the U.S. Supreme Court defined a security, subject to regulation under the Securities Act, as "an investment of money in a common enterprise with the profits to come solely from the efforts of others."

The heart of the Securities Act is Section 5, which prohibits the offer of securities to anyone unless a "registration statement" (including a prospectus or business plan describing the securities and the company issuing them) is on file with and has been declared "effective" by the SEC. Section 5 also prohibits the delivery of the securities to a purchaser or investor unless accompanied or preceded by a prospectus that complies with the requirements of the Securities Act.

The Securities Act, like all securities laws, is basically a consumer protection law. The idea is that securities should not be sold to anyone unless the company issuing them educates the purchaser about the company, the business, the securities, and the risks involved in an investment. Failure to do so, or false or misleading statements in the offering documents, are severely punished under the Securities Act. The investor, of course, does not have to read all the documentation but must be given a reasonable opportunity to do so before the rule of *caveat emptor* kicks in and he is faulted for making a bad investment.

Section 5 basically says that if you want to make a public offering of securities in the United States, you must—*must*—go through the public offering process: you must prepare a registration statement and prospectus, file it, have it approved (or "declared effective") by the SEC, and deliver it to prospective investors. The size of the offering or the company issuing the securities do not matter. Under the Securities Act, every offering of securities is a "public" offering unless it is specifically exempted from the registration requirements of Section 5.

From the beginning, it was recognized that the requirements of Section 5 would be too onerous for many small companies making small or limited offerings of securities to people they knew well who could handle the risks of investing in an unproven, early-stage company. Thus the Securities Act contains several exemptions from the Section 5 registration requirement, two of which are especially important when dealing with crowdfunded offerings:

1. Section 3(b) of the Securities Act gives the SEC authority to exempt small offerings of securities (defined by the SEC as offerings that do not exceed

$1 million during a rolling twelve-month period, less other offerings by that same company during the same period).

2. Section 4(a)(2) of the Securities Act, which exempts from Section 5 "any transaction by an issuer not involving any public offering."

In determining whether an offering is nonpublic under Section 4(a)(2), the Supreme Court has looked at whether the class of people being offered the securities needs the protection of the Securities Act or otherwise is sophisticated and has access to the type of information that would be contained in a registration statement filed with the SEC.

Thus, for an offering of securities to be other than a public offering requiring compliance with the Securities Act's registration requirements, the offering must:

- Not be made "publicly" or in a public manner (for example, by a general solicitation or general advertising)

- Not be made "to the public" (that is, the crowd, the hoi polloi, aka "the great unwashed") indiscriminately but only to selected people who by virtue of their sophistication and wealth do not need the protection of the federal securities laws

In 1934, Congress passed the Securities and Exchange Act of 1934, containing rules for companies that have registered one or more public offerings with the SEC and have thereby become "public companies." Various sections of the 1934 act require public companies to file annual and quarterly financial reports with the SEC, regulate how public companies can be governed, describe illegal "market manipulation" activities, and contain detailed rules for broker-dealers and other players in the securities markets.

Section 12 of the 1934 act provided that even if a company had not registered a public offering with the SEC, it could become a public company subject to the act's requirements if it had more than five hundred shareholders or more than $10 million in total assets at the end of its last fiscal year. Title V of the JOBS Act (discussed in Chapter 13) raised those limits to two thousand shareholders, five hundred shareholders who are not accredited investors, and $25 million in total assets.

1964: The SEC Adopts Regulation A

Fast-forward to 1964, the era of Camelot, the rise of Madison Avenue, and colossal tail fins (on automobiles). In that year, the SEC issued Regulation A, consisting of thirteen rules that make up, in effect, a shortened form of registration for a securities offering.

Regulation A exempts from Section 5 of the Securities Act an offering of securities in an aggregate amount of $1,500,000 in any twelve-month period, reduced by the amount of any other securities that the issuer sold during that period under any other exemption.

Relatively few companies over the years have taken advantage of a Regulation A offering, but two aspects of Regulation A are still relevant for crowdfunded offerings:

1. Regulation A contains provisions disqualifying "bad" companies from using the regulation; these are basically companies whose owners, key executives, or promoters have been convicted of securities offenses, been subject to SEC disciplinary proceedings, or been involved in certain other types of proceedings (these are commonly referred to by securities professionals as "bad boy" provisions, sexist language notwithstanding).

2. Compliance with Regulation A requires the filing, generally in the regional SEC office where the issuer has its principal place of business, of a notification and an offering circular on SEC Form 1-A, which must be approved by the SEC prior to the offering.

Also, companies that are subject to the bad boy disqualification rules are not eligible to make crowdfunded offerings under Title III.

Title IV of the JOBS Act and SEC Release No. 33-9741, adopted March 25, 2015 (the text can be found online at www.sec.gov/rules/final/2015/33-9741.pdf), made numerous amendments to Regulation A designed to make it a more attractive option for early-stage companies than previously, with mixed results. Issuers interested in Regulation A should also consult the SEC's "Small Entity Compliance Guide" (available at www.sec.gov/info/smallbus/secg/regulation-a-amendments-secg.shtml).

1970: The SEC Adopts Rule 146 for Private Placements

Fast-forward to 1970: Richard Nixon, tie-dyed shirts, Vietnam, and "All you need is love." In that year, the SEC adopted Rule 146 in an attempt to create a "safe harbor" under Section 4(a)(2). Safe harbor means that if a company issuing securities complied with all of the rule's requirements, it was engaged in a "private placement" that did not have to be registered with the SEC under Section 5 of the Securities Act.

If a company substantially complies with the safe harbor rules in Rule 146 but fails to nail them 100 percent, it might still be exempt from registration under the Securities Act by virtue of the Section 4(a)(2) private placement exemption, but it might have to prove it in court if challenged by angry investors, the SEC, or state securities regulators. Securities lawyers refer to this as the "residual" Section 4(a)(2) exemption. Of course, whether a company has "substantially complied" with a rule is often a matter for the courts to decide, an expensive and time-consuming proposition for any early-stage company.

Rule 146 imposed a number of hoops for companies to jump through in order to qualify for the safe harbor, but three specifically are relevant to crowdfunded offerings:

1. The offering must be limited to thirty-five purchasers overall.

2. The offering must not be made by "general solicitation" or "general advertising."

3. The company must have "reasonable grounds to believe" prior to making an offer that (1) either the offeree or her investment representative has such knowledge and experience in financial and business matters that she is capable of using the information contained in the company's offering statement to evaluate the risks of the prospective investment and of making an informed investment decision, and (2) the offeree is a person who is able to bear the economic risks of investment.

In other words, for an offering to qualify as a private placement under Rule 146, it must be made discreetly to a limited number of people who are both sophisticated and rich—people who do not need the protection of the federal securities laws because they can fend for themselves.

1982: The SEC Adopts Regulation D, Adding More Exemptions

Fast-forward to the early 1980s: Ronald Reagan, Michael Jackson, Madonna, MTV, big hair for men, and bigger shoulder pads for women. After a decade of wrestling with the "sophistication" and "rich" definitions to determine which investors qualify as offerees under Rule 146, the SEC decided to throw the rule out and start from scratch. Also, there was a growing consensus in the securities industry and the SEC that exemptions from the Securities Act's registration requirement should be available for offerings under $1 million that don't deserve the federal government's time and attention (and/or which could be more easily regulated by state governments under their blue-sky laws).

What emerged was Regulation D, containing three separate exemptions from the registration requirements in Section 5 of the Securities Act: two (Rules 504 and 505) under Section 3(b) of the Securities Act dealing with small offerings, and one (Rule

506) under Section 4(a)(2) of the Securities Act dealing with private placements to accredited investors (and some others).

Rule 504 exempts an offering of securities not in excess of $1 million in any twelve-month period (less all other exempt offerings during that period by the same company).

Rule 505 exempts an offering of securities not in excess of $5 million in any twelve-month period (less all other exempt offerings during that period by the same company).

Rule 506 exempts the sale of an unlimited amount of the securities if the company issuing them reasonably believes the sale is being made to not more than thirty-five nonaccredited investors. Sales under Rule 506 may also be made to an unlimited number of people whom the issuer reasonably believes are accredited investors. In addition, the issuer must reasonably believe that each nonaccredited investor, alone or with a purchaser representative, has such knowledge and experience in financial and business matters as to be capable of evaluating the merits and risk of the investment (in other words, is a sophisticated investor).

Rule 501 of Regulation D defined "accredited investors" as:

- Certain institutional investors, such as banks, employee benefit plans, and venture capital firms

- Insiders, such as directors, executive officers, or general partners of the issuing company

- Wealthy individuals—people who have a net worth, or a joint net worth with a spouse, in excess of $1 million, or who had an individual income in excess of $200,000, or a joint income with a spouse in excess of $300,000, in each of the last two years and anticipated in the current year

- Entities—all of whose beneficial owners meet the above three criteria of "accredited investors"

Whether an offering of securities is made under Rule 504, 505, or 506, it must also meet a number of other conditions under Regulation D. For example:

- Rule 502(b) requires that specific information be made available to non-accredited investors in a Rule 505 or 506 offering (for offerings up to $2 million, the information required is the same as would be required by Part II of SEC Form 1-A), and copies of that information be given as well to all accredited investors in the offering.

- Rule 502(c) requires that a Regulation D offering be made with no "general solicitation" or "general advertising."

- Rule 502(d) requires the issuing company to make reasonable inquiry to determine if the purchaser is acquiring the securities for his or her own account, generally by requiring the investor to sign an investment-intent letter or subscription agreement that contains a representation that the purchaser is buying for his or her own account for investment and not with a view to distribution or for resale to others.

- Rule 503 specifies that five copies, one manually signed, of a notice of sale on SEC Form D be filed with the SEC not later than fifteen days after the first sale of the securities.

Although issuers may be disqualified from using Rule 505 if there is a violation of the bad actor disqualification provisions set forth in Regulation A, there is no such disqualification procedure in connection with Rule 504 or 506 offerings.

Regulation D is still the dominant rule for determining whether an offering of securities is exempt from the registration requirements of Section 5 of the Securities Act. If an offering qualifies for exemption under Title II or Title III of the federal JOBS Act of 2012 and the SEC regulations contained in Regulation Crowdfunding, it does not have to qualify separately for exemption under Regulation D. An offering that does not meet all of the conditions of Title II or Title III may, however, still be exempt from registration under the Securities Act if it separately meets the conditions of Rule 504, 505, or 506 of Regulation D.

Thus a Title III crowdfunded offering that closes with twenty-five accredited investors and five nonaccredited investors, all of whom had access to the offering documents prepared by the issuing company and posted to the funding portal, but one of whom invested more than $2,000 in private offerings of securities during the past year, may still qualify for exemption under Rule 506 if all the nonaccredited investors who purchased securities in the offering meet the "sophistication" criteria of that rule. Of course, the offering of the securities via a crowdfunding portal constituted a general solicitation or general advertising that might deny the offering exemption under the Rule 506 safe harbor, but the offering may still qualify under the residual exemption in Section 4(a)(2) of the Securities Act (for offerings that substantially comply with the safe harbor rules). That will be a case for the courts to decide if and when the time comes.

1996: The National Securities Markets Improvement Act

Fast-forward to 1996: Bill and Hillary Clinton, corduroys and grunge music, and the dawn of the Internet. Congress passes the National Securities Markets Improvement Act (NSMIA), which eliminates state registration requirements for "covered securities," including shares sold in a private placement under Rule 506 of Regulation D.

The NSMIA, however, left the other exemptions untouched. Offerings relying on Regulation A, Rules 504 and 505 of Regulation D, and private placements under Section 4(a)(2) of the Securities Act that do not meet the requirements of the Rule 506 safe harbor remained subject to state registration requirements.

The states also retained the power to enforce the antifraud provisions in their blue-sky laws, bringing actions against fraudulent offerings and establishing registration violations for offerings improperly made under Rule 506.

2012: The Jumpstart Our Business Startups Act

Fast-forward to today: Barack Obama, Lady Gaga, the Great Recession, social media networks, reality television, and Kickstarter. And the Jumpstart Our Business Startups (JOBS) Act of 2012, discussed in the next chapter.

CHAPTER 13

The JOBS Act and Regulation Crowdfunding Rules

O n April 5, 2012, President Barack Obama signed into law the Jumpstart Our Business Startups Act (JOBS Act, for short, which gives you an idea of what the government seeks to achieve with this statute).[*]

The act, described by one early commentator as a "dog's breakfast," is an eclectic combination of law changes designed to make it easier for emerging growth companies to raise capital without having to deal with the sometimes onerous requirements of federal and state securities laws.

The JOBS Act is divided into six sections, or titles, each of which addresses a specific area of securities law compliance for different types of companies. Some of these titles do not refer directly to crowdfunded offerings of securities, the primary topic of this book, but are discussed briefly in order to give a reader a better understanding of the JOBS Act's scope and impact on the marketplace for private offerings of securities.

Title I: The IPO On-Ramp

Title I of the JOBS Act established a new process and disclosure regime for IPOs of securities. The statute creates a new class of companies called emerging growth companies (EGCs); an emerging growth company is defined as an issuer with total annual gross revenues of less than $1 billion (subject to inflationary adjustment by the SEC every five years) during its most recently completed fiscal year.

For those companies that qualify as EGCs, Title I creates a simplified IPO process, or IPO on-ramp. Instead of preparing and filing a formal IPO registration statement and prospectus, EGCs can obtain confidential SEC staff review of draft IPO registration statements, scaled disclosure requirements, no restrictions on "test the waters"

---

[*] Pub.L. 112-206, 126 Stat. 306, codified at 15 U.S.C. § 78a (at www.gpo.gov/fdsys/pkg/PLAW-112publ106/pdf/PLAW-112publ106.pdf).

communications with qualified institutional buyers and institutional accredited investors before and after filing a registration statement, and fewer restrictions on research (including research by participating underwriters) around the time of an offering.

Title I does not relate directly to crowdfunding and is not discussed elsewhere in this book. Interested readers should review the frequently asked questions about Title I posted by the SEC staff at www.sec.gov/divisions/corpfin/guidance/cfjjobsactfaq-title-i-general.htm.

Title II: Private Placements and New Rule 506(c)

Title II of the JOBS Act directs the SEC to eliminate the ban on general solicitation and general advertising for certain offerings under Rule 506 of Regulation D, provided that the securities are sold only to accredited investors.

Rule 506 of Regulation D, discussed in Chapter 12, has traditionally been the most popular means for conducting a private offering because it permitted issuers to raise an unlimited amount of money and preempts state securities laws, as long as all purchasers in the offering were accredited investors (very wealthy and/or sophisticated people) and up to thirty-five nonaccredited investors (everyone else). No general solicitation or general advertising was allowed in a traditional Rule 506 offering.

Title II directs the SEC to revise Rule 506 to provide that the prohibition against general solicitation or general advertising in Rule 502(c) shall not apply to offers and sales of securities made pursuant to Rule 506, provided that all purchasers of the securities are accredited investors or the issuer "reasonably believes" them to be accredited investors. Title II further requires that issuers using general solicitation or general advertising in connection with Rule 506 offerings take reasonable steps to verify that purchasers of securities are accredited investors, using methods to be determined by the SEC. If an issuer is not comfortable making this effort, it can still use a traditional Rule 506 offering (no general solicitation or advertising, purchasers limited to accredited investors, and up to thirty-five other investors).

On July 10, 2013, the SEC approved final rules under Title II that eliminate the prohibition against general solicitation and general advertising in certain offerings of securities pursuant to Rule 506 of Regulation D. The rules create a new form of offering under Rule 506(c) that permits issuers to use general solicitation in connection with the sale of securities in private placements if the purchasers of all securities are accredited investors, and the issuer takes reasonable steps to verify that the purchasers are accredited investors.

The new rules leave intact Section 4(a)(2) of the Securities Act, which exempts from registration transactions by an issuer "not involving any public offering," and existing Rule 506(b), which provides a safe harbor under Section 4(a)(2) for offerings conducted without general solicitation.

Under Rule 506(c), issuers will be permitted to approach prospective investors even without a preexisting relationship. Advertisements, articles, notices, or other public communications will be permitted, as will public seminars and meetings to promote the offering. The bad news here is that there will be a greater risk of running afoul of federal and state antifraud rules while engaging in general solicitation activities under Rule 506(c), such as live speaking engagements and webinars where it may be difficult if not impossible for company founders and promoters to hold their tongues when necessary.

Rule 506(c) requires issuers to take "reasonable steps" to verify accredited investor status. Unlike Rule 506 offerings, where general solicitation is not used, an investor will not be able to self-certify his status by filling out an accredited-investor questionnaire such as that included as Appendix 10. While such questionnaires will no doubt continue to be used, an issuer under Rule 506(c) will have to perform some due diligence on each of her investors, such as reviewing federal income tax returns, personal financial statements, bank and brokerage statements, credit reports, and other financial information, and/or requesting certification letters from the investor's brokers, lawyers, and accountants confirming the information in the questionnaire.

An issuer relying on Rule 506(c) will have to fill out and File SEC Form D (a sales report) no later than fifteen calendar days before commencing general solicitation and general advertising, and include specific disclosures in its general solicitation and advertising materials. In a traditional Rule 506 offering involving no general solicitation, Form D is not due until fifteen calendar days after the first sale of securities in the offering. On Form D, an issuer must state whether it is relying on Rule 506(c) or a traditional private placement under Rule 506 (one without general solicitation) and will not be able to change it later if it makes a mistake.

Because of its anticipated impact on angel investor offerings, the text of new Rule 506(c) deserves to be quoted in full:

(c) *Conditions to be met in offerings not subject to limitation on manner of offering*—(1) *General conditions.* To qualify for exemption under this section, sales must satisfy all the terms and conditions of §§230.501 and 230.502(a) and (d).

(2) *Specific conditions*—(i) *Nature of purchasers.* All purchasers of securities sold in any offering under paragraph (c) of this section are accredited investors.

(ii) *Verification of accredited investor status.* The issuer shall take reasonable steps to verify that purchasers of securities sold in any offering under paragraph (c) of this section are accredited investors. The issuer shall be deemed to take reasonable steps to verify if the issuer uses, at its option, one of the following non-exclusive and non-mandatory methods of verifying that a natural person who purchases securities in such offering is an accredited investor; provided, however, that the issuer does not have knowledge that such person is not an accredited investor:

(A) In regard to whether the purchaser is an accredited investor on the basis of income, reviewing any Internal Revenue Service form that reports the purchaser's income for the two most recent years (including, but not limited to, Form W-2, Form 1099, Schedule K-1 to Form 1065, and Form 1040) and obtaining a written representation from the purchaser that he or she has a reasonable expectation of reaching the income level necessary to qualify as an accredited investor during the current year;

(B) In regard to whether the purchaser is an accredited investor on the basis of net worth, reviewing one or more of the following types of documentation dated within the prior three months and obtaining a written representation from the purchaser that all liabilities necessary to make a determination of net worth have been disclosed:

(1) With respect to assets: Bank statements, brokerage statements and other statements of securities holdings, certificates of deposit, tax assessments, and appraisal reports issued by independent third parties; and

(2) With respect to liabilities: A consumer report from at least one of the nationwide consumer reporting agencies; or

(C) Obtaining a written confirmation from one of the following persons or entities that such person or entity has taken reasonable steps to verify that the purchaser is an accredited investor within the prior three months and has determined that such purchaser is an accredited investor:

(1) A registered broker-dealer;

(2) An investment adviser registered with the Securities and Exchange Commission;

(3) A licensed attorney who is in good standing under the laws of the jurisdictions in which he or she is admitted to practice law; or

(4) A certified public accountant who is duly registered and in good standing under the laws of the place of his or her residence or principal office.

(D) In regard to any person who purchased securities in an issuer's Rule 506(b) offering as an accredited investor prior to September 23, 2013 and continues to hold such securities, for the same issuer's Rule 506(c) offering, obtaining a certification by such person at the time of sale that he or she qualifies as an accredited investor.

The SEC also created new Rules 506(d) and (e), providing that companies that have run afoul of the securities laws in the past (by committing one or more of the "bad acts" that disqualify issuers from offering securities under Regulation A) could not avail themselves of the new unlimited "accredited investor only" offerings. Basically, a company cannot take advantage of a Rule 506(c) offering if it, or any of its directors, officers, or principals:

- Has been convicted, within ten years before such sale (or five years, in the case of issuers, their predecessors, and affiliated issuers) of any felony or misdemeanor in connection with the purchase or sale of any security; involving the making of any false filing with the SEC; or arising out of the conduct of the business of an underwriter, broker, dealer, municipal securities dealer, investment adviser, or paid solicitor of purchasers of securities

- Is subject to any order, judgment, or decree of any court of competent jurisdiction, entered within five years before such sale, that, at the time of such sale, restrains or enjoins such person from engaging or continuing to engage in any conduct or practice in connection with the purchase or sale of any security; involving the making of any false filing with the SEC; or arising out of the conduct of the business of an underwriter, broker, dealer, municipal securities dealer, investment adviser, or paid solicitor of purchasers of securities

- Is subject to a final order of a state securities commission (or an agency or officer of a state performing like functions); a state authority that supervises or examines banks, savings associations, or credit unions; a state insurance commission (or an agency or officer of a state performing like functions); an appropriate federal banking agency; the U.S. Commodity Futures Trading Commission; or the National Credit Union Administration that at the time of such sale (i) bars the person from association with an entity regulated by such commission, authority, agency, or officer; engaging in the business of securities, insurance, or banking; or engaging in savings association or credit union activities, or (ii) constitutes a final order based on a violation of any law or regulation that prohibits fraudulent, manipulative, or deceptive conduct entered within ten years before such sale

- Is subject to an SEC order that, at the time of such sale, suspends or revokes such person's registration as a broker, dealer, municipal securities dealer, or investment adviser; places limitations on the activities, functions, or operations of such person; or bars such person from being associated with any entity or from participating in the offering of any penny stock

- Is subject to any order of the commission entered within five years before such sale that, at the time of such sale, orders the person to cease and desist from committing or causing a violation or future violation of Section 5 of the Securities Act or the antifraud provisions of any federal securities law

- Is suspended or expelled from membership in, or suspended or barred from association with a member of, a registered national securities exchange or a registered national or affiliated securities association for any act or omission to act constituting conduct inconsistent with just and equitable principles of trade

- Has filed (as a registrant or issuer), or was named as an underwriter in, any registration statement or Regulation A offering statement filed with the commission that, within five years before such sale, was the subject of a refusal order, stop order, or order suspending the Regulation A exemption, or is, at the time of such sale, the subject of an investigation or proceeding to determine whether a stop order or suspension order should be issued; or

- Is subject to a U.S. Postal Service false representation order entered within five years before such sale, or is, at the time of such sale, subject to a temporary restraining order or preliminary injunction with respect to conduct alleged by the United States Postal Service to constitute a scheme or device for obtaining money or property through the mail by means of false representations

Under new SEC Rule 506(e), the issuer is required to furnish to each purchaser, during a reasonable time prior to sale, a description in writing of any matters that would have triggered disqualification under Rule 506(d) but occurred before September 23, 2013. The failure to furnish such information in a timely fashion will not prevent an issuer from relying on Rule 506(c) if the issuer establishes that it did not know and, in the exercise of reasonable care, could not have known of the existence of the undisclosed matter or matters.

As I will state in this book's Afterword, I believe it is Title II of the JOBS Act—as opposed to the crowdfunding provisions in Title III—that will actually facilitate crowdfunding, at least by the more seasoned early-stage private companies that tend to attract accredited investors.

That said, there are a few "gotchas" in Title II.

First, Title II leaves intact the general solicitation and general advertising prohibition for offerings that include any "non-accredited" investors, such as employees, product developers, and other people contributing sweat equity for their shares. These people would have to be brought on board as founders (and their number would be strictly limited as under previous law) well before a company offers securities under Title II.

Second, an issuer who plans to rely on Rule 506(c) but fails to comply to the letter with the rule's requirements may not be able to rely on the residual exemption under Section 4(a)(2) of the Securities Act, as issuers who rely on the traditional Rule 506 offering have always been able to do, because of that section's express prohibition on general solicitation and general advertising.

Third, while the JOBS Act expressly preempted state securities laws that might otherwise prevent or restrict an offering under the Title III crowdfunding provisions of the JOBS Act, the same blanket preemption does not apply to offerings under new Rule 506(c). While the National Securities Markets and Improvements Act of 1996, discussed in the previous chapter, generally preempts state securities laws requiring registration at the state level of Rule 506 offerings (including offerings under Rule 506(c)), offerings under Rule 506(c) may still be subject to notice filing requirements (and possibly fees) in some states. Determining whether a Rule 506(c) offering triggers notice-filing requirements and payment of fees will likely involve additional diligence for issuers currently relying on blue-sky exemptions conditioned on the prohibition of general solicitation, with attention to the specific rules of each state.

Finally, while the JOBS Act preempts any state blue-sky laws requiring registration of securities at the state level, the states are still allowed to enforce their antifraud rules to target Rule 506(c) private placements, as well as crowdfunded offerings, for fraud. Crowdfunded offerings will often involve a high degree of risk. Start-ups have a high rate of failure, and—let's face it—some offerings will likely involve fraud, or at least sloppiness in complying with the securities laws. Given the $1 million limit on the size of the offering, the SEC will not be likely to engage in significant enforcement activities. So the burden of enforcing the crowdfunding marketplace for securities may well fall to the states, and there may be fifty different sets of rules and fifty different regulators.

Given that the states have also been given responsibility for overseeing funding portals, as discussed in Chapter 11, the message Titles II and III send to issuers may well be, "You register with the feds, but you answer to your state regulator(s) if anything goes wrong."

Title III: Crowdfunded Offerings of Securities

Title III is the heart of the JOBS Act, containing the provisions that will allow crowdfunded offerings of securities on the Internet. On October 23, 2013, the SEC issued a proposed Regulation Crowdfunding containing rules and regulations implementing Title III. After a period of public comment, the final version of Regulation Crowdfunding was approved by the SEC on October 30, 2015, with an effective date of May 16, 2016.

Title III added a new Section 4(a)(6) to the Securities Act to permit companies to engage in crowdfunded offerings of securities without having to go through the public offering registration process. The exemption is subject to the following conditions:

- The aggregate amount an issuer may sell to all investors in reliance on the new exemption may not exceed $1 million in any twelve-month period (offerings made under other exemptions such as Regulation A do not count toward the $1 million limit).

- An investor is limited in the amount he or she may invest in crowdfunding securities in any twelve-month period.

  - If either the annual income or the net worth of the investor is less than $100,000, the investor is limited to the greater of $2,000 or 5 percent of his or her annual income or net worth.
  - If the annual income or net worth of the investor is $100,000 or more, the investor is limited to 10 percent of the lesser of his or her annual income or net worth, to a maximum of $100,000 (the SEC justified this approach by expressing concern about the number of U.S. households—approximately 20 percent—where there is a sizable gap between net worth and annual income, and the ability of these households to withstand the risk of loss).
  - Regulation Crowdfunding treats investors who fall within both of these definitions as being able to take advantage of the higher investment limit.

- The transaction must be made through a broker-dealer registered with the SEC or through a funding portal (a new designation under the Securities and Exchange Act of 1934) that meets the requirements described in detail in Chapter 11.

- The issuer must comply with numerous disclosure and other requirements, described in detail elsewhere in this book.

Title III of the JOBS Act also added new Section 4A to the Securities Act of 1933, containing numerous hoops that issuers, funding portals, and investors will need to jump through to launch a successful crowdfunded offering. Regulation Crowdfunding, which implemented these requirements, contains nearly seven hundred pages of new regulations.

The author has spread discussion of Regulation Crowdfunding over several chapters. See the last section of Chapter 2 for the location of the discussions of the Regulation Crowdfunding provisions that apply at each stage of the crowdfunded offering process.

The bottom line on Title III of the JOBS Act and Regulation Crowdfunding is that companies desiring to use the crowdfunding option will have to go through much of the paperwork involved in an IPO or an offering of securities under the "simplified public offering" rules in the SEC's Regulation A, although on a streamlined scale. Once a successful Title III crowdfunded offering is completed, the issuing company will have to file annual reports with the SEC and deal with dozens, or perhaps hundreds, of investors whose level of sophistication and maturity will be all over the map, just like public companies do.

Title IV: **Expanded Availability of Regulation A**

Title IV of the JOBS Act created a new Section 3(b)(2) of the Securities Act to allow companies to issue up to $50 million in securities under Regulation A (up from $5 million). Although the details of certain provisions of the new exemption must be decided by future SEC rule making, Title IV of the JOBS Act does specify several important requirements of the new exemption:

- *Offering Limitation.* The new exemption will allow companies to issue up to $50 million in securities under Regulation A (up from the $5 million currently available) within the prior twelve-month period. Unlike the $5 million limitation under Regulation A, which has remained in place since 1992, the SEC is required every two years to consider raising the $50 million limitation.

- *Unrestricted Resales.* Similar to offerings under Regulation A, securities sold under the new exemption will be freely tradable upon issuance to investors in the offering.

- *Testing the Waters.* Similar to offerings under Regulation A, issuers that rely on the new exemption may confidentially solicit investor interest prior to filing offering statements with the SEC. However, the SEC must conduct further rule making to determine the terms and conditions placed on such solicitation.

- *Audited Financial Statements.* Unlike issuers who conduct offerings under Regulation A, issuers relying on the new exemption must file audited financial statements with the SEC on an annual basis upon completion of the offering. The SEC must conduct further rule making to determine whether audited financial statements should also be required as part of the offering statement.

- *Liability.* The civil liability provisions of Section 12(a)(2) of the Securities Act apply to people offering or selling such securities pursuant to the new exemption.

- *Offering Statement.* Companies relying on the new exemption may need to file an offering statement with the SEC. However, the SEC must conduct further rule making to determine the requirements of any such offering statement.

- *Periodic SEC Reporting.* Unlike Regulation A, companies relying on the new exemption may be subject to periodic SEC reporting upon completion of the offering. However, the SEC must conduct further rule making to determine specific filing requirements, if any. Specifically, the SEC must consider requiring periodic disclosure about a company's business operations, financial condition, corporate governance principles, and use of investor funds.

The SEC approved regulations under Title IV of the JOBS Act in SEC Release No. 33-9741, effective March 25, 2015 (www.sec.gov/rules/final/2015/33-9741.pdf).

Title V: Changes to Definition of "Public Company" in the Securities and Exchange Act of 1934

Title V of the JOBS Act amends Section 12(g) of the 1934 Securities and Exchange Act, which governs the annual reports and other documents required to be filed with the SEC by publicly traded companies. The amendments raise the threshold number of shareholders required to trigger securities registration requirements with the SEC.

Registration under the 1934 act has significant consequences. Registered companies must file periodic reports, adhere to the proxy rules, prohibit short-swing profits, and comply with other requirements of the federal securities laws. These provisions protect investors but also add significant cost to a company's operations.

Title V changed the requirements for registration in a complicated fashion. The amendment increased the threshold for registration from five hundred holders of record to two thousand. But it provided that companies with five hundred nonaccredited investors must register. The JOBS Act also excluded from the total those employees who acquired shares through certain compensation plans.

Title V of the JOBS Act increased the threshold for registration in Section 12(g) to two thousand people of record or five hundred people "who are not accredited investors." In addition, the provision excluded from the definition of "holder of record" those people who received securities through employee compensation plans. The legislation instructed the SEC to adopt a safe harbor implementing the provision and to examine whether it needed additional enforcement authority to prevent evasion of the requirement.

Title VI: Special Provisions for Banks and Bank Holding Companies

Title VI of the JOBS Act raises the threshold for banks and bank holding companies for mandatory 1934 act registration from five hundred shareholders of record to two thousand (and unlike Title V, there is no limitation to the number of nonaccredited investors). Since passage of the JOBS Act, a bank or a bank holding company is required to register its securities when its total assets exceed $10 million and any class of its equity securities is held of record by two thousand or more people. As with other types of issuers, this number does not include employees who acquired their securities through an exempt employee compensation plan or holders who acquired their securities through crowdfunding offerings.

Title VI also amended Section 12(g)(4) of the 1934 act, which provides a mechanism for deregistration. Issuers may terminate the registration of certain securities by filing a certification with the SEC that the number of holders of record of the class of securities in question has fallen to fewer than three hundred people. Title VI sets the threshold at one thousand two hundred for banks and bank holding companies. (It remains three hundred for other types of issuers.)

AFTERWORD

What the Author Really Thinks
of Crowdfunding

Throughout this book I have taken great pains not to editorialize or give my personal views of crowdfunding, its future potential as a means of raising capital for entrepreneurs and small businesses, or the likelihood that crowdfunding will revolutionize the securities industry.

As I stated in Chapter 1, I am an attorney in private practice and not privy to inside information about the federal JOBS Act of 2012, Regulation Crowdfunding, or the lobbying efforts that made equity crowdfunding the law of the land.

Since many readers will want to know my views, however, I thought it prudent to devote a few pages to my—admittedly biased and uninformed—opinion as to how crowdfunding will play out over the next few years.

First, the Bad News

Although Title III of the JOBS Act and Regulation Crowdfunding are excellent attempts at loosening the restrictions that have held back small business capital raising since the Great Depression, they do not go far enough to ensure that crowdfunding will be the revolutionary new financing tool its promoters intended it to be.

There are a number of reasons for this.

The Cost of Crowdfunding

Crowdfunding was intended to give access to start-ups and early-stage companies that are under the radar screen and invisible to traditional venture capitalists, angels, and other professional investors. The way Regulation Crowdfunding is written, however, these are the very entrepreneurs who—with three possible exceptions, which I will discuss in the following pages—will be unable to take full advantage of Title III crowdfunding.

The cost of preparing a written and detailed business plan, together with the legal and accounting fees necessary to convert the plan into an offering statement meeting the requirements of Regulation Crowdfunding, will be prohibitive for many if not most start-up companies. I have joked with friends in the financial world that the JOBS Act should really have been titled the Attorneys' and Accountants' Full Employment Act of 2012 because of the extensive professional work that will be required to get even the simplest crowdfunded offering to market. Not that I'm complaining, mind you!

The more established and mature private companies that have the capital and management time to devote to these tasks are precisely the companies that probably are already on investors' radar screens and can take advantage of more traditional private placement offerings and angel investments. While crowdfunded offerings may provide additional capital, especially if tied to a targeted project to which the proceeds of the offering can be dedicated, it may well be easier and less costly for emerging companies to work a little harder to find traditional sources of capital. After all, as someone once pointed out, "It is always easier to raise the second million dollars than the first hundred thousand."

Liability of Issuing Companies (and Their Professional Advisers)

As any attorney can tell you, the cost of obtaining malpractice insurance for securities law work is astronomical. Securities law is the obstetrics and gynecology of the legal malpractice world: it requires the most expensive malpractice coverage and faces the highest probability of claims of any legal specialty. Most securities lawyers I know tell me that their insurance premiums for securities law coverage are 50 to 75 percent of their total annual malpractice insurance premiums, often in the range of $5,000 to $10,000 a year (or more if there has been a claim against the attorney).

Why is that? Because when investors get angry, investors sue. And the first people they sue are the lawyers, accountants, and other professionals who made possible what they perceive (often incorrectly) as a fraudulent investment.

Although I have helped put together friends-and-family offerings for my clients for more than thirty-five years, I would hate to be the first attorney to prepare an offering statement under Regulation Crowdfunding. One small mistake and I would be toast.

With crowdfunding, an attorney's or accountant's malpractice risk will be even greater than it has been. Most attorney malpractice insurance policies are capped at $1 million per lawsuit, with a maximum cap of $2 million to $3 million per year. When there are only a handful of investors in an offering, they can't bring a class-action lawsuit for millions of dollars that would exceed the policy limits. With dozens or hundreds of investors in a Regulation Crowdfunding investment, they can, and you can bet there will be plaintiffs' lawyers aplenty looking to cash in when a crowdfunded company crashes and burns. From a litigation perspective, Title III has the potential to replace mesotheliomia (also known as "asbestos-related injuries") as the number one moneymaker for plaintiffs' attorneys.

Funding Portal Liability

Now let's consider the funding portals authorized by Regulation Crowdfunding. Under Regulation Crowdfunding, these portals assume liability if either or both:

- An offering statement they have reviewed and promoted online contains any material misstatement of fact or omission

- An investor the portal has certified as an accredited investor turns out not to be so because of misstatements or errors in the documents

As a middleman or facilitator of the crowdfunding process, the funding portal has double the risk and potential legal liability of either the issuing company or the investor(s). If I were advising a funding portal under the current Regulation Crowdfunding, I would advise it to:

- Tighten its terms and conditions so they are even more restrictive than Regulation Crowdfunding—for example, by requiring additional backup and support that Regulation Crowdfunding does not currently require (the "investment due diligence" that is commonly performed by investment banks when engaged in an IPO

- Require collateral from a company and its founders (such as personal guarantees backed by mortgages on the founders' homes) for securities-law-related claims before taking on that company as a new crowdfunding client.

- Make sure its fees and commissions are high enough to justify taking on the extensive legal risks posed by a Regulation Crowdfunding offering

As I stated in Chapter 11, why would anyone in their right mind want to start and operate a funding portal? Because of the high risk of liability, portals will be extremely capital intensive to set up and extremely labor intensive to operate. How many clerks (some of whom will require at least paralegal if not actual legal training) will a portal need to review offering documents from five different issuers looking to launch their offerings at the same time? How much will the portal have to pay these people for their salaries, employee benefits, payroll taxes, and liability insurance? Will the portal be able to outsource these activities to companies in India or elsewhere in the developing world?

Those additional costs, needless to say, will be reflected in the fees and commissions the portals will unquestionably charge their issuers and investors.

Don't Get Me Wrong

There will certainly be crowdfunded offerings of securities under Title III and Regulation Crowdfunding —just not as many as crowdfunding's promoters and cheerleaders think there will be.

As currently drafted, there is a risk that Title III will end up in the same place as the SEC's Regulation A, which has been around since 1964 but has generated only a handful of successful offerings as compared to those under the SEC's Regulation D.

Now for the Good News

Before my readers get out their pitchforks and torches and start "doxing" me as a heretic on their social media pages, let me say there is one aspect of the new crowdfunding scheme that is truly groundbreaking and has the potential to revolutionize at least one corner of the securities industry.

That aspect is Title II of the JOBS Act, relating to offerings made by general solicitation and advertising to accredited investors only, which I predict will totally transform the angel investor industry.

Traditionally, angel investors—millionaire-next-door types of individuals who provide capital and advice to start-up and very early-stage companies—are an isolated bunch of loners. Their investments tend to be purely local, to companies based in their home towns or counties. The most social of them belong to an angel club consisting of not more than ten people who meet once a month at a local country club or restaurant.

They are often ignorant of investment opportunities in other states (or countries), especially in industries other than the one they know thoroughly from their years of working in corporate America.

Probably the greatest challenge in the entire venture capital industry is introducing promising new start-up companies to the right angel investors.

One of the goals I and my colleagues had when we put together the *MoneyHunt* television show in the early 1990s was to create a portal—yes, we actually used that word back then—to help isolated angel investors around the country identify the most promising start-ups, no matter where they were geographically based or what industry they were in.

Title II crowdfunding, which enables websites dedicated to accredited-investor-only offerings to reach out to investors via general solicitation and general advertising methods, has the potential to be precisely that portal, opening up angel investment to scores of start-up and early-stage companies that today don't even have a clue where to begin looking for such folks.

Even better, Title II crowdfunding will enable these websites to build up a database of qualified accredited-investor angel investors that they can share to find the perfect fit for a particular start-up or entrepreneur.

And for Some Even Better News

There are three situations in which I think an early-stage company should consider an offering under Regulation Crowdfunding as it is currently drafted, even with all its faults and limitations:

The Small Business with a Huge Following

Let's say you are the owner of a well-known restaurant in your area, a manufacturing or distribution business serving a primarily local or regional market, or a company selling a particular line of antiques, collectibles, or household items on eBay or Amazon. Because your company doesn't have tons of equipment or other assets, and cash flows vary from quarter to quarter, you are not eligible to obtain a traditional or Small Business Administration-guaranteed loan from a bank. You might qualify for a microloan of up to $50,000, but you need more than that to finance working capital or expand your business. There is, however, something you do have: a large number of customers and other fans in your Outlook contacts, hundreds if not thousands of friends on Facebook, and hundreds if not thousands of followers on Twitter. People love your business, but few of them qualify as "accredited investors."

If that describes your business, you may be a candidate for Regulation Crowdfunding.

Keep in mind that crowdfunding was originally established as a way for people and businesses to tap into their social media followers in order to raise money for personal or business projects. Let's face it: it's highly unlikely that someone surfing Kickstarter or one of the other crowdfunding websites will stumble across a total stranger's project and decide, on the spur of the moment, to invest in it (unless it's generating lots of buzz elsewhere in online and off-line media). But if you know the people or company that launched the crowdfunding campaign, or have received notice of the campaign via your Facebook, Twitter, and other social media connections, you might take a look at it, and you might invest a small amount of money.

Success under Regulation Crowdfunding, as in crowdfunding generally, will depend on the quantity and quality of a company's existing contacts, on social media and elsewhere, who can be leveraged into becoming actual investors.

The Start-Up Looking for Market Validation

A number of commentators on the JOBS Act have pointed out (I think correctly) that many early-stage companies will be fearful of raising money via Regulation Crowdfunding for fear they will alienate the well-heeled accredited investors they will need for future, and much larger, rounds of financing. It is well-known that sophisticated angel investors are reluctant to invest in companies with many friends-and-family shareholders already in place.

I see one possible exception to that argument, though: the company that is looking to validate either its market or its technology and has had difficulty attracting angel and venture capital investors for that reason.

Let's say, for example, that your company has created a new consumer product. You've scrounged up the money to develop a prototype and get a patent on the product, but you're far short of the capital needed to manufacture the product in large quantities and line up a distribution deal with Walmart and other major retailers.

Here's what you could do: you could get someone to manufacture one thousand units of the product, and then launch an offering under Regulation Crowdfunding where investors would receive X shares in your company per $100 (or $1,000) of investment plus one of the units of your product. (Again, your presence on social media and ability to network online will be crucial to the success of the offering.)

If your offering sells out, it will demonstrate to later, more sophisticated investors that your product has market potential and deserves to be manufactured in larger quantities. After all, what better market research is there than people who have demonstrated they will buy not only your product but your company as well? It will really help if (1) your crowdfunded offering closes out extremely quickly, showing strong market demand, and (2) some of your investors are players in your industry, for example, executives of distributors or retailers who would carry your product if it were available in sufficient quantities. This would demonstrate to potential investors that the market, distribution, and other factors are there, if only you could manufacture the product in sufficient quantities, buy the necessary equipment, and so forth.

The Upstairs-Downstairs Offering

One thought that occurred to me (and, to be fair, other commentators on the JOBS Act as well) is that an early-stage company might want to launch two offerings simultaneously:

- An accredited-investor-only offering of preferred shares under Title II (using general solicitation and advertising) for most of the money needed to grow

- A Title III crowdfunded offering of common shares for nonaccredited investors such as friends, family, customers, and other people sourced online who do not qualify as accredited investors

I discussed this two-tiered approach to crowdfunding in Chapter 9. For it to work, you would have to make sure not to include in the general solicitation of the Title II offering an advertisement of the terms of the Regulation Crowdfunding offering, unless that advertisement follows the tombstone format authorized by Regulation Crowdfunding and otherwise complies with the advertising restrictions for a Title III offering. You will need to satisfy yourself (and the SEC) that the purchasers in the Regulation Crowdfunding offering were not solicited by means of the Title II offering, to avoid "integration" of the two offerings under Rule 502(a) of Regulation D. Of course, if the total of the two offerings is less than $1 million, and you do not contemplate a follow-on offering within the next twelve months, the integration question may not matter.

It may well be that Title III crowdfunding will perform best as a plug-in or add-on capital source for a company that is raising capital using more traditional means.

The Longer-Term Picture

Looking at the longer-term picture, crowdfunded investments have a potential to become the norm for private equity investment in early-stage companies. The people who promoted Title III were absolutely right in pointing out to Congress and the SEC that investors today are a lot more savvy and have access to lots more information at their fingertips (literally) than investors in early-twentieth-century America could even imagine, making the investor protections of the federal and state securities laws much less necessary than they were in Franklin D. Roosevelt's day.

It's just that I think it will take longer to get there than the current wisdom says it will. Change, especially in an industry so tradition bound and cautious as the securities industry (yes, I am saying that without irony), happens only slowly and incrementally. It will take longer than a few years for the industry, and its regulators, to accept the hypothesis that the crowd knows more collectively than the individuals within it.

Then again, I could be wrong. We'll see.

ACKNOWLEDGMENTS

Just as it takes a village to raise a child, it takes an awful lot of mentors to raise a lawyer, especially in the corporate and securities law field.

I owe a special debt to my law school faculty adviser, Thomas McCoy (now retired), of Vanderbilt University School of Law in Nashville, Tennessee, for helping to set me on the right path and preventing me from chucking it all to join the circus.

While I have worked with many attorneys during my three decades plus in practice, three individuals stand out as having shaped my approach to the world of venture capital and start-up companies:

Raymond W. Merritt, now retired, formerly partner with Willkie Farr & Gallagher LLP in New York City.

Stephen T. Whelan, partner with Blank Rome LLP in New York City, formerly partner with Thacher Proffitt & Wood.

William A. Perrone, managing partner of the Stamford, Connecticut, office of Wiggin & Dana LLP, formerly partner with Kleban & Samor PC in Southport, Connecticut.

In performing research for this book, I am thankful for all of the help and support offered by the New York State Bar Association (www.nysba.gov/cle), especially my good friends Jean E. Nelson II, Mark Belkin, and Kathy Suchocki. I am especially grateful to my good friend Jim Blasingame, host of the *Small Business Advocate* radio program (www.smallbusinessadvocate.com) and author (most recently) of *The Age of the Customer: Prepare for the Moment of Relevance*, for his personal tales of friends-and-family offerings, both good and bad.

I am also deeply indebted to my good friend John M. D'Aquila, CPA, of Jacksonville, Florida (www.daquilallp.com), for offering his perspective on the accounting and financial management aspects of crowdfunded securities offerings. In our twenty years of working together, he and I have helped launch more start-ups than Helen of Troy launched ships.

In thirty-five-plus years of helping launch start-up companies, I have worked with hundreds of entrepreneurs and their families to put together friends-and-family offerings. They have taught me everything I know, and I'm grateful to all of them, especially the ones who didn't "make it" but still managed to keep their friendships and family relationships intact. In the end, that's a lot more important than having a successful business.

Thanks to my editors at AMACOM Books, Bob Nirkind and Stephen S. Power, for believing in this project from the very start, for their almost-weekly email messages asking, "Have they passed the regulations yet?", for shepherding a time-sensitive manuscript through the publication process, and—especially—for not suggesting that I seek crowdfunded investment for the book in lieu of a standard author's royalty.

A special shout-out to the U.S. government, especially the Securities and Exchange Commission, for finally recognizing, after more than eighty years, that advertising and promoting a start-up company through a "general solicitation" and "general advertising" will not inevitably lead to the decline of Western civilization. (For the record, I tried to persuade your staff of that in 1994, when we were launching the *MoneyHunt* television show on PBS.)

Finally, to D.J., my soul mate, without whose patience nothing would be possible.

Fairfield, Connecticut
December 31, 2015

APPENDIX 1

Form C

UNITED STATES

SECURITIES AND EXCHANGE COMMISSION

Washington, D.C. 20549

FORM C

UNDER THE SECURITIES ACT OF 1933

(Mark one.)
- ☐ Form C: Offering Statement
- ☐ Form C-U: Progress Update
- ☐ Form C/A: Amendment to Offering Statement
- ☐ Check box if Amendment is material and investors must reconfirm within five business days.
- ☐ Form C-AR: Annual Report
- ☐ Form C-AR/A: Amendment to Annual Report
- ☐ Form C-TR: Termination of Reporting

Name of issuer:

Legal status of issuer:

Form:

Jurisdiction of Incorporation/Organization:

Date of organization):

Physical address of issuer:

Website of issuer:

Name of intermediary through which the offering will be conducted:

CIK number of intermediary:

SEC file number of intermediary:

CRD number, if applicable, of intermediary:

Amount of compensation to be paid to the intermediary, whether as a dollar amount or a percentage of the offering amount, or a good faith estimate if the exact amount is not available at the time of the filing, for conducting the offering, including the amount of referral and any other fees associated with the offering:

Any other direct or indirect interest in the issuer held by the intermediary, or any arrangement for the intermediary to acquire such an interest:

Type of security offered:

Target number of securities to be offered:

Price (or method for determining price):

Target offering amount:

Oversubscriptions accepted: ☐ Yes ☐ No

If yes, disclose how oversubscriptions will be allocated: ☐ Pro-rata basis ☐ First-come, first-served basis

☐ Other—provide a description:

Maximum offering amount (if different from target offering amount):

Deadline to reach the target offering amount:

NOTE: If the sum of the investment commitments does not equal or exceed the target offering amount at the offering deadline, no securities will be sold in the offering, investment commitments will be cancelled, and committed funds will be returned.

Current number of employees: _____

Total Assets:	Most recent fiscal year-end:	Prior fiscal year-end:
Cash & Cash Equivalents:	Most recent fiscal year-end:	Prior fiscal year-end:
Accounts Receivable:	Most recent fiscal year-end:	Prior fiscal year-end:
Short-term Debt:	Most recent fiscal year-end:	Prior fiscal year-end:
Long-term Debt:	Most recent fiscal year-end:	Prior fiscal year-end:
Revenues/Sales:	Most recent fiscal year-end:	Prior fiscal year-end:
Cost of Goods Sold:	Most recent fiscal year-end:	Prior fiscal year-end:
Taxes Paid:	Most recent fiscal year-end:	Prior fiscal year-end:
Net Income:	Most recent fiscal year-end:	Prior fiscal year-end:

Using the list below, select the jurisdictions in which the issuer intends to offer the securities:

[The list—which appears only in the XML version of Form C online— includes all U.S. jurisdictions, with an option to add and remove them individually, add all and remove all.]

GENERAL INSTRUCTIONS

I. Eligibility Requirements for Use of Form C

This Form shall be used for the offering statement, and any related amendments and progress reports, required to be filed by any issuer offering or selling securities in reliance on the exemption in Securities Act Section 4(a)(6) and in accordance with Section 4A and Regulation Crowdfunding (§ 227.100 *et seq.*). This Form also shall be used for an annual report required pursuant to Rule 202 of Regulation Crowdfunding (§ 227.202) and for the termination of reporting required pursuant to Rule 203(b)(2) of Regulation Crowdfunding (§ 227.203(b)(2)). Careful attention should be directed to the terms, conditions and requirements of the exemption.

II. Preparation and Filing of Form C

Information on the cover page will be generated based on the information provided in XML format. Other than the cover page, this Form is not to be used as a blank form to be filled in, but only as a guide in the preparation of Form C. General information regarding the preparation, format and how to file this Form is contained in Regulation S-T (§ 232 *et seq.*).

III. Information to be Included in the Form

Item 1. Offering Statement Disclosure Requirements

An issuer filing this Form for an offering in reliance on Section 4(a)(6) of the Securities Act and pursuant to Regulation Crowdfunding (§ 227.100 *et seq.*) must file the Form prior to the commencement of the offering and include the information required by Rule 201 of Regulation Crowdfunding (§ 227.201).

An issuer must include in the XML-based portion of this Form: the information required by paragraphs (a), (e), (g), (h), (l), (n), and (o) of Rule 201 of Regulation Crowdfunding (§ 227.201(a), (e), (g), (h), (l), (n), and (o)); selected financial data for the prior two fiscal years (including total assets, cash and cash equivalents, accounts receivable, short-term debt, long-term debt, revenues/sales, cost of goods sold, taxes paid and net income); the jurisdictions in which the issuer intends to offer the securities; and any information required by Rule 203(a)(3) of Regulation Crowdfunding (§ 227.203(a)(3)).

Other than the information required to be provided in XML format, an issuer may provide the required information in the optional Question and Answer format included herein or in any other format included on the intermediary's platform, by filing such information as an exhibit to this Form, including copies of screen shots of the relevant information, as appropriate and necessary.

If disclosure in response to any paragraph of Rule 201 of Regulation Crowdfunding (§ 227.201) or Rule 203(a)(3) is responsive to one or more other paragraphs of Rule 201 of Regulation Crowdfunding (§ 227.201) or to Rule 203(a)(3) of Regulation Crowdfunding (§ 227.203(a)(3)), issuers are not required to make duplicate disclosures.

Item 2. Legends

(a) An issuer filing this Form for an offering in reliance on Section 4(a)(6) of the Securities Act and pursuant to Regulation Crowdfunding (§ 227.100 *et seq.*) must include the following legends:

A crowdfunding investment involves risk. You should not invest any funds in this offering unless you can afford to lose your entire investment.

In making an investment decision, investors must rely on their own examination of the issuer and the terms of the offering, including the merits and risks involved. These securities have not been recommended or approved by any federal or state securities commission or regulatory authority. Furthermore, these authorities have not passed upon the accuracy or adequacy of this document.

The U.S. Securities and Exchange Commission does not pass upon the merits of any securities offered or the terms of the offering, nor does it pass upon the accuracy or completeness of any offering document or literature.

These securities are offered under an exemption from registration; however, the U.S. Securities and Exchange Commission has not made an independent determination that these securities are exempt from registration.

(b) An issuer filing this Form for an offering in reliance on Section 4(a)(6) of the Securities Act and pursuant to Regulation Crowdfunding (§ 227.100 *et seq.*) must disclose in the offering statement that it will file a report with the Commission annually and post the report on its website, no later than 120 days after the end of each fiscal year covered by the report. The issuer must also disclose how an issuer may terminate its reporting obligations in the future in accordance with Rule 202(b) of Regulation Crowdfunding (§ 227.202(b)).

Item 3. Annual Report Disclosure Requirements

An issuer filing this Form for an annual report, as required by Regulation Crowdfunding (§ 227.100 *et seq.*), must file the Form no later than 120 days after the issuer's fiscal year end covered by the report and include the information required by Rule 201(a), (b), (c), (d), (e), (f), (m), (p), (q), (r), (s), (t), (x) and (y) of Regulation Crowdfunding (§§ 227.201(a), (b), (c), (d), (e), (f), (m), (p), (q), (r), (s), (t), (x) and (y)). For purposes of paragraph (t), the issuer shall provide financial statements certified by the principal executive officer of the issuer to be true and complete in all material respects. If, however, the issuer has available financial statements prepared in accordance with U.S. generally accepted accounting principles (U.S. GAAP) that have been reviewed or audited by an independent certified public accountant, those financial statements must be provided and the principal executive officer certification will not be required.

An issuer must include in the XML-based portion of this Form: the information required by paragraphs (a), and (e) of Rule 201 of Regulation Crowdfunding (§ 227.201(a) and (e)); and selected financial data for the prior two fiscal years (including total assets, cash and cash equivalents, accounts receivable, short-term debt, long-term debt, revenues/sales, cost of goods sold, taxes paid and net income).

Pursuant to the requirements of Sections 4(a)(6) and 4A of the Securities Act of 1933 and Regulation Crowdfunding (§ 227.100 et seq.), the issuer certifies that it has reasonable grounds to believe that it meets all of the requirements for filing on Form C and has duly caused this Form to be signed on its behalf by the duly authorized undersigned.

(Issuer)

By:

(Signature and Title)

Pursuant to the requirements of Sections 4(a)(6) and 4A of the Securities Act of 1933 and Regulation Crowdfunding (§ 227.100 *et seq.*), this Form C has been signed by the following persons in the capacities and on the dates indicated.

(Signature)

(Title)

(Date)

Instructions.

1. The form shall be signed by the issuer, its principal executive officer or officers, its principal financial officer, its controller or principal accounting officer and at least a majority of the board of directors or persons performing similar functions.

2. The name of each person signing the form shall be typed or printed beneath the signature. Intentional misstatements or omissions of facts constitute federal criminal violations. *See* 18 U.S.C. 1001.

APPENDIX 2

OPTIONAL QUESTION & ANSWER FORMAT
FOR AN OFFERING STATEMENT

Respond to each question in each paragraph of this part. Set forth each question and any notes, but not any instructions thereto, in their entirety. If disclosure in response to any question is responsive to one or more other questions, it is not necessary to repeat the disclosure. If a question or series of questions is inapplicable or the response is available elsewhere in the Form, either state that it is inapplicable, include a cross-reference to the responsive disclosure, or omit the question or series of questions.

Be very careful and precise in answering all questions. Give full and complete answers so that they are not misleading under the circumstances involved. Do not discuss any future performance or other anticipated event unless you have a reasonable basis to believe that it will actually occur within the foreseeable future. If any answer requiring significant information is materially inaccurate, incomplete or misleading, the Company, its management and principal shareholders may be liable to investors based on that information.

THE COMPANY

1. Name of issuer: _____

ELIGIBILITY

2. ☐ Check this box to certify that all of the following statements are true for the issuer:
   - Organized under, and subject to, the laws of a State or territory of the United States or the District of Columbia.
   - Not subject to the requirement to file reports pursuant to Section 13 or Section 15(d) of the Securities Exchange Act of 1934.
   - Not an investment company registered or required to be registered under the Investment Company Act of 1940.
   - Not ineligible to rely on this exemption under Section 4(a)(6) of the Securities Act as a result of a disqualification specified in Rule 503(a) of Regulation Crowdfunding. (For more information about these disqualifications, see Question 30 of this Question and Answer format).
   - Has filed with the Commission and provided to investors, to the extent required, the ongoing annual reports required by Regulation Crowdfunding during the two years immediately preceding the filing of this offering statement (or for such shorter period that the issuer was required to file such reports).

- Not a development stage company that (a) has no specific business plan or (b) has indicated that its business plan is to engage in a merger or acquisition with an unidentified company or companies.

INSTRUCTION TO QUESTION 2: If any of these statements is not true, then you are NOT eligible to rely on this exemption under Section 4(a)(6) of the Securities Act.

3. Has the issuer or any of its predecessors previously failed to comply with the ongoing reporting requirements of Rule 202 of Regulation Crowdfunding? ☐ Yes ☐ No

Explain: _____

DIRECTORS OF THE COMPANY

4. Provide the following information about each director (and any persons occupying a similar status or performing a similar function) of the issuer:

Name: _____ Dates of Board Service: _____

Principal Occupation: _____

Employer: _____ Dates of Service: _____

Employer's Principal Business: _____

List all positions and offices that the issuer held and the period of time in which the director served in the position or office:

Position: _____ Dates of Service: _____

Position: _____ Dates of Service: _____

Position: _____ Dates of Service: _____

Business Experience: List the employers, titles, and dates of positions held during past three years with an indication of job responsibilities:

Employer: _____

Employer's Principal Business: _____

Title: _____ Dates of Service: _____

Responsibilities: _____

Employer: _____

Employer's Principal Business: _____

Title: _____ Dates of Service: _____

Responsibilities: _____

Employer: _____

Employer's Principal Business: _____

Title: _____ Dates of Service: _____

Responsibilities: _____

OFFICERS OF THE COMPANY

5. Provide the following information about each officer (and any persons occupying a similar status or performing a similar function) of the issuer:

Name: _____

Title: _____ Dates of Service: _____

Responsibilities: _____

List any prior positions and offices held with the issuer and the period of time in which the officer served in the position or office:

Position: _____ Dates of Service: _____

Responsibilities: _____

Position: _____ Dates of Service: _____

Responsibilities: _____

Position: _____ Dates of Service: _____

Responsibilities: _____

Business Experience: List any other employers, titles, and dates of positions held during the past three years with an indication of job responsibilities:

Employer: _____

Employer's Principal Business: _____

Title: _____ Dates of Service: _____

Responsibilities: _____

Employer: _____

Employer's Principal Business: _____

Title: _____ Dates of Service: _____

Responsibilities: _____

Employer: _____

Employer's Principal Business: _____

Title: _____ Dates of Service: _____

Responsibilities: _____

INSTRUCTION TO QUESTION 5: For purposes of this Question 5, the term officer means a president, vice president, secretary, treasurer or principal financial officer, comptroller or principal accounting officer, and any person routinely performing similar functions.

PRINCIPAL SECURITY HOLDERS

6. Provide the name and ownership level of each person, as of the most recent practicable date, who is the beneficial owner of 20 percent or more of the issuer's outstanding voting equity securities, calculated on the basis of voting power.

Name of Holder	No. and Class of Securities Now Held	% of Voting Power Prior to Offering

INSTRUCTION TO QUESTION 6: The above information must be provided as of a date that is no more than 120 days prior to the date of filing of this offering statement.

To calculate total voting power, include all securities for which the person directly or indirectly has or shares the voting power, which includes the power to vote or to direct the voting of such securities. If the person has the right to acquire voting power of such securities within 60 days, including through the exercise of any option, warrant or right, the conversion of a security, or other arrangement, or if securities are held by a member of the family, through corporations or partnerships, or otherwise in a manner that would allow a person to direct or control the voting of the securities (or share in such direction or control—as, for example, a co-trustee) they should be included as being "beneficially owned." You should include an explanation of these circumstances in a footnote to the "Number of and Class of Securities Now Held." To calculate outstanding voting equity securities, assume all outstanding options are exercised and all outstanding convertible securities converted.

BUSINESS AND ANTICIPATED BUSINESS PLAN

7. Describe in detail the business of the issuer and the anticipated business plan of the issuer.

RISK FACTORS

A crowdfunding investment involves risk. You should not invest any funds in this offering unless you can afford to lose your entire investment.

In making an investment decision, investors must rely on their own examinations of the issuer and the terms of the offering, including the merits and risks involved. These securities have not been recommended or approved by any federal or state securities commission or regulatory authority. Furthermore, these authorities have not passed upon the accuracy or adequacy of this document.

The U.S. Securities and Exchange Commission does not pass upon the merits of any securities offered or the terms of the offering, nor does it pass upon the accuracy or completeness of any offering document or literature.

These securities are offered under an exemption from registration; however, the U.S. Securities and Exchange Commission has not made an independent determination that these securities are exempt from registration.

8. Discuss the material factors that make an investment in the issuer speculative or risky:

(1) _____

(2) _____

(3) _____

(4) _____

(5) _____

(6) _____

(7) _____

(8) _____

(9) _____

(10) _____

INSTRUCTION TO QUESTION 8: Avoid generalized statements and include only those factors that are unique to the issuer. Discussion should be tailored to the issuer's business and the offering and should not repeat the factors addressed in the legends set forth above. No specific number of risk factors is required to be identified. Add additional lines and number as appropriate.

THE OFFERING

9. What is the purpose of this offering?

10. How does the issuer intend to use the proceeds of this offering?

	If Target Offering Amount Sold	If Maximum
Amount Sold		
Total Proceeds	$	$
Less Offering Expenses		
(A)		
(B)		
(C)		
Net Proceeds	$	$
Use of Proceeds		
(A)		
(B)		
(C)		
Total Use of Net Proceeds	$	$

INSTRUCTION TO QUESTION 10: An issuer must provide a reasonably detailed description of any intended use of proceeds, such that investors are provided with an adequate amount of information to understand how the offering proceeds will be used. If an issuer has identified a range of possible uses, the issuer should identify and describe each probable use and the factors the issuer may consider in allocating proceeds among the potential uses. If the issuer will accept proceeds in excess of the target offering amount, the issuer must describe the purpose, method for allocating oversubscriptions, and intended use of the excess proceeds with similar specificity.

11. How will the issuer complete the transaction and deliver securities to the investors?

12. How can an investor cancel an investment commitment?

NOTE: Investors may cancel an investment commitment until 48 hours prior to the deadline identified in these offering materials.

The intermediary will notify investors when the target offering amount has been met.

If the issuer reaches the target offering amount prior to the deadline identified in the offering materials, it may close the offering early if it provides notice about the new offering deadline

at least five business days prior to such new offering deadline (absent a material change that would require an extension of the offering and reconfirmation of the investment commitment).

If an investor does not cancel an investment commitment before the 48-hour period prior to the offering deadline, the funds will be released to the issuer upon closing of the offering and the investor will receive securities in exchange for his or her investment.

If an investor does not reconfirm his or her investment commitment after a material change is made to the offering, the investor's investment commitment will be cancelled and the committed funds will be returned.

OWNERSHIP AND CAPITAL STRUCTURE

The Offering

13. Describe the terms of the securities being offered.

14. Do the securities offered have voting rights? ☐ Yes ☐ No

15. Are there any limitations on any voting or other rights identified above? ☐ Yes ☐ No

Explain: _____

16. How may the terms of the securities being offered be modified?

Restrictions on Transfer of the Securities Being Offered

The securities being offered may not be transferred by any purchaser of such securities during the one-year period beginning when the securities were issued, unless such securities are transferred:

(1) to the issuer;

(2) to an accredited investor;

(3) as part of an offering registered with the U.S. Securities and Exchange Commission; or

(4) to a member of the family of the purchaser or the equivalent, to a trust controlled by the purchaser, to a trust created for the benefit of a member of the family of the purchaser or the equivalent, or in connection with the death or divorce of the purchaser or other similar circumstance.

NOTE: The term "accredited investor" means any person who comes within any of the categories set forth in Rule 501(a) of Regulation D, or who the seller reasonably believes comes within any of such categories, at the time of the sale of the securities to that person.

The term "member of the family of the purchaser or the equivalent" includes a child, stepchild, grandchild, parent, stepparent, grandparent, spouse or spousal equivalent, sibling, mother-in-law, father-in-law, son-in-law, daughter-in-law, brother-in-law, or sister-in-law of the purchaser, and includes adoptive relationships. The term "spousal equivalent" means a cohabitant occupying a relationship generally equivalent to that of a spouse.

Description of Issuer's Securities

17. What other securities or classes of securities of the issuer are outstanding? Describe the material terms of any other outstanding securities or classes of securities of the issuer.

Class of Security	Securities (or Amount) Authorized	Securities (or Amount) Authorized	Voting Rights	Other Rights
Preferred Stock (list each class in order of preference)				
_____			___Yes ___No	___Yes ___No Specify:
_____			___Yes ___No	___Yes ___No Specify:
Common Stock:			___Yes ___No	___Yes ___No Specify:
Debt Securities:			___Yes ___No	___Yes ___No Specify:
Other:				
_____			___Yes ___No	___Yes ___No Specify:
_____			___Yes ___No	___Yes ___No Specify:

Class of Security or Conversion	Securities Reserved for Issuance upon Exercise		
Warrants:			
Options:			
Other Rights:			
_____			

18. How may the rights of the securities being offered be materially limited, diluted, or qualified by the rights of any other class of security identified above?

19. Are there any differences not reflected above between the securities being offered and each other class of security of the issuer? ☐ Yes ☐ No

Explain: _____

20. How could the exercise of rights held by the principal shareholders identified in Question 6 affect the purchasers of the securities being offered?

21. How are the securities being offered being valued? Include examples of methods for how such securities may be valued by the issuer in the future, including during subsequent corporate actions.

22. What are the risks to purchasers of the securities relating to minority ownership in the issuer?

23. What are the risks to purchasers associated with corporate actions including:
- additional issuances of securities,
- issuer repurchases of securities,
- a sale of the issuer or of assets of the issuer, or
- transactions with related parties?

24. Describe the material terms of any indebtedness of the issuer:

Creditor(s) Terms	Amount Outstanding	Interest Rate	Maturity Date	Other Material
	$	%		
	$	%		
	$	%		

25. What other exempt offerings has the issuer conducted within the past three years?

Date of Offering	Exemption Relied Upon	Securities Offered	Amount Sold	Use of Proceeds
			$	
			$	
			$	

26. Was or is the issuer or any entities controlled by or under common control with the issuer a party to any transaction since the beginning of the issuer's last fiscal year, or any currently proposed transaction, where the amount involved exceeds five percent of the aggregate amount of capital raised by the issuer in reliance on Section 4(a)(6) of the Securities Act during the preceding 12-month period, including the amount the issuer seeks to raise in the current offering, in which any of the following persons had or is to have a direct or indirect material interest:

(1) any director or officer of the issuer;

(2) any person who is, as of the most recent practicable date, the beneficial owner of 20 percent or more of the issuer's outstanding voting equity securities, calculated on the basis of voting power;

(3) if the issuer was incorporated or organized within the past three years, any promoter of the issuer; or

(4) any immediate family member of any of the foregoing persons.

If yes, for each such transaction, disclose the following:

Specified Person	Relationship to Issuer	Nature of Interest	Amount of Interest
$			
$			
$			

INSTRUCTIONS TO QUESTION 26:

The term "transaction" includes, but is not limited to, any financial transaction, arrangement or relationship (including any indebtedness, or guarantee of indebtedness) or any series of similar transactions, arrangements, or relationships.

Beneficial ownership for purposes of paragraph (2) shall be determined as of a date that is no more than 120 days prior to the date of filing of this offering statement and using the same calculation described in Question 6 of this Question and Answer format.

The term "member of the family" includes any child, stepchild, grandchild, parent, stepparent, grandparent, spouse or spousal equivalent, sibling, mother-in-law, father-in-law, son-in-law, daughter-in-law, brother-in-law, or sister-in-law of the person, and includes adoptive relationships. The term "spousal equivalent" means a cohabitant occupying a relationship generally equivalent to that of a spouse.

Compute the amount of a related party's interest in any transaction without regard to the amount of the profit or loss involved in the transaction. Where it is not practicable to state the approximate amount of the interest, disclose the approximate amount involved in the transaction.

FINANCIAL CONDITION OF THE ISSUER

27. Does the issuer have an operating history? ☐ Yes ☐ No

28. Describe the financial condition of the issuer, including, to the extent material, liquidity, capital resources, and historical results of operations.

INSTRUCTIONS TO QUESTION 28:

The discussion must cover each year for which financial statements are provided. Include a discussion of any known material changes or trends in the financial condition and results of operations of the issuer during any time period subsequent to the period for which financial statements are provided.

For issuers with no prior operating history, the discussion should focus on financial milestones and operational, liquidity, and other challenges.

For issuers with an operating history, the discussion should focus on whether historical results and cash flows are representative of what investors should expect in the future.

Take into account the proceeds of the offering and any other known or pending sources of capital. Discuss how the proceeds from the offering will affect liquidity, whether receiving these funds and any other additional funds is necessary to the viability of the business, and how quickly the issuer anticipates using its available cash. Describe the other available sources of capital to the business, such as lines of credit or required contributions by shareholders.

References to the issuer in this Question 28 and these instructions refer to the issuer and its predecessors, if any.

FINANCIAL INFORMATION

29. Include the financial information specified below covering the two most recently completed fiscal years or the period(s) since inception, if shorter:

Aggregate Offering Amount (defined below)	Financial Information Required	Financial Statement Requirements
(a) $100,000 or less:	• The following information or their equivalent line items as reported on the federal income tax return filed by the issuer for the most recently completed year (if any): • Total income • Taxable income; and • Total tax; certified by the principal executive officer of the issuer to reflect accurately the information reported on the issuer's federal income tax returns; and • Financial statements of the issuer and its predecessors, if any.	Financial statements must be **certified** by the principal executive officer of the issuer as set forth below. If financial statements are available that have either been reviewed or audited by a public accountant that is independent of the issuer, the issuer must provide those financial statements instead along with a signed audit or review report and need not include the information reported on the federal income tax returns or the certification of the principal executive officer.

Aggregate Offering Amount (defined below):	Financial Information Required:	Financial Statement Requirements:
(b) More than $100,000, but not more than $500,000:	• Financial statements of the issuer and its predecessors, if any.	Financial statements must be **reviewed** by a public accountant that is independent of the issuer and must include a signed review report. If financial statements of the issuer are available that have been audited by a public accountant that is independent of the issuer, the issuer must provide those financial statements instead along with a signed audit report and need not include the reviewed financial statements.
(c) More than $500,000:	• Financial statements of the issuer and its predecessors, if any.	If the issuer **has** previously sold securities in reliance on Regulation Crowdfunding: Financial statements must be **audited** by a public accountant that is independent of the issuer and must include a signed audit report. If the issuer **has not** previously sold securities in reliance on Regulation Crowdfunding and it is offering more than $500,000 but not more than $1,000,000: Financial statements must be reviewed by a public accountant that is independent of the issuer and must include a signed review report. If financial statements of the issuer are available that have been audited by a public accountant that is independent of the issuer, the issuer must provide those financial statements instead along with a signed audit report and need not include the reviewed financial statements.

INSTRUCTIONS TO QUESTION 29:

To determine the financial statements required, the Aggregate Offering amount for purposes of this Question 29 means the aggregate amounts offered and sold by the issuer, all entities controlled by or under common control with the issuer, and all predecessors of the issuer in reliance on Section 4(a)(6) of the Securities Act within the preceding 12-month period plus the current maximum offering amount provided on the cover of this Form.

To determine whether the issuer has previously sold securities in reliance on Regulation Crowdfunding for purposes of paragraph (c) of this Question 29, "issuer" means the issuer, all entities controlled by or under common control with the issuer, and all predecessors of the issuer.

Financial statements must be prepared in accordance with generally accepted U.S. accounting principles and must include balance sheets, statements of comprehensive income, statements of cash flows, statements of changes in stockholders' equity and notes to the financial statements. If the financial statements are not audited, they shall be labeled as "unaudited."

Issuers offering securities and required to provide the information set forth in row (a) before filing a tax return for the most recently completed fiscal year may provide information from the tax return filed for the prior year (if any), provided that the issuer provides information from the tax return for the most recently completed fiscal year when it is filed, if filed during the offering period. An issuer that requested an extension of the time to file would not be required to provide information from the tax return until the date when the return is filed, if filed during the offering period.

A principal executive officer certifying financial statements as described above must provide the following certification**:

I, [identify the certifying individual], certify that:

(1) the financial statements of [identify the issuer] included in this Form are true and complete in all material respects; and

(2) the tax return information of [identify the issuer] included in this Form reflects accurately the information reported on the tax return for [identify the issuer] filed for the fiscal year ended [date of most recent tax return].

[Signature] _____

[Title] _____

** Intentional misstatements or omissions of facts constitute federal criminal violations. *See* 18 U.S.C. 1001.

To qualify as a public accountant that is independent of the issuer for purposes of this Question 29, the accountant must satisfy the independence standards of either:

(i) Rule 2-01 of Regulation S-X or

(ii) the AICPA.

The public accountant that audits or reviews the financial statements provided by an issuer must be (1) duly registered and in good standing as a certified public accountant under the laws of the place of his or her residence or principal office or (2) in good standing and entitled to practice as a public accountant under the laws of his or her place of residence or principal office.

An issuer will not be in compliance with the requirement to provide reviewed financial statements if the issuer received a review report that includes modifications. An issuer will not be in compliance with the requirement to provide audited financial statements if the issuer received a qualified opinion, an adverse opinion, or a disclaimer of opinion.

The issuer must notify the public accountant of the issuer's intended use of the public accountant's audit or review report in the offering.

For an offering conducted in the first 120 days of a fiscal year, the financial statements provided may be for the two fiscal years prior to the issuer's most recently completed fiscal year; however, financial statements for the two most recently completed fiscal years must be provided if they are otherwise available. If more than 120 days have passed since the end of the issuer's most recently completed fiscal year, the financial statements provided must be for the issuer's two most recently completed fiscal years. If the 120th day falls on a Saturday, Sunday, or holiday, the next business day shall be considered the 120th day for purposes of determining the age of the financial statements.

An issuer may elect to delay complying with any new or revised financial accounting standard until the date that a company that is not an issuer (as defined under section 2(a) of the Sarbanes-Oxley Act of 2002 is required to comply with such new or revised accounting standard, if such standard also applies to companies that are not issuers. Issuers electing such extension of time accommodation must disclose it at the time the issuer files its offering statement and apply the election to all standards. Issuers electing not to use this accommodation must forgo this accommodation for all financial accounting standards and may not elect to rely on this accommodation in any future filings.

30. With respect to the issuer, any predecessor of the issuer, any affiliated issuer, any director, officer, general partner or managing member of the issuer, any beneficial owner of 20 percent or more of the issuer's outstanding voting equity securities, calculated in the same form as described in Question 6 of this Question and Answer format, any promoter connected with the issuer in any capacity at the time of such sale, any person who has been or will be paid (directly or indirectly) remuneration for solicitation of purchasers in connection with such sale of securities, or any general partner, director, officer or managing member of any such solicitor, prior to May 16, 2016:

(1) Has any such person been convicted, within 10 years (or five years, in the case of issuers, their predecessors and affiliated issuers) before the filing of this offering statement, of any felony or misdemeanor:

(i) in connection with the purchase or sale of any security? ☐ Yes ☐ No

(ii) involving the making of any false filing with the Commission? ☐ Yes ☐ No

(iii) arising out of the conduct of the business of an underwriter, broker, dealer, municipal securities dealer, investment adviser, funding portal or paid solicitor of purchasers of securities? ☐ Yes ☐ No

If Yes to any of the above, explain: _____

(2) Is any such person subject to any order, judgment or decree of any court of competent jurisdiction, entered within five years before the filing of the information required by Section 4A(b) of the Securities Act that, at the time of filing of this offering statement, restrains or enjoins such person from engaging or continuing to engage in any conduct or practice:

(i) in connection with the purchase or sale of any security? ☐ Yes ☐ No

(ii) involving the making of any false filing with the Commission? ☐ Yes ☐ No

(iii) arising out of the conduct of the business of an underwriter, broker, dealer, municipal securities dealer, investment adviser, funding portal or paid solicitor of purchasers of securities? ☐ Yes ☐ No

If Yes to any of the above, explain: _____

(3) Is any such person subject to a final order of a state securities commission (or an agency or officer of a state performing like functions); a state authority that supervises or examines banks, savings associations or credit unions; a state insurance commission (or an agency or officer of a state performing like functions); an appropriate federal banking agency; the U.S. Commodity Futures Trading Commission; or the National Credit Union Administration that:

(i) at the time of the filing of this offering statement bars the person from:

(A) association with an entity regulated by such commission, authority, agency or officer?

(B) engaging in the business of securities, insurance or banking? ☐ Yes ☐ No

(C) engaging in savings association or credit union activities? ☐ Yes ☐ No

(ii) constitutes a final order based on a violation of any law or regulation that prohibits fraudulent, manipulative or deceptive conduct and for which the order was entered within the 10-year period ending on the date of the filing of this offering statement? ☐ Yes ☐ No

If Yes to any of the above, explain: _____

(4) Is any such person subject to an order of the Commission entered pursuant to Section 15(b) or 15B(c) of the Exchange Act or Section 203(e) or (f) of the Investment Advisers Act of 1940 that, at the time of the filing of this offering statement:

(i) suspends or revokes such person's registration as a broker, dealer, municipal securities dealer, investment adviser or funding portal? ☐ Yes ☐ No

(ii) places limitations on the activities, functions or operations of such person? ☐ Yes ☐ No

(iii) bars such person from being associated with any entity or from participating in the offering of any penny stock? ☐ Yes ☐ No

If Yes to any of the above, explain: _____

(5) Is any such person subject to any order of the Commission entered within five years before the filing of this offering statement that, at the time of the filing of this offering

statement, orders the person to cease and desist from committing or causing a violation or future violation of:

(i) any scienter-based anti-fraud provision of the federal securities laws, including without limitation Section 17(a)(1) of the Securities Act, Section 10(b) of the Exchange Act, Section 15(c)(1) of the Exchange Act and Section 206(1) of the Investment Advisers Act of 1940 or any other rule or regulation thereunder? ☐ Yes ☐ No

(ii) Section 5 of the Securities Act? ☐ Yes ☐ No

If Yes to any of the above, explain: _____

(6) Is any such person suspended or expelled from membership in, or suspended or barred from association with a member of, a registered national securities exchange or a registered national or affiliated securities association for any act or omission to act constituting conduct inconsistent with just and equitable principles of trade? ☐ Yes ☐ No

If Yes, explain: _____

(7) Has any such person filed (as a registrant or issuer), or was any such person named as an underwriter in, any registration statement or Regulation A offering statement filed with the Commission that, within five years before the filing of this offering statement, was the subject of a refusal order, stop order, or order suspending the Regulation A exemption, or is any such person, at the time of such filing, the subject of an investigation or proceeding to determine whether a stop order or suspension order should be issued? ☐ Yes ☐ No

If Yes, explain: _____

(8) Is any such person subject to a United States Postal Service false representation order entered within five years before the filing of the information required by Section 4A(b) of the Securities Act, or is any such person, at the time of filing of this offering statement, subject to a temporary restraining order or preliminary injunction with respect to conduct alleged by the United States Postal Service to constitute a scheme or device for obtaining money or property through the mail by means of false representations? ☐ Yes ☐ No

If Yes, explain: _____

If you would have answered "Yes" to any of these questions had the conviction, order, judgment, decree, suspension, expulsion or bar occurred or been issued after May 16, 2016, then you are NOT eligible to rely on this exemption under Section 4(a)(6) of the Securities Act.

INSTRUCTIONS TO QUESTION 30:

Final order means a written directive or declaratory statement issued by a federal or state agency, described in Rule 503(a)(3) of Regulation Crowdfunding, under applicable statutory authority that provides for notice and an opportunity for hearing, which constitutes a final disposition or action by that federal or state agency.

No matters are required to be disclosed with respect to events relating to any affiliated issuer that occurred before the affiliation arose if the affiliated entity is not (i) in control of the issuer or (ii) under common control with the issuer by a third party that was in control of the affiliated entity at the time of such events.

OTHER MATERIAL INFORMATION

31. In addition to the information expressly required to be included in this Form, include:

(1) any other material information presented to investors; and

(2) such further material information, if any, as may be necessary to make the required statements, in the light of the circumstances under which they are made, not misleading.

INSTRUCTIONS TO QUESTION 31:

If information is presented to investors in a format, media or other means not able to be reflected in text or portable document format, the issuer should include

(a) a description of the material content of such information;

(b) a description of the format in which such disclosure is presented; and

(c) in the case of disclosure in video, audio or other dynamic media or format, a transcript or description of such disclosure.

ONGOING REPORTING

The issuer will file a report electronically with the Securities & Exchange Commission annually and post the report on its website, no later than: _____

(120 days after the end of each fiscal year covered by the report).

Once posted, the annual report may be found on the issuer's website at:

_____

The issuer must continue to comply with the ongoing reporting requirements until:

(1) the issuer is required to file reports under Section 13(a) or Section 15(d) of the Exchange Act;

(2) the issuer has filed at least one annual report pursuant to Regulation Crowdfunding and has fewer than 300 holders of record and has total assets that do not exceed $10,000,000;

(3) the issuer has filed at least three annual reports pursuant to Regulation Crowdfunding;

(4) the issuer or another party repurchases all of the securities issued in reliance on Section 4(a)(6) of the Securities Act, including any payment in full of debt securities or any complete redemption of redeemable securities; or

(5) the issuer liquidates or dissolves its business in accordance with state law.

APPENDIX 3

Amended and Restated Certificate of Incorporation Creating Classes of Voting and Nonvoting Common Stock and Convertible Preferred Stock [Delaware form]

AMENDED AND RESTATED
CERTIFICATE OF INCORPORATION

OF

_____ , INC.

**(Pursuant to Sections 242 and 245 of the
General Corporation Law of the State of Delaware)**

_____ , INC., a corporation organized and existing under and by virtue of the provisions of the General Corporation Law of the State of Delaware (the "General Corporation Law"),

DOES HEREBY CERTIFY:

1. That the name of this corporation is _____ , INC., and that this corporation was originally incorporated pursuant to the General Corporation Law on [*date of incorporation*] under the name_____ , INC.

2. That the Board of Directors duly adopted resolutions proposing to amend and restate the Certificate of Incorporation of this corporation, declaring said amendment and restatement to be advisable and in the best interests of this corporation and its stockholders, and authorizing the appropriate officers of this corporation to solicit the consent of the stockholders therefor, which resolution setting forth the proposed amendment and restatement is as follows:

RESOLVED, that the Certificate of Incorporation of this corporation be amended and restated in its entirety to read as follows:

FIRST: The name of this corporation is _____ , INC. (the "Corporation").

SECOND: The address of the registered office of the Corporation in the State of Delaware is [*address of registered agent*], in the City of Dover, County of Kent. The name of its registered agent at such address is [*name of registered agent*].

THIRD: The nature of the business or purposes to be conducted or promoted is to engage in any lawful act or activity for which corporations may be organized under the General Corporation Law.

1. The total number of shares of all classes of stock which the Corporation shall have authority to issue is 10,000,000, of which 6,000,000 of such shares shall be common stock having a par value of $0.001 per share ("Voting Common Stock"), 2,000,000 of such shares shall be non-voting common stock having a par value of $0.001 per share ("Nonvoting Common Stock"), and 2,000,000 of such shares shall

be Series A Preferred Stock, having a par value of $0.001 per share ("Preferred Stock"). The number of authorized shares of capital stock of the Corporation may be increased or decreased (but not below the number of shares thereof then outstanding) by (in addition to any vote of the holders of one or more series of Preferred Stock that may be required by the terms of the Certificate of Incorporation) the affirmative vote of the holders of shares of capital stock of the Corporation representing a majority of the votes represented by all outstanding shares of capital stock of the Corporation entitled to vote, irrespective of the provisions of Section 242(b)(2) of the General Corporation Law.

FOURTH: The following is a statement of the designations and the powers, privileges and rights, and the qualifications, limitations or restrictions thereof in respect of each class of capital stock of the Corporation.

A. COMMON STOCK

1. *General.* The voting, dividend and liquidation rights of the holders of the Common Stock are subject to and qualified by the rights, powers and preferences of the holders of the Preferred Stock set forth herein. Except as expressly provided by this Article FOURTH, Voting Common Stock and Nonvoting Common Stock (collectively, the "Common Stock") shall be pari passu in all respects.

2. *Voting.* Except as required by law, Nonvoting Common Stock shall not be entitled to vote on any mater submitted for approval by the Corporation's stockholders. The holders of the Common Stock are entitled to one vote for each share of Common Stock held at all meetings of stockholders (and written actions in lieu of meetings); provided, however, that, except as otherwise required by law, holders of Common Stock, as such, shall not be entitled to vote on any amendment to the Certificate of Incorporation that relates solely to the terms of one or more outstanding series of Preferred Stock if the holders of such affected series are entitled, either separately or together with the holders of one or more other such series, to vote thereon pursuant to the Certificate of Incorporation or pursuant to the General Corporation Law. There shall be no cumulative voting.

3. *Dividends.* If the Corporation shall in any manner subdivide (by stock split, stock dividend or otherwise) or combine (by reverse stock split or otherwise) the outstanding shares of Voting Common Stock, the outstanding shares of Nonvoting Common Stock shall be proportionally subdivided or combined, and vice versa. No dividends shall be declared and paid on Voting Common Stock unless equivalent dividends are simultaneously paid on Nonvoting Common Stock, and vice versa; provided, however, that in the case of a dividend payable in shares of Voting Common Stock, the holders of Voting Common Stock shall receive additional shares of Voting Common Stock and the holders of Nonvoting Common Stock shall receive additional shares of Nonvoting Common Stock.

4. *Rights Upon Liquidation.* In the event of any dissolution, liquidation or winding up of the Corporation, whether voluntary or involuntary, the holders of the Common Stock, and holders of any class or series of stock entitled to participate therewith, in whole or in part, as to the distribution of assets in such event, shall become entitled to participate in the distribution of any assets of the Corporation

remaining after the Corporation shall have paid, or provide for payment of, all debts and liabilities of the Corporation and after the Corporation shall have paid, or set aside for payment, to the holders of any class of stock having preference over the Common Stock in the event of dissolution, liquidation or winding up the full preferential amounts if any) to which they are entitled.

A. PREFERRED STOCK

1,000,000 shares of the authorized and unissued Preferred Stock of the Corporation are hereby designated "Series A Preferred Stock" with the following rights, preferences, powers, privileges and restrictions, qualifications and limitations. Unless otherwise indicated, references to "sections" or "subsections" in this Part B of this Article Fourth refer to sections and subsections of Part B of this Article Fourth.

1. *Dividends.*

The Corporation shall not declare, pay or set aside any dividends on shares of any other class or series of capital stock of the Corporation (other than dividends on shares of Common Stock payable in shares of Common Stock) unless (in addition to the obtaining of any consents required elsewhere in the Certificate of Incorporation) the holders of the Series A Preferred Stock then outstanding shall first receive, or simultaneously receive, a dividend on each outstanding share of Series A Preferred Stock in an amount at least equal to (i) in the case of a dividend on Common Stock or any class or series that is convertible into Common Stock, that dividend per share of Series A Preferred Stock as would equal the product of (A) the dividend payable on each share of such class or series determined, if applicable, as if all shares of such class or series had been converted into Common Stock and (B) the number of shares of Common Stock issuable upon conversion of a share of Series A Preferred Stock, in each case calculated on the record date for determination of holders entitled to receive such dividend or (ii) in the case of a dividend on any class or series that is not convertible into Common Stock, at a rate per share of Series A Preferred Stock determined by (A) dividing the amount of the dividend payable on each share of such class or series of capital stock by the original issuance price of such class or series of capital stock (subject to appropriate adjustment in the event of any stock dividend, stock split, combination or other similar recapitalization with respect to such class or series) and (B) multiplying such fraction by an amount equal to the Series A Original Issue Price (as defined below); provided that, if the Corporation declares, pays or sets aside, on the same date, a dividend on shares of more than one class or series of capital stock of the Corporation, the dividend payable to the holders of Series A Preferred Stock pursuant to this *Section 1* shall be calculated based upon the dividend on the class or series of capital stock that would result in the highest Series A Preferred Stock dividend. The "Series A Original Issue Price" shall mean $0.8358 per share, subject to appropriate adjustment in the event of any stock dividend, stock split, combination or other similar recapitalization with respect to the Series A Preferred Stock.

2. *Liquidation, Dissolution or Winding Up; Certain Mergers, Consolidations and Asset Sales.*
　　2.1 *Preferential Payments to Holders of Series A Preferred Stock.* In the event of any voluntary or involuntary liquidation, dissolution or winding up of the Corporation or Deemed Liquidation Event, the holders of shares of Series A Preferred Stock

then outstanding shall be entitled to be paid out of the assets of the Corporation available for distribution to its stockholders before any payment shall be made to the holders of Common Stock by reason of their ownership thereof, an amount per share equal to the greater of (i) the Series A Original Issue Price, plus any dividends declared but unpaid thereon, or (ii) such amount per share as would have been payable had all shares of Series A Preferred Stock been converted into Common Stock pursuant to *Section 4* immediately prior to such liquidation, dissolution, winding up or Deemed Liquidation Event (the amount payable pursuant to this sentence is hereinafter referred to as the "Series A Liquidation Amount"). If upon any such liquidation, dissolution or winding up of the Corporation or Deemed Liquidation Event, the assets of the Corporation available for distribution to its stockholders shall be insufficient to pay the holders of shares of Series A Preferred Stock the full amount to which they shall be entitled under this *Subsection 2.1*, the holders of shares of Series A Preferred Stock shall share ratably in any distribution of the assets available for distribution in proportion to the respective amounts which would otherwise be payable in respect of the shares held by them upon such distribution if all amounts payable on or with respect to such shares were paid in full.

2.2 *Payments to Holders of Common Stock.* In the event of any voluntary or involuntary liquidation, dissolution or winding up of the Corporation or Deemed Liquidation Event, after the payment of all preferential amounts required to be paid to the holders of shares of Series A Preferred Stock, the remaining assets of the Corporation available for distribution to its stockholders shall be distributed among the holders of shares of Common Stock, pro rata based on the number of shares held by each such holder.

2.3 *Deemed Liquidation Events.*

2.3.1 Definition. Each of the following events shall be considered a "Deemed Liquidation Event" unless the holders of at least a majority of the outstanding shares of Series A Preferred Stock elect otherwise by written notice sent to the Corporation at least 10 days prior to the effective date of any such event:

    (a) a merger or consolidation in which

        (i) the Corporation is a constituent party or

        (ii) a subsidiary of the Corporation is a constituent party and the Corporation issues shares of its capital stock pursuant to such merger or consolidation, except any such merger or consolidation involving the Corporation or a subsidiary in which the shares of capital stock of the Corporation outstanding immediately prior to such merger or consolidation continue to represent, or are converted into or exchanged for shares of capital stock that represent, immediately following such merger or consolidation, at least a majority, by voting power, of the capital stock of (1) the surviving or resulting corporation; or (2) if the surviving or resulting corporation is a wholly owned subsidiary of another corporation immediately following such merger or consolidation, the parent corporation of such surviving or resulting corporation; or

(b) the sale, lease, transfer, exclusive license or other disposition, in a single transaction or series of related transactions, by the Corporation or any subsidiary of the Corporation of all or substantially all the assets of the Corporation and its subsidiaries taken as a whole, or the sale or disposition (whether by merger, consolidation or otherwise) of one or more subsidiaries of the Corporation if substantially all of the assets of the Corporation and its subsidiaries taken as a whole are held by such subsidiary or subsidiaries, except where such sale, lease, transfer, exclusive license or other disposition is to a wholly owned subsidiary of the Corporation.

2.3.2 *Effecting a Deemed Liquidation Event.*

(a) The Corporation shall not have the power to effect a Deemed Liquidation Event referred to in Subsection *2.3.1(a)(i)* unless the agreement or plan of merger or consolidation for such transaction (the "Merger Agreement") provides that the consideration payable to the stockholders of the Corporation shall be allocated among the holders of capital stock of the Corporation in accordance with *Subsections 2.1* and *2.2.*

(b) In the event of a Deemed Liquidation Event referred to in *Subsection 2.3.1(a)(ii)* or *2.3.1(b)*, if the Corporation does not effect a dissolution of the Corporation under the General Corporation Law within ninety (90) days after such Deemed Liquidation Event, then (i) the Corporation shall send a written notice to each holder of Series A Preferred Stock no later than the ninetieth (90th) day after the Deemed Liquidation Event advising such holders of their right (and the requirements to be met to secure such right) pursuant to the terms of the following clause; (ii) to require the redemption of such shares of Series A Preferred Stock, and (iii) if the holders of at least a majority of the then outstanding shares of Series A Preferred Stock so request in a written instrument delivered to the Corporation not later than one hundred twenty (120) days after such Deemed Liquidation Event, the Corporation shall use the consideration received by the Corporation for such Deemed Liquidation Event (net of any retained liabilities associated with the assets sold or technology licensed, as determined in good faith by the Board of Directors of the Corporation), together with any other assets of the Corporation available for distribution to its stockholders, all to the extent permitted by Delaware law governing distributions to stockholders (the "Available Proceeds"), on the one hundred fiftieth (150th) day after such Deemed Liquidation Event, to redeem all outstanding shares of Series A Preferred Stock at a price per share equal to the Series A Liquidation Amount. Notwithstanding the foregoing, in the event of a redemption pursuant to the preceding sentence, if the Available Proceeds are not sufficient to redeem all outstanding shares of Series A Preferred Stock, the Corporation shall ratably redeem each holder's shares of Series A Preferred Stock to the fullest extent of such Available Proceeds, and shall redeem the remaining shares as soon as it may lawfully do so under Delaware law governing distributions to stockholders. The provisions of Section 6 shall apply, with such necessary changes in the details thereof as are necessitated by the context, to the redemption of the Series A Preferred Stock pursuant to this *Subsection 2.3.2(b)*. Prior to the distribution or redemption provided for in this *Subsection 2.3.2(b)*, the Corporation shall not expend or dissipate the consideration received for such Deemed Liquidation Event, except to discharge expenses incurred in connection with such Deemed Liquidation Event or in the ordinary course of business.

2.3.3 *Amount Deemed Paid or Distributed.* The amount deemed paid or distributed to the holders of capital stock of the Corporation upon any such merger, consolidation, sale, transfer, exclusive license, other disposition or redemption shall be the cash or the value of the property, rights or securities paid or distributed to such holders by the Corporation or the acquiring person, firm or other entity. The value of such property, rights or securities shall be determined in good faith by the Board of Directors of the Corporation.

2.3.4 *Allocation of Escrow and Contingent Consideration.* In the event of a Deemed Liquidation Event pursuant to *Subsection 2.3.1(a)(i)*, if any portion of the consideration payable to the stockholders of the Corporation is payable only upon satisfaction of contingencies (the "Additional Consideration"), the Merger Agreement shall provide that (a) the portion of such consideration that is not Additional Consideration (such portion, the "Initial Consideration") shall be allocated among the holders of capital stock of the Corporation in accordance with *Subsections 2.1* and *2.2* as if the Initial Consideration were the only consideration payable in connection with such Deemed Liquidation Event; and (b) any Additional Consideration which becomes payable to the stockholders of the Corporation upon satisfaction of such contingencies shall be allocated among the holders of capital stock of the Corporation in accordance with *Subsections 2.1* and *2.2* after taking into account the previous payment of the Initial Consideration as part of the same transaction. For the purposes of this *Subsection 2.3.4*, consideration placed into escrow or retained as holdback to be available for satisfaction of indemnification or similar obligations in connection with such Deemed Liquidation Event shall be deemed to be Initial Consideration.

3. *Voting.*

3.1 *General.* On any matter presented to the stockholders of the Corporation for their action or consideration at any meeting of stockholders of the Corporation (or by written consent of stockholders in lieu of meeting), each holder of outstanding shares of Series A Preferred Stock shall be entitled to cast the number of votes equal to the number of whole shares of Common Stock into which the shares of Series A Preferred Stock held by such holder are convertible as of the record date for determining stockholders entitled to vote on such matter. Except as provided by law or by the other provisions of the Certificate of Incorporation, holders of Series A Preferred Stock shall vote together with the holders of Voting Common Stock as a single class.

3.2 *Election of Directors.* The holders of record of the shares of Series A Preferred Stock, exclusively and as a separate class, shall be entitled to elect one director of the Corporation (the "Series A Director") and the holders of record of the shares of Voting Common Stock, exclusively and as a separate class, shall be entitled to elect two directors of the Corporation. Any director elected as provided in the preceding sentence may be removed without cause by, and only by, the affirmative vote of the holders of the shares of the class or series of capital stock entitled to elect such director or directors, given either at a special meeting of such stockholders duly called for that purpose or pursuant to a written consent of stockholders. If the holders of shares of Series A Preferred Stock or Voting Common Stock, as the case may be, fail to elect a sufficient number of directors to fill all directorships for which they are entitled to elect directors, voting exclusively and as a separate class, pursuant to the first sentence of this *Subsection 3.2*, then any directorship not so filled shall remain vacant until such time as the holders of the Series A Preferred Stock or Voting Common Stock, as the case may be, elect a person to fill such directorship by vote or written consent in lieu of a meeting; and no such directorship may be filled by stockholders of the Corporation other than by the stockholders of the Corporation that are entitled to elect a person to fill such directorship, voting exclusively and as a separate class. The holders of record of the shares of Voting Common Stock and of any other class or series of voting stock (including the Series A Preferred Stock), exclusively and voting together as a single class, shall be entitled to elect the balance of the total number of directors of the Corporation. At any meeting held for the purpose of electing a director, the presence in person or by proxy of the holders of a majority of the outstanding shares of the class or series entitled to elect such director shall constitute a quorum for the purpose of electing such director. Except as otherwise provided in this *Subsection 3.2*, a vacancy in any directorship filled by the holders of any class or series shall be filled only by vote or written consent in lieu of a meeting of the holders of such class or series or by any remaining director or directors elected by the holders of such class or series pursuant to this *Subsection 3.2*.

3.3 *Series A Preferred Stock Protective Provisions*. At any time when at least 500,000 shares of Series A Preferred Stock (subject to appropriate adjustment in the event of any stock dividend, stock split, combination or other similar recapitalization with respect to the Series A Preferred Stock) are outstanding, the Corporation shall not, either directly or indirectly by amendment, merger, consolidation or otherwise, do any of the following without (in addition to any other vote required by law or the Certificate of Incorporation) the written consent or affirmative vote of the holders of at least a majority of the then outstanding shares of Series A Preferred Stock, given in writing or by vote at a meeting, consenting or voting (as the case may be) separately as a class, and any such act or transaction entered into without such consent or vote shall be null and void *ab initio*, and of no force or effect.

3.3.1 liquidate, dissolve or wind-up the business and affairs of the Corporation, effect any merger or consolidation or any other Deemed Liquidation Event, or consent to any of the foregoing;

3.3.2 amend, alter or repeal any provision of the Certificate of Incorporation or Bylaws of the Corporation in a manner that adversely affects the powers, preferences or rights of the Series A Preferred Stock;

3.3.3 create, or authorize the creation of any additional class or series of capital stock unless the same ranks junior to the Series A Preferred Stock with respect to the distribution of assets on the liquidation, dissolution or winding up of the Corporation, the payment of dividends and rights of redemption, or increase the authorized number of shares of Series A Preferred Stock or increase the authorized number of shares of any additional class or series of capital stock unless the same ranks junior to the Series A Preferred Stock with respect to the distribution of assets on the liquidation, dissolution or winding up of the Corporation, the payment of dividends and rights of redemption;

3.3.4 purchase or redeem (or permit any subsidiary to purchase or redeem) or pay or declare any dividend or make any distribution on, any shares of capital stock of the Corporation other than (i) redemptions of or dividends or distributions on the Series A Preferred Stock as expressly authorized herein, (ii) dividends or other distributions payable on the Common Stock solely in the form of additional shares of Common Stock and (iii) repurchases of stock from former employees, officers, directors, consultants or other persons who performed services for the Corporation or any subsidiary in connection with the cessation of such employment or service at the lower of the original purchase price or the then-current fair market value thereof or (iv) as approved by the Board of Directors;

3.3.5 create, or authorize the creation of, or issue, or authorize the issuance of any debt security, or permit any subsidiary to take any such action with respect to any debt security, unless such debt security has received the prior approval of the Board of Directors;

3.3.6 create, or hold capital stock in, any subsidiary that is not wholly owned (either directly or through one or more other subsidiaries) by the Corporation, or sell, transfer or otherwise dispose of any capital stock of any direct or indirect subsidiary of the Corporation, or permit any direct or indirect subsidiary to sell, lease, transfer, exclusively license or otherwise dispose (in a single transaction or series of related transactions) of all or substantially all of the assets of such subsidiary; or

3.3.7 increase or decrease the authorized number of directors constituting the Board of Directors.

4. *Optional Conversion.* The holders of the Series A Preferred Stock shall have conversion rights as follows (the "Conversion Rights"):

4.1 *Right to Convert.*

4.1.1 *Conversion Ratio.* Each share of Series A Preferred Stock shall be convertible, at the option of the holder thereof, at any time and from time to time, and without the payment of additional consideration by the holder thereof, into such number of fully paid and non-assessable shares of Voting Common Stock as is determined by dividing the Series A Original Issue Price by the Series A Conversion Price (as defined below) in effect at the time of conversion. The "Series A Conversion Price" shall initially be equal to $[*initial conversion price of preferred stock*]. Such initial Series A Conversion Price, and the rate at which shares of Series A Preferred Stock may be converted into shares of Voting Common Stock, shall be subject to adjustment as provided below.

4.1.2 *Termination of Conversion Rights.* In the event of a notice of redemption of any shares of Series A Preferred Stock pursuant to Section 6, the Conversion Rights of the shares designated for redemption shall terminate at the close of business on the last full day preceding the date fixed for redemption, unless the redemption price is not fully paid on such redemption date, in which case the Conversion Rights for such shares shall continue until such price is paid in full. In the event of a liquidation, dissolution or winding up of the Corporation or a Deemed Liquidation Event, the Conversion Rights shall terminate at the close of business on the last full day preceding the date fixed for the payment of any such amounts distributable on such event to the holders of Series A Preferred Stock.

4.2 *Fractional Shares.* No fractional shares of Voting Common Stock shall be issued upon conversion of the Series A Preferred Stock. In lieu of any fractional shares to which the holder would otherwise be entitled, the Corporation shall pay cash equal to such fraction multiplied by the fair market value of a share of Voting Common Stock as determined in good faith by the Board of Directors of the Corporation. Whether or not fractional shares would be issuable upon such conversion shall be determined on the basis of the total number of shares of Series A Preferred Stock the holder is at the time converting into Voting Common Stock and the aggregate number of shares of Voting Common Stock issuable upon such conversion.

4.3 *Mechanics of Conversion.*

4.3.1 *Notice of Conversion.* In order for a holder of Series A Preferred Stock to voluntarily convert shares of Series A Preferred Stock into shares of Voting Common Stock, such holder shall (a) provide written notice to the Corporation's transfer agent at the office of the transfer agent for the Series A Preferred Stock (or at the principal office of the Corporation if the Corporation serves as its own transfer agent) that such holder elects to convert all or any number of such holder's shares of Series A Preferred Stock and, if applicable, any event on which such conversion is contingent and (b), if such holder's shares are certificated, surrender the certificate or certificates for such shares of Series A Preferred Stock (or, if such registered holder alleges that such certificate has been lost, stolen or destroyed, a lost certificate affidavit and agreement reasonably acceptable to the Corporation to indemnify the Corporation against any claim that may be made against the Corporation on account of the alleged loss, theft or destruction of such certificate), at the office of the transfer agent for the Series A Preferred Stock (or at the principal office of the Corporation if the Corporation serves as its own transfer agent). Such notice shall state such holder's name or the names of the nominees in which such holder wishes the shares of Voting Common Stock to be issued. If required by the Corporation, any certificates surrendered for conversion shall be endorsed or accompanied by a written instrument or instruments of transfer, in form satisfactory to the Corporation, duly executed by the registered holder or his, her or its attorney duly authorized in writing. The close of business on the date of receipt by the transfer agent (or by the Corporation if the Corporation serves as its own transfer agent) of such notice and, if applicable, certificates (or lost certificate affidavit and agreement) shall be the time of conversion (the "Conversion Time"), and the shares of Voting Common Stock issuable upon conversion of the specified shares shall be deemed to be outstanding of record as of such date. The Corporation shall, as soon as practicable after the Conversion Time (i) issue and deliver to such holder of Series A Preferred Stock, or to his, her or its nominees, a certificate or certificates for the number of full shares of Voting Common Stock issuable upon such conversion in accordance with the provisions hereof and a certificate for the number (if any) of the shares of Series A Preferred Stock represented by the surrendered certificate that were not converted into Voting Common Stock, (ii) pay in cash such amount as provided in Subsection 4.2 in lieu of any fraction of a share of Voting Common Stock otherwise issuable upon such conversion and (iii) pay all declared but unpaid dividends on the shares of Series A Preferred Stock converted.

4.3.2 *Reservation of Shares.* The Corporation shall at all times when the Series A Preferred Stock shall be outstanding, reserve and keep available out of its authorized but unissued capital stock, for the purpose of effecting the conversion of the Series A Preferred Stock, such number of its duly authorized shares of Voting Common Stock as shall from time to time be sufficient to effect the conversion of all outstanding Series A Preferred Stock; and if at any time the number of authorized but unissued shares of Voting Common Stock shall not be sufficient to effect the conversion of all then outstanding shares of the Series A Preferred Stock, the Corporation shall take such corporate action as may be necessary to increase its authorized but unissued shares of Voting Common Stock to such number of shares as shall be sufficient for such purposes, including, without limitation, engaging in best efforts to obtain the requisite stockholder approval of any necessary amendment to the Certificate of Incorporation. Before taking any action which would cause an adjustment reducing the Series A Conversion Price below the then par value of the shares of Voting Common Stock issuable upon conversion of the Series A Preferred Stock, the Corporation will take any corporate action which may, in the opinion of its counsel, be necessary in order that the Corporation may validly and legally issue fully paid and non-assessable shares of Voting Common Stock at such adjusted Series A Conversion Price.

4.3.3 *Effect of Conversion.* All shares of Series A Preferred Stock which shall have been surrendered for conversion as herein provided shall no longer be deemed to be outstanding and all rights with respect to such shares shall immediately cease and terminate at the Conversion Time, except only the right of the holders thereof to receive shares of Voting Common Stock in exchange therefor, to receive payment in lieu of any fraction of a share otherwise issuable upon such conversion as provided in Subsection 4.2 and to receive payment of any dividends declared but unpaid thereon. Any shares of Series A Preferred Stock so converted shall be retired and cancelled and may not be reissued as shares of such series, and the Corporation may thereafter take such appropriate action (without the need for stockholder action) as may be necessary to reduce the authorized number of shares of Series A Preferred Stock accordingly.

4.3.4 *No Further Adjustment.* Upon any such conversion, no adjustment to the Series A Conversion Price shall be made for any declared but unpaid dividends on the Series A Preferred Stock surrendered for conversion or on the Voting Common Stock delivered upon conversion.

4.3.5 *Taxes.* The Corporation shall pay any and all issue and other similar taxes that may be payable in respect of any issuance or delivery of shares of Voting Common Stock upon conversion of shares of Series A Preferred Stock pursuant to this Section 4. The Corporation shall not, however, be required to pay any tax which may be payable in respect of any transfer involved in the issuance and delivery of shares of Voting Common Stock in a name other than that in which the shares of Series A Preferred Stock so converted were registered, and no such issuance or delivery shall be made unless and until the person or entity requesting such issuance has paid to the Corporation the amount of any such tax or has established, to the satisfaction of the Corporation, that such tax has been paid.

4.4 *Adjustments to Series A Conversion Price for Diluting Issues.*

4.4.1 Special Definitions. For purposes of this Article Fourth, the following definitions shall apply:

(a) "Option" shall mean rights, options or warrants to subscribe for, purchase or otherwise acquire Common Stock or Convertible Securities.

(b) "Series A Original Issue Date" shall mean the date on which the first share of Series A Preferred Stock was issued.

(c) "Convertible Securities" shall mean any evidences of indebtedness, shares or other securities directly or indirectly convertible into or exchangeable for Common Stock, but excluding Options.

(d) "Additional Shares of Common Stock" shall mean all shares of Common Stock issued (or, pursuant to Subsection 4.4.3 below, deemed to be issued) by the Corporation after the Series A Original Issue Date, other than (1) the following shares of Common Stock and (2) shares of Common Stock deemed issued pursuant to the following Options and Convertible Securities (clauses (1) and (2), collectively, "Exempted Securities"):

(i) shares of Common Stock, Options or Convertible Securities issued as a dividend or distribution on Series A Preferred Stock;

(ii) shares of Common Stock, Options or Convertible Securities issued by reason of a dividend, stock split, split-up or other distribution on shares of Common Stock that is covered by Subsection 4.5, 4.6, 4.7 or 4.8;

(iii) shares of Common Stock or Options issued to employees or directors of, or consultants or advisers to, the Corporation or any of its subsidiaries pursuant to a plan, agreement or arrangement approved by the Board of Directors of the Corporation; or

(iv) shares of Common Stock or Convertible Securities actually issued upon the exercise of Options or shares of Common Stock actually issued upon the conversion or exchange of Convertible Securities, in each case provided such issuance is pursuant to the terms of such Option or Convertible Security;

(v) shares of Common Stock, Options or Convertible Securities issued to banks, equipment lessors or other financial institutions, or to real property lessors, pursuant to a debt financing, equipment leasing or real property leasing transaction approved by the Board of Directors of the Corporation; or

(vi) shares of Common Stock, Options or Convertible Securities issued pursuant to the acquisition of another corporation by the Corporation by merger, purchase of substantially all of the assets or other reorganization or to a joint venture agreement, provided that such issuances are approved by the Board of Directors of the Corporation.

4.4.2 *No Adjustment of Series A Conversion Price.* No adjustment in the Series A Conversion Price shall be made as the result of the issuance or deemed issuance of Additional Shares of Common Stock if the Corporation receives written notice from the holders of at least a majority of the then outstanding shares of Series A Preferred Stock agreeing that no such adjustment shall be made as the result of the issuance or deemed issuance of such Additional Shares of Common Stock.

4.4.3 *Deemed Issue of Additional Shares of Common Stock.*

(a) If the Corporation at any time or from time to time after the Series A Original Issue Date shall issue any Options or Convertible Securities (excluding Options or Convertible Securities which are themselves Exempted Securities) or shall fix a record date for the determination of holders of any class of securities entitled to receive any such Options or Convertible Securities, then the maximum number of shares of Common Stock (as set forth in the instrument relating thereto, assuming the satisfaction of any conditions to exercisability, convertibility or exchangeability but without regard to any provision contained therein for a subsequent adjustment of such number) issuable upon the exercise of such Options or, in the case of Convertible Securities and Options therefor, the conversion or exchange of such Convertible Securities, shall be deemed to be Additional Shares of Common Stock issued as of the time of such issue or, in case such a record date shall have been fixed, as of the close of business on such record date.

(b) If the terms of any Option or Convertible Security, the issuance of which resulted in an adjustment to the Series A Conversion Price pursuant to the terms of Subsection 4.4.4, are revised as a result of an amendment to such terms or any other adjustment pursuant to the provisions of such Option or Convertible Security (but excluding automatic adjustments to such terms pursuant to anti-dilution or similar provisions of such Option or Convertible Security) to provide for either (1) any increase or decrease in the number of shares of Common Stock issuable upon the exercise, conversion and/or exchange of any such Option or Convertible Security or (2) any increase or decrease in the consideration payable to the Corporation upon such exercise, conversion and/or exchange, then, effective upon such increase or decrease becoming effective, the Series A Conversion Price computed upon the original issue of such Option or Convertible Security (or upon the occurrence of a record date with respect thereto) shall be readjusted to such Series A Conversion Price as would have obtained had such revised terms been in effect upon the original date of issuance of such Option or Convertible Security. Notwithstanding the foregoing, no readjustment pursuant to this clause (b) shall have the effect of increasing the Series A Conversion Price to an amount which exceeds the lower of (i) the Series A Conversion Price in effect immediately prior to the original adjustment made as a result of the issuance of such Option or Convertible Security, or (ii) the Series A Conversion Price that would have resulted from any issuances of Additional Shares of Common Stock (other than deemed issuances of Additional Shares of Common Stock as a result of the issuance of such Option or Convertible Security) between the original adjustment date and such readjustment date.

(c) If the terms of any Option or Convertible Security (excluding Options or Convertible Securities which are themselves Exempted Securities), the issuance of which did not result in an adjustment to the Series A Conversion Price pursuant to the terms of Subsection 4.4.4 (either because the consideration per share (determined pursuant to Subsection 4.4.5) of the Additional Shares of Common Stock subject thereto was equal to or greater than the Series A Conversion Price then in effect, or because such Option or Convertible Security was issued before the Series A Original Issue Date), are revised after the Series A Original Issue Date as a result of an amendment to such terms or any other adjustment pursuant to the provisions of such Option or Convertible Security (but excluding automatic adjustments to such terms pursuant to anti-dilution or similar provisions of such Option or Convertible Security) to provide for either (1) any increase in the number of shares of Common Stock issuable upon the exercise, conversion or exchange of any such Option or Convertible Security or (2) any decrease in the consideration payable to the Corporation upon such exercise, conversion or exchange, then such Option or Convertible Security, as so amended or adjusted, and the Additional Shares of Common Stock subject thereto (determined in the manner provided in Subsection 4.4.3(a) shall be deemed to have been issued effective upon such increase or decrease becoming effective.

(d) Upon the expiration or termination of any unexercised Option or unconverted or unexchanged Convertible Security (or portion thereof) which resulted (either upon its original issuance or upon a revision of its terms) in an adjustment to the Series A Conversion Price pursuant to the terms of Subsection 4.4.4, the Series A Conversion Price shall be readjusted to such Series A Conversion Price as would have obtained had such Option or Convertible Security (or portion thereof) never been issued.

(e) If the number of shares of Common Stock issuable upon the exercise, conversion and/or exchange of any Option or Convertible Security, or the consideration payable to the Corporation upon such exercise, conversion and/or exchange, is calculable at the time such Option or Convertible Security is issued or amended but is subject to adjustment based upon subsequent events, any adjustment to the Series A Conversion Price provided for in this Subsection 4.4.3 shall be effected at the time of such issuance or amendment based on such number of shares or amount of consideration without regard to any provisions for subsequent adjustments (and any subsequent adjustments shall be treated as provided in clauses (b) and (c) of this Subsection 4.4.3). If the number of shares of Common Stock issuable upon the exercise, conversion and/or exchange of any Option or Convertible Security, or the consideration payable to the Corporation upon such exercise, conversion and/or exchange, cannot be calculated at all at the time such Option or Convertible Security is issued or amended, any adjustment to the Series A Conversion Price that would result under the terms of this Subsection 4.4.3 at the time of such issuance or amendment shall instead be effected at the time such number of shares and/or amount of consideration is first calculable (even if subject to subsequent adjustments), assuming for purposes of calculating such adjustment to the Series A Conversion Price that such issuance or amendment took place at the time such calculation can first be made.

4.4.4 *Adjustment of Series A Conversion Price Upon Issuance of Additional Shares of Common Stock*. In the event the Corporation shall at any time after the Series A Original Issue Date issue Additional Shares of Common Stock (including Additional Shares of Common Stock deemed to be issued pursuant to Subsection 4.4.3), without consideration or for a consideration per share less than the Series A Conversion Price in effect immediately prior to such issue, then the Series A Conversion Price shall be reduced, concurrently with such issue, to a price (calculated to the nearest one-hundredth of a cent) determined in accordance with the following formula:

$$CP2 = CP1 * (A + B) \div (A + C)$$

For purposes of the foregoing formula, the following definitions shall apply:

(a) "CP2" shall mean the Series A Conversion Price in effect immediately after such issue of Additional Shares of Common Stock

(b) "CP1" shall mean the Series A Conversion Price in effect immediately prior to such issue of Additional Shares of Common Stock;

(c) "A" shall mean the number of shares of Common Stock outstanding immediately prior to such issue of Additional Shares of Common Stock (treating for this purpose as outstanding all shares of Common Stock issuable upon exercise of Options outstanding immediately prior to such issue or upon conversion or exchange of Convertible Securities (including the Series A Preferred Stock) outstanding (assuming exercise of any outstanding Options therefor) immediately prior to such issue);

(d) "B" shall mean the number of shares of Common Stock that would have been issued if such Additional Shares of Common Stock had been issued at a price per share equal to CP1 (determined by dividing the aggregate consideration received by the Corporation in respect of such issue by CP1); and

(e) C shall mean the number of such Additional Shares of Common Stock issued in such transaction.

4.4.5 *Determination of Consideration.* For purposes of this Subsection 4.4, the consideration received by the Corporation for the issue of any Additional Shares of Common Stock shall be computed as follows:

(a) *Cash and Property:* Such consideration shall:

(i) insofar as it consists of cash, be computed at the aggregate amount of cash received by the Corporation, excluding amounts paid or payable for accrued interest;

(ii) insofar as it consists of property other than cash, be computed at the fair market value thereof at the time of such issue, as determined in good faith by the Board of Directors of the Corporation; and

(iii) in the event Additional Shares of Common Stock are issued together with other shares or securities or other assets of the Corporation for consideration which covers both, be the proportion of such consideration so received, computed as provided in clauses (i) and (ii) above, as determined in good faith by the Board of Directors of the Corporation.

(b) *Options and Convertible Securities.* The consideration per share received by the Corporation for Additional Shares of Common Stock deemed to have been issued pursuant to Subsection 4.4.3, relating to Options and Convertible Securities, shall be determined by dividing:

(i) The total amount, if any, received or receivable by the Corporation as consideration for the issue of such Options or Convertible Securities, plus the minimum aggregate amount of additional consideration (as set forth in the instruments relating thereto, without regard to any provision contained therein for a subsequent adjustment of such consideration) payable to the Corporation upon the exercise of such Options or the conversion or exchange of such Convertible Securities, or in the case of Options for Convertible Securities, the exercise of such Options for Convertible Securities and the conversion or exchange of such Convertible Securities, by

(ii) the maximum number of shares of Common Stock (as set forth in the instruments relating thereto, without regard to any provision contained therein for a subsequent adjustment of such number) issuable upon the exercise of such Options or the conversion or exchange of such Convertible Securities, or in the case of Options for Convertible Securities, the exercise of such Options for Convertible Securities and the conversion or exchange of such Convertible Securities.

4.4.6 *Multiple Closing Dates.* In the event the Corporation shall issue on more than one date Additional Shares of Common Stock that are a part of one transaction or a series of related transactions and that would result in an adjustment to the Series A Conversion Price pursuant to the terms of Subsection 4.4.4, and such issuance dates occur within a period of no more than ninety (90) days from the first such issuance to the final such issuance, then, upon the final such issuance, the Series A Conversion Price shall be readjusted to give effect to all such issuances as if they occurred on the date of the first such issuance (and without giving effect to any additional adjustments as a result of any such subsequent issuances within such period).

4.5 *Adjustment for Stock Splits and Combinations.* If the Corporation shall at any time or from time to time after the Series A Original Issue Date effect a subdivision of the outstanding Common Stock, the Series A Conversion Price in effect immediately before that subdivision shall be proportionately decreased so that the number of shares of Voting Common Stock issuable on conversion of each share of such series shall be increased in proportion to such increase in the aggregate number of shares of Common Stock outstanding. If the Corporation shall at any time or from time to time after the Series A Original Issue Date combine the outstanding shares of Common Stock, the Series A Conversion Price in effect immediately before the combination shall be proportionately increased so that the number of shares of Common Stock issuable on conversion of each share of such series shall be decreased in proportion to such decrease in the aggregate number of shares of Common Stock outstanding. Any adjustment under this subsection shall become effective at the close of business on the date the subdivision or combination becomes effective.

4.6 *Adjustment for Certain Dividends and Distributions.* In the event the Corporation at any time or from time to time after the Series A Original Issue Date shall make or issue, or fix a record date for the determination of holders of Common Stock entitled to receive, a dividend or other distribution payable on the Common Stock in additional shares of Common Stock, then and in each such event the Series A Conversion Price in effect immediately before such event shall be decreased as of the time of such issuance or, in the event such a record date shall have been fixed, as of the close of business on such record date, by multiplying the Series A Conversion Price then in effect by a fraction:

(1) the numerator of which shall be the total number of shares of Common Stock issued and outstanding immediately prior to the time of such issuance or the close of business on such record date, and

(2) the denominator of which shall be the total number of shares of Common Stock issued and outstanding immediately prior to the time of such issuance or the close of business on such record date plus the number of shares of Common Stock issuable in payment of such dividend or distribution.

Notwithstanding the foregoing (a) if such record date shall have been fixed and such dividend is not fully paid or if such distribution is not fully made on the date fixed therefor, the Series A Conversion Price shall be recomputed accordingly as of the close of business on such record date and thereafter the Series A Conversion Price shall be adjusted pursuant to this subsection as of the time of actual payment of such dividends or distributions; and (b) that no such adjustment shall be made if the holders of Series A Preferred Stock simultaneously receive a dividend or other distribution of shares of Common Stock in a number equal to the number of shares of Common Stock as they would have received if all outstanding shares of Series A Preferred Stock had been converted into Common Stock on the date of such event.

4.7 *Adjustments for Other Dividends and Distributions.* In the event the Corporation at any time or from time to time after the Series A Original Issue Date shall make or issue, or fix a record date for the determination of holders of Common Stock entitled to receive, a dividend or other distribution payable in securities of the Corporation (other than a distribution of shares of Common Stock in respect of outstanding shares of Common Stock) or in other property and the provisions of Section 1 do not apply to such dividend or distribution, then and in each such event the holders of Series A Preferred Stock shall receive, simultaneously with the distribution to the holders of Common Stock, a dividend or other distribution of such securities or other property in an amount equal to the amount of such securities or other property as they would have received if all outstanding shares of Series A Preferred Stock had been converted into Voting Common Stock on the date of such event.

4.8 *Adjustment for Merger or Reorganization, etc.* Subject to the provisions of *Subsection 2.3,* if there shall occur any reorganization, recapitalization, reclassification, consolidation or merger involving the Corporation in which the Common Stock (but not the Series A Preferred Stock) is converted into or exchanged for securities, cash or other property (other than a transaction covered by Subsections 4.4, 4.6 or 4.7), then, following any such reorganization, recapitalization, reclassification, consolidation or merger, each share of Series A Preferred Stock shall thereafter be convertible in lieu of the Voting Common Stock into which it was convertible prior to such event into the kind and amount of securities, cash or other property which a holder of the number of shares of Voting Common Stock of the Corporation issuable upon conversion of one share of Series A Preferred Stock immediately prior to such reorganization, recapitalization, reclassification, consolidation or merger would have been entitled to receive pursuant to such transaction; and, in such case, appropriate adjustment (as determined in good faith by the Board of Directors of the Corporation) shall be made in the application of the provisions in this Section 4 with respect to the rights and interests thereafter of the holders of the Series A Preferred Stock, to the end that the provisions set forth in this Section 4 (including provisions with respect to changes in and other adjustments of the Series A Conversion Price) shall thereafter be applicable, as nearly as reasonably may be, in relation to any securities or other property thereafter deliverable upon the conversion of the Series A Preferred Stock.

4.9 Certificate as to Adjustments. Upon the occurrence of each adjustment or readjustment of the Series A Conversion Price pursuant to this Section 4, the Corporation at its expense shall, as promptly as reasonably practicable but in any event not later than ten (10) days thereafter, compute such adjustment or readjustment in accordance with the terms hereof and furnish to each holder of Series A Preferred Stock a certificate setting forth such adjustment or readjustment (including the kind and amount of securities, cash or other property into which the Series A Preferred Stock is convertible) and showing in detail the facts upon which such adjustment or readjustment is based. The Corporation shall, as promptly as reasonably practicable after the written request at any time of any holder of Series A Preferred Stock (but in any event not later than ten (10) days thereafter), furnish or cause to be furnished to such holder a certificate setting forth (i) the Series A Conversion Price then in effect, and (ii) the number of shares of Voting Common Stock and the amount, if any, of other securities, cash or property which then would be received upon the conversion of Series A Preferred Stock.

4.10 Notice of Record Date. In the event:

(a) the Corporation shall take a record of the holders of its Common Stock (or other capital stock or securities at the time issuable upon conversion of the Series A Preferred Stock) for the purpose of entitling or enabling them to receive any dividend or other distribution, or to receive any right to subscribe for or purchase any shares of capital stock of any class or any other securities, or to receive any other security; or

(b) of any capital reorganization of the Corporation, any reclassification of the Common Stock of the Corporation, or any Deemed Liquidation Event; or

(c) of the voluntary or involuntary dissolution, liquidation or winding-up of the Corporation, then, and in each such case, the Corporation will send or cause to be sent to the holders of the Series A Preferred Stock a notice specifying, as the case may be, (i) the record date for such dividend, distribution or right, and the amount and character of such dividend, distribution or right, or (ii) the effective date on which such reorganization, reclassification, consolidation, merger, transfer, dissolution, liquidation or winding-up is proposed to take place, and the time, if any is to be fixed, as of which the holders of record of Common Stock (or such other capital stock or securities at the time issuable upon the conversion of the Series A Preferred Stock) shall be entitled to exchange their shares of Common Stock (or such other capital stock or securities) for securities or other property deliverable upon such reorganization, reclassification, consolidation, merger, transfer, dissolution, liquidation or winding-up, and the amount per share and character of such exchange applicable to the Series A Preferred Stock and the Common Stock. Such notice shall be sent at least ten (10) days prior to the record date or effective date for the event specified in such notice.

5. *Mandatory Conversion.*

5.1 *Trigger Events.* Upon either (a) the closing of the sale of shares of Common Stock to the public in a firm-commitment underwritten public offering pursuant to an effective registration statement under the Securities Act of 1933, as amended, resulting in at least $25,000,000 of gross proceeds to the Corporation or (b) the date and time, or the occurrence of an event, specified by vote or written consent of the holders of at least a majority of the then outstanding shares of Series A Preferred Stock (the time of such closing or the date and time specified or the time of the event specified in such vote or written consent is referred to herein as the "Mandatory Conversion Time"), then (i) all outstanding shares of Series A Preferred Stock shall automatically be converted into shares of Voting Common Stock, at the then effective conversion rate as calculated pursuant to *Subsection 4.1.1.* and (ii) such shares may not be reissued by the Corporation.

5.2 *Procedural Requirements.* All holders of record of shares of Series A Preferred Stock shall be sent written notice of the Mandatory Conversion Time and the place designated for mandatory conversion of all such shares of Series A Preferred Stock pursuant to this Section 5. Such notice need not be sent in advance of the occurrence of the Mandatory Conversion Time. Upon receipt of such notice, each holder of shares of Series A Preferred Stock in certificated form shall surrender his, her or its certificate or certificates for all such shares (or, if such holder alleges that such certificate has been lost, stolen or destroyed, a lost certificate affidavit and agreement reasonably acceptable to the Corporation to indemnify the Corporation against any claim that may be made against the Corporation on account of the alleged loss, theft or destruction of such certificate) to the Corporation at the place designated in such notice. If so required by the Corporation, any certificates surrendered for conversion shall be endorsed or accompanied by written instrument or instruments of transfer, in form satisfactory to the Corporation, duly executed by the registered holder or by his, her or its attorney duly authorized in writing. All rights with respect to the Series A Preferred Stock converted pursuant to *Subsection 5.1*, including the rights, if any, to receive notices and vote (other than as a holder of Voting Common Stock), will terminate at the Mandatory Conversion Time (notwithstanding the failure of the holder or holders thereof to surrender any certificates at or prior to such time), except only the rights of the holders thereof, upon surrender of any certificate or certificates of such holders (or lost certificate affidavit and agreement) therefor, to receive the items provided for in the next sentence of this *Subsection 5.2*. As soon as practicable after the Mandatory Conversion Time and, if applicable, the surrender of any certificate or certificates (or lost certificate affidavit and agreement) for Series A Preferred Stock, the Corporation shall (a) issue and deliver to such holder, or to his, her or its nominees, a certificate or certificates for the number of full shares of Voting Common Stock issuable on such conversion in accordance with the provisions hereof and (b) pay cash as provided in *Subsection 4.2* in lieu of any fraction of a share of Voting Common Stock otherwise issuable upon such conversion and the payment of any declared but unpaid dividends on the shares of Series A Preferred

Stock converted. Such converted Series A Preferred Stock shall be retired and cancelled and may not be reissued as shares of such series, and the Corporation may thereafter take such appropriate action (without the need for stockholder action) as may be necessary to reduce the authorized number of shares of Series A Preferred Stock accordingly.

6. *Redeemed or Otherwise Acquired Shares.* Any shares of Series A Preferred Stock that are redeemed or otherwise acquired by the Corporation or any of its subsidiaries shall be automatically and immediately cancelled and retired and shall not be reissued, sold or transferred. Neither the Corporation nor any of its subsidiaries may exercise any voting or other rights granted to the holders of Series A Preferred Stock following redemption.

7. *Waiver.* Any of the rights, powers, preferences and other terms of the Series A Preferred Stock set forth herein may be waived on behalf of all holders of Series A Preferred Stock by the affirmative written consent or vote of the holders of at least a majority of the shares of Series A Preferred Stock then outstanding.

8. *Notices.* Any notice required or permitted by the provisions of this Article Fourth to be given to a holder of shares of Series A Preferred Stock shall be mailed, postage prepaid, to the post office address last shown on the records of the Corporation, or given by electronic communication in compliance with the provisions of the General Corporation Law, and shall be deemed sent upon such mailing or electronic transmission.

SECOND: Subject to any additional vote required by the Certificate of Incorporation or Bylaws, in furtherance and not in limitation of the powers conferred by statute, the Board of Directors is expressly authorized to make, repeal, alter, amend and rescind any or all of the Bylaws of the Corporation.

THIRD: Subject to any additional vote required by the Certificate of Incorporation, the number of directors of the Corporation shall be determined in the manner set forth in the Bylaws of the Corporation.

FOURTH: Elections of directors need not be by written ballot unless the Bylaws of the Corporation shall so provide.

FIFTH: Meetings of stockholders may be held within or without the State of Delaware, as the Bylaws of the Corporation may provide. The books of the Corporation may be kept outside the State of Delaware at such place or places as may be designated from time to time by the Board of Directors or in the Bylaws of the Corporation.

SIXTH: To the fullest extent permitted by law, a director of the Corporation shall not be personally liable to the Corporation or its stockholders for monetary damages for breach of fiduciary duty as a director. If the General Corporation Law or any other law of the State of Delaware is amended after approval by the stockholders of this Article Ninth to authorize corporate action further eliminating or limiting the personal liability of directors, then the liability of a director of the Corporation shall be eliminated or limited to the fullest extent permitted by the General Corporation Law as so amended.

Any repeal or modification of the foregoing provisions of this Article Ninth by the stockholders of the Corporation shall not adversely affect any right or protection of a director of the Corporation existing at the time of, or increase the liability of any director of the Corporation with respect to any acts or omissions of such director occurring prior to, such repeal or modification.

SEVENTH: To the fullest extent permitted by applicable law, the Corporation is authorized to provide indemnification of (and advancement of expenses to) directors, officers and agents of the Corporation (and any other persons to which General Corporation Law permits the Corporation to provide indemnification) through Bylaw provisions, agreements with such agents or other persons, vote of stockholders or disinterested directors or otherwise, in excess of the indemnification and advancement otherwise permitted by Section 145 of the General Corporation Law.

Any amendment, repeal or modification of the foregoing provisions of this Article Tenth shall not adversely affect any right or protection of any director, officer or other agent of the Corporation existing at the time of such amendment, repeal or modification.

EIGHTH: The Corporation renounces, to the fullest extent permitted by law, any interest or expectancy of the Corporation in, or in being offered an opportunity to participate in, any Excluded Opportunity. An "Excluded Opportunity" is any matter, transaction or interest that is presented to, or acquired, created or developed by, or which otherwise comes into the possession of (i) any director of the Corporation who is not an employee of the Corporation or any of its subsidiaries, or (ii) any holder of Series A Preferred Stock or any partner, member, director, stockholder, employee or agent of any such holder, other than someone who is an employee of the Corporation or any of its subsidiaries (collectively, "Covered Persons"), unless such matter, transaction or interest is presented to, or acquired, created or developed by, or otherwise comes into the possession of, a Covered Person expressly and solely in such Covered Person's capacity as a director of the Corporation.

NINTH: Unless the Corporation consents in writing to the selection of an alternative forum, the Court of Chancery in the State of Delaware shall be the sole and exclusive forum for any stockholder (including a beneficial owner) to bring (i) any derivative action or proceeding brought on behalf of the Corporation, (ii) any action asserting a claim of breach of fiduciary duty owed by any director, officer or other employee of the Corporation to the Corporation or the Corporation's stockholders, (iii) any action asserting a claim against the Corporation, its directors, officers or employees arising pursuant to any provision of the Delaware General Corporation Law or the Corporation's certificate of incorporation or bylaws or (iv) any action asserting a claim against the Corporation, its directors, officers or employees governed by the internal affairs doctrine, except for, as to each of (i) through (iv) above, any claim as to which the Court of Chancery determines that there is an indispensable party not subject to the jurisdiction of the Court of Chancery (and the indispensable party does not consent to the personal jurisdiction of the Court of Chancery within ten days following such determination), which is vested in the exclusive jurisdiction of a court or forum other than the Court of Chancery, or for which the Court of Chancery does not have subject matter jurisdiction. If any provision or provisions of this Article Twelfth shall be held to be invalid, illegal or unenforceable as applied to any person or entity or circumstance for any reason whatsoever, then, to the fullest extent permitted by law, the validity, legality and enforceability of such provisions in any other circumstance and of the remaining provisions of this Article Twelfth (including, without limitation, each portion of any sentence of this Article Twelfth containing any such provision held to be invalid, illegal or unenforceable that is not itself held to be invalid, illegal or unenforceable) and the application of such provision to other persons or entities and circumstances shall not in any way be affected or impaired thereby.

     TENTH: For purposes of Section 500 of the California Corporations Code (to the extent applicable), in connection with any repurchase of shares of Common Stock permitted under this Certificate of Incorporation from employees, officers, directors or consultants of the Company in connection with a termination of employment or services pursuant to agreements or arrangements approved by the Board of Directors (in addition to any other consent required under this Certificate of Incorporation), such repurchase may be made without regard to any "preferential dividends arrears amount" or "preferential rights amount" (as those terms are defined in Section 500 of the California Corporations Code). Accordingly, for purposes of making any calculation under California Corporations Code Section 500 in connection with such repurchase, the amount of any "preferential dividends arrears amount" or "preferential rights amount" (as those terms are defined therein) shall be deemed to be zero (0).

◆ ◆ ◆

     5. That the foregoing amendment and restatement was approved by the holders of the requisite number of shares of this corporation in accordance with Section 228 of the General Corporation Law.

     6. That this Amended and Restated Certificate of Incorporation, which restates and integrates and further amends the provisions of this Corporation's Certificate of Incorporation, has been duly adopted in accordance with Sections 242 and 245 of the General Corporation Law.

IN WITNESS WHEREOF, this Amended and Restated Certificate of Incorporation has been executed by a duly authorized officer of this corporation on this _____ day of _____, 20___ .

                                     _____ , INC.

          By: _____

          Print Name: _____

          Title: _____

APPENDIX 4

Provision of LLC Operating Agreement Creating Classes of Voting and Nonvoting Membership Interest, with Nonvoting Preferred Interests

____1. *Definitions.* For purposes of this Section:

"Class A Member" shall mean the holder of one or more Class A Voting Units.

"Class B Member" shall mean the holder of one or more Class B Non-Voting Units.

"Class A Voting Units" shall mean Units entitling the owner thereof to all rights set forth in the definition of "Membership Interest" below, including but not limited to the right to vote on matters affecting the business or operations of the Company that require an affirmative vote of the Members.

"Class B Non-Voting Units" shall mean Units entitling the owner thereof to all rights set forth in the definition of "Membership Interest" below except for the right to vote on matters affecting the business or operations of the Company that require an affirmative vote of the Members, and shall include both Class B Common Equity Units and Class B Preferred Equity Units.

"Class B Preferred Equity Member" shall mean each owner of one or more Class B Preferred Equity Units.

"Class B Preferred Equity Units" shall mean all issued and outstanding Class B Non-Voting Units designated by the Managers as "Class B Preferred Equity Units" pursuant to Sections __.2 and __.3 of this Agreement at the time of issuance, the holders of which shall have the rights and preferences as shall be determined by the Managers and approved by majority vote of the Class A Members at the time of issuance.

"Class B Common Equity Units" shall mean all issued and outstanding Class B Non-Voting Units other than Class B Preferred Equity Units.

"Membership Interest" means all of the rights of a Member in the Company, including a Member's: (i) Interest; (ii) right to inspect the Company's books and records; (iii) with respect to Members owning Class A Voting Rights only, the right to participate in the management of and vote on matters coming before the Company; and (iv) unless this Agreement or the Articles of Organization provide to the contrary, right to act as an agent of the Company.

____2. *Units; Classes of Units.* Ownership rights and Membership Interests in the Company are reflected in capital membership units ("Units" or "Units of Membership Interest"), all as recorded in the books and records of the Company. Units may be issued in two classes: Class A Voting Units and Class B Non-Voting Units. Class B Non-Voting Units may be either Class B Preferred Equity Units or Class B Common Equity Units, and the Managers shall designate each Class B Non-Voting Unit as either a Class B Preferred Equity Unit or a Class B Common Equity Unit in writing at the time of issuance. The holders of Class B Preferred Equity Units shall have such rights, benefits and preferences as shall be determined by the Managers and approved by the Class A Members at the time of designation. Unless otherwise set forth in this Agreement, each Unit: (a) if a Class A Voting Unit, has equal governance rights with every other Class A Voting Unit and in matters subject to a vote of the Class A Members has one (1) vote and (b) has equal rights with every other Unit with respect to sharing of profits and losses and with respect to Distributions attributable to the Units.

_____3. *Authorized and Issued Units; Classes of Units.* (a) The aggregate number of Units that may be issued by the Company shall be One Million (1,000,000) (the "Authorized Units"). Of the Authorized Units, 800,000 shall be designated as Class A Voting Units and 200,000 shall be designated as Class B Non-Voting Units. One Hundred Thousand (100,000) Units shall be issued to the Initial Members as set forth in paragraph (b) below, with the remaining Nine Hundred Thousand (900,000) Units being reserved for issuance by affirmative vote of the Class A Members to new and existing Members as provided in this Agreement.

(b) The number of Units issued by the Company to the Initial Members as of the date hereof, and their designation as Class A Voting Units and Class B Non-Voting Units, shall be as set forth on Exhibit A hereto, which exhibit may be amended from time to time by the Managers to reflect the then existing Unit ownership of record.

(c) The Managers are hereby authorized to issue options to officers, employees, agents and consultants of or to the Company in exchange for services rendered to acquire Class B Common Equity Units in amounts (including but not limited to themselves and other Members) in such amount as the Class A Members may approve from time to time pursuant to Section 5.1.3 hereof ("Bonus Units"), provided that any person, firm or entity receiving any additional Units or Bonus Units under this paragraph, if not already a Member of the Company, shall be required to execute and deliver this Operating Agreement and agree in writing to be bound by its terms as a condition to receiving such Bonus Units. The issuance of any such options or Bonus Units may be subject to such vesting periods and other conditions as the Managers may determine in accordance with Section 3.5 of this Agreement. A true and correct list of all Persons currently entitled to options to acquire Class B Common Equity Units for services rendered to the Company is attached to this Agreement as Exhibit "D" and made a part hereof.

(d)The number of Authorized Units may be increased by such amounts as shall be determined by the affirmative vote of a majority in interest of the Class A Members pursuant to Section _____ of this Agreement.

_____4. *Certificates Evidencing Units.* (a) The Company may, with the approval of the Managers, issue certificates reflecting Units (each, a "Certificate") held by a Member. Additionally, at the written request of a Member, the Company will provide certified statements of ownership interests, stating the number of Units owned, as well as (i) the percentage that such Units represent of the respective class of Units and (ii) any effective assignments of rights under those Units, as of the date the statement is provided. Certificates, if issued, shall be signed by a Manager and shall certify the number of Units held by that Member. Certificates for Units shall be issued only when the Units are fully paid. All Certificates shall bear a legend substantially in the form set forth below reflecting that (x) they are subject to the terms and conditions of this Agreement, if and as amended, and (y) they represent "restricted securities" within the meaning of the Securities Act of 1933, as amended, specifically reading as follows:

"TRANSFER OF THE SECURITIES EVIDENCED BY THIS CERTIFICATE IS SUBJECT TO THE TERMS AND CONDITIONS SET FORTH IN THE LIMITED LIABILITY COMPANY OPERATING AGREEMENT OF _____ , LLC (THE "COMPANY"), AS AMENDED. THAT AGREEMET PROVIDES FOR VARIOUS LIMITATIONS AND OBLIGATIONS AND ALL THE TERMS THEREOF ARE INCORPORATED HEREIN. THE COMPANY WILL FURNISH A COPY OF THE AGREEMENT WITHOUT CHARGE TO THE HOLDER HEREOF UPON WRITTEN REQUEST.

THE SECURITIES EVIDENCED BY THIS CERTIFICATE HAVE NOT BEEN REGISTERED UNDER THE SECURITIES ACT OF 1933, AS AMENDED (THE "SECURITIES ACT"), OR UNDER THE SECURITIES ACT OF ANY STATE OR JURISDICTION (THE "STATE ACTS"). THESE SECURITIES MAY NOT BE OFFERED, SOLD OR OTHERWISE TRANSFERRED UNLESS SUCH OFFER, SALE OR TRANSFER IS PURSUANT TO AN EFFECTIVE REGISTRATION STATEMENT UNDER THE SECURITIES ACT, OR IN THE OPINION OF COUNSEL TO THE COMPANY, THE PROPOSED DISPOSITION FALLS WITHIN A VALID EXEMPTION FROM THE REGISTRATION PROVISIONS OF THE SECURITIES ACT AND THE STATE ACTS."

All such Certificates shall be transferable upon the books of the Company upon, in addition to compliance with other applicable provisions of this Agreement, surrender and cancellation of Certificate(s) for a like number of Units, with duly executed assignment and power of transfer endorsed thereon or attached thereto, and with such proof of the authenticity of the signatures to such assignment and power of transfer as the Company or its agents may reasonably require.

(b) The Company may issue a new Certificate in place of any Certificate previously issued by it and alleged to have been lost, stolen or destroyed. The Company may require the owner or the owner's legal representative to give the Company a bond containing such terms as the Company may require to protect the Company or any Person injured by the 7execution and delivery of a new Certificate.

____5. *Consideration for Units; Conditions on Membership Rights.* (a) The determination of when and for what consideration the Company will issue additional Units to new Members shall be made by the Managers. The books and records of the Company shall state the value and nature of the contribution received by the Company and the number and classification of Units received in return by any and all new Members.

(b) Notwithstanding anything to the contrary in this Agreement, the Managers may in their sole discretion, prior to the issuance of any Units (other than any issuance to the Initial Member as contemplated by this Agreement), impose conditions or restrictions, in the manner set forth below, on the ownership rights inuring to such Units. These conditions or restrictions may include, but shall not be limited to:

(i) *Vesting Requirements.* The vesting of ownership rights in the Units may be conditioned upon the attaining quantified benchmarks based on time of service, financial performance, etc.

(ii) *Transferability Restrictions.* The transferability of the Units may be subject to special restrictions.

(iii) *Other Restrictions.* Other rights afforded the Units under this Agreement may be limited or otherwise restricted (i.e., voting rights, Distribution rights, etc.).

(c) The Managers' discretion to restrict ownership rights under this Section may only be imposed in connection with the initial issuance of the affected Units. Each Member receiving Units subject to this Section shall receive a written notice of restriction (the "Restriction Notice") executed by the Managers setting forth in detail the nature of the restriction and the duration of time for which it is effective. The affected Member's prior acceptance, execution and delivery of the Restriction Notice to the Company shall be a condition precedent to the issuance of the Units subject to the Restriction Notice.

APPENDIX 5

SOME RIGHTS OF SHAREHOLDERS UNDER STATE CORPORATION LAWS

1. Issuance of Shares

The following rules prevail in most states.

A corporation's Certificate of Incorporation must prescribe the classes of shares and the number of shares of each class that the corporation is authorized to issue. If more than one class of shares is authorized, the Certificate of Incorporation must prescribe a distinguishing designation for each class, and prior to the issuance of shares of a class the preferences, limitations, and relative rights of that class must be described in the Certificate of Incorporation. All shares of a class must have preferences, limitations, and relative rights identical with those of other shares of the same class.

The Articles of Incorporation must authorize (1) one or more classes of shares that together have unlimited voting rights, and (2) one or more classes of shares (which may be the same class or classes as those with voting rights) that together are entitled to receive the net assets of the corporation upon dissolution.

The Articles of Incorporation may authorize one or more classes of shares that:

1. Have special, conditional, or limited voting rights, or no right to vote, except to the extent prohibited elsewhere in the state corporation statute

2. Are redeemable or convertible as specified in the Articles of Incorporation (i) at the opinion of the corporation, the shareholder, or another person or upon the occurrence of a designated event; (ii) for cash, indebtedness, securities, or other property; (iii) in a designated amount or in an amount determined in accordance with a designated formula or by reference to extrinsic data or events

3. Entitle the holders to distributions calculated in any manner, including dividends that may be cumulative, noncumulative, or partially cumulative

4. Have preferences over any other class of shares with respect to distributions upon the dissolution of the corporation

Note especially the requirement that each class of securities a "distinguishing designation, such as "Class A Common Stock," or "Series P Convertible Preferred Stock." It is customary, although not legally required, for the class title to reflect the key privileges and rights of the holders of that class of stock, so for example "Series A Cumulative Redeemable Exchangeable Participatory Preferred Stock" (although I would advise any client not to use a title that would unavoidably lead to the acronym "CREEP," "CRAP," or any variation thereof).

Shares may but need not be represented by certificates. Unless the state corporation statute or another state law expressly provides otherwise, the rights and obligations of shareholders are identical whether or not their shares are represented by certificates. If the issuing corporation is authorized to issue different classes of shares, the designations, relative rights, preferences, and limitations applicable to each class must be summarized on the front or back of each certificate. Alternatively, each certificate may state conspicuously on its front or back that the corporation will furnish the shareholder this information on request in writing and without charge.

2. Shareholders' Preemptive Rights

The following rules apply in virtually all states.

The shareholders of a corporation do not have a preemptive right to acquire the corporation's unissued shares except to the extent the Articles of Incorporation so provide. A statement included in the Articles of Incorporation that "the corporation elects to have preemptive rights" (or words of similar import) means that the following principles apply except to the extent the Articles of Incorporation expressly provide otherwise:

The shareholders of the corporation have a preemptive right, granted on uniform terms and conditions prescribe by the board of directors, to provide a fair and reasonable opportunity to exercise the right, to acquire proportional amounts of the corporation's unissued shares upon the decision of the board of directors to issue them.

There is no preemptive right with respect to:

1. Shares issued as compensation to directors, officers, agents, or employees of the corporation

2. Shares issued to satisfy conversion or option rights created to provide compensation to directors, officers, agents or employees of the corporation

3. Shares authorized in the Articles of Incorporation that are issued within six months from the effective date of incorporation

4. Shares sold otherwise than for money

Holders of nonvoting preferred stock have no preemptive rights with respect to shares of any class.

Holders of shares of common stock have no preemptive rights with respect to shares of any class of preferred stock, unless the preferred stock is convertible into common stock.

Preemptive rights cannot be exercised for a period of one year after issuance for a subsequent offering of securities at the same price or a higher price than the price set for the exercise of preemptive rights. An offering at a lower price during the one-year period, or an offering at any price after the expiration of one year, is subject to the preemptive rights.

The following provide preemptive rights to shareholders unless denied in the Articles of Incorporation: Alabama, Alaska, Arkansas, Connecticut, the District of Columbia, Hawaii, Maine, Minnesota, Missouri, Nevada, North Dakota, Ohio, Puerto Rico, Rhode Island, South Carolina, South Dakota, Texas, Virginia, Washington (state), and West Virginia.

3. Rights of Nonvoting Shareholders

Generally, only voting shareholders are required to receive notice of annual and special meetings of a corporation's shareholders. Where the matter to be voted on is a major corporate transaction, however, most states require notice of the meeting to be given to nonvoting as well as voting shareholders. For example, notice of shareholder meetings to approve merger and acquisition transaction, the sale of all or substantially all of the corporation's assets, amendment of the Articles of Incorporation, or the dissolution and liquidation of the corporation, should be given to both nonvoting as well as voting shareholders.

4. Shareholder Right to Compel Dissolution of Corporation

In Alaska, one-third of a corporation's outstanding shares can petition for judicial dissolution.

In Georgia, the holders of 20 percent or more of the outstanding shares can petition for dissolution on the grounds of illegal or fraudulent conduct by the directors or others in control of the corporation.

In Maryland, the holders of 25 percent of a corporation's outstanding shares can petition for judicial dissolution on the grounds of director or shareholder deadlock (inability to reach decisions).

In Massachusetts, the holders of 40 percent of a corporation's outstanding shares can petition for judicial dissolution on grounds of director or shareholder deadlock.

In Nevada, the holders of 10 percent of a corporation's outstanding shares can petition for judicial dissolution on the grounds of director or shareholder deadlock.

In New York, the holders of 50 percent of a corporation's outstanding shares can petition for judicial dissolution on the grounds of director or shareholder deadlock.

In New York, the holders of 20 percent or more of the outstanding shares can petition for judicial dissolution on the grounds of "harsh or oppressive misconduct" by the majority of shareholders or others in control of the corporation.

5. Shareholder Liability for Unpaid Wage Claims if Corporation Dissolves

In New York, the ten largest shareholders of a corporation are personally liable for wage claims of employees of the corporation, if the corporation fails to satisfy those claims.

In Wisconsin, shareholders are personally liable for unpaid wage claims of employees of the corporation, if the corporation fails to satisfy those claims, up to an amount equal to the par value of the shareholders owned by a shareholder for debts owing to employees for services for a period not to exceed six months.

APPENDIX 6

Term Sheet for Crowdfunded Offering of Debt Securities

(CONVERTIBLE PROMISSORY NOTES)

_____ , INC.

TERM SHEET

FOR CONVERTIBLE NOTE FINANCING

_____ , 20 ____

This Term Sheet sets forth the principal terms proposed for the sale and issuance of Convertible Promissory Notes of _____ , Inc., a Delaware corporation (the "Company"). No legally binding obligations will be created by this Term Sheet until definitive agreements are executed and delivered by all parties. This Term Sheet is not a commitment to invest or issue any promissory note, and is conditioned on the completion of due diligence, legal review and documentation that is satisfactory to the Investors. This Term Sheet shall be governed in all respects by the laws of the State of Delaware.

OFFERING TERMS

Type of Security:	Convertible Promissory Notes, bearing interest at A simple interest rate of ____% (the "Notes").
Amount of Financing:	$_____
Closing:	A first closing will be held on or before _____ , 20____ or such other date that the Company and the investor(s) participating in such closing (each a "Note Holder") mutually decide upon (the "Initial Closing"). Additional closings may be held up to 90 days after the Initial Closing at the option of the Company.
Minimum Investment:	$_____
Terms of Conversion:	*Mandatory Conversion:* The Notes and any accrued interest will be converted into the Company's next issued series of preferred stock (the "Preferred Shares") resulting in new money of not less than $_____ (the "Preferred Financing") at a discount to the per-share price of such Preferred Shares of ___% (the "Conversion Price").

Terms of Conversion (cont.):	*Voluntary Conversion:* The Notes and any accrued interest shall be convertible, at the option of the Company, on the __-month anniversary of the Initial Closing (the "Maturity Date"), into shares of Class B (Nonvoting) Common Stock, $____ par value per share, at a conversion price equivalent to a pre-money valuation of $_____ .
Term of Payment:	If the Company has not elected a Voluntary Conversion, then all outstanding principal and accrued interest under the Note is due and payable to each Note Holder on the Maturity Date.
Payment:	The Notes may be prepaid only upon prior written approval of the holders of a majority in interest of the outstanding principal amount of the Notes ("Majority Holders"). Any prepayment must be made in connection with the prepayment of all Notes issued under the Note Purchase Agreement, as amended.
Change of Control:	If an acquisition or similar change of control transaction occurs prior to the Preferred Financing or the Maturity Date, then upon the closing of such transaction, the Notes will, at the election of the Majority Holders, become (1) payable upon demand as of the closing of such transaction; or (2) redeemable for a prepayment equal to the amount each Note Holder would have received had the Note converted immediately prior to the transaction to (i) Preferred Stock (if a Preferred Financing is pending at the time of the transaction) or, (ii) if no Preferred Financing is pending, to Common Stock at a price per share equivalent to a fully diluted pre-month valuation of $_____ , to be paid in the same form of consideration (e.g. a mix of cash and stock) received by other equity holders in the transaction.
Documentation:	The transaction will be documented by counsel to the Company with the documents containing the provisions described above and consisting of the following: Note Purchase Agreement, Convertible Promissory Note(s), and Investor Questionnaire.
Note Purchase Agreement:	The Notes will be issued pursuant to a definitive Note Purchase Agreement containing customary covenants, representations and warranties of the Company.
Expiration Date:	This offer will expire on _____ , 20__ unless extended in writing by the Company.
Expenses:	The Company and the Investors will each bear their own legal and other expenses with respect to the transactions contemplated herein.

APPENDIX 7

Term Sheet for Crowdfunded Offering of Series B (Nonvoting) Preferred Shares in Corporation

TERM SHEET

FOR PRIVATE PLACEMENT OF

SERIES B CONVERTIBLE PREFERRED STOCK OF

[Name of Corporation]

[Date of Issue]

This term sheet summarizes the principal terms of the "Series B" round of financing for [Name of Corporation].

OFFERING TERMS

Issuer:	[Name of Corporation], a [jurisdiction of incorporation] corporation (the "Company")
Securities to be Issued:	[Number of Shares to be issued] shares of Series B Convertible Preferred Stock (the "Preferred Stock")
Aggregate Proceeds:	$[aggregate proceeds of offering, in dollars]
Price:	$[offering price per share] per share
Pre-money valuation:	$[pre-money valuation of corporation]
Expected Closing Date:	[closing date of offering]
Investors:	[name of each investor and amount of each investor's commitment]
Option Pool:	A stock option pool of [percentage of common shares allocated for corporation's employees] of the outstanding shares of Common Stock on a post-financing basis, on a fully diluted basis, shall be reserved for distribution to employees, directors, and consultants. An option pool of shares is factored into the pre-money valuation set forth above.

RIGHTS, PREFERENCES, PRIVILEGES AND RESTRICTIONS OF SERIES B CONVERTIBLE PREFERRED STOCK:

Dividend Provisions: Dividends shall be payable pro rata on the Series B Convertible Preferred Stock based on the number of shares of Common Stock in to which they are convertible, but only if and when declared by the Company's Board of Directors. No dividends shall be paid on any Common Stock unless comparable dividends are paid on all of the Series B Convertible Preferred Stock and all shares of the Series A Preferred Stock (the "Series A Preferred Stock") based on the number of shares of Common Stock in to which they are convertible.

Liquidation Preference: In the event of any liquidation or winding up of the Company, the holders of the Series B Convertible Preferred Stock, pari passu with the holders of the "Series A Preferred Stock, shall be entitled to receive in preference to the holders of Common Stock the amount at which the Series B Convertible Preferred Stock and the Series A Preferred Stock, as the case may be, was purchased from the Company plus any accrued but unpaid dividends. The remaining balance of the proceeds from the liquidation will then be allocated to the Series B Convertible Preferred Stock, the Series A Preferred Stock, and the Common Stock holders on an as-converted basis. At the option of the holders of the Series B Convertible Preferred Stock and the Series A Preferred Stock, a merger, sale of all or substantially all of the assets of the Company, reorganization or other transaction in which control of the Company is transferred may be treated as a liquidation, dissolution or winding up for purpose of the liquidation preference. This liquidation preference will expire if the Company is liquidated at a value of greater than $48 million. In the event of liquidation above $48 million, proceeds from the liquidation will then be allocated to Series B Convertible Preferred Stock, Series A Preferred Stock and Common Stock holders on an as-converted basis.

Redemption: Commencing five (5) years after the original date of issuance of the Series A Preferred Stock, the Company shall redeem the Series B Convertible Preferred Stock in three equal annual amounts, one-third of the invested amount per year. Accrued, but unpaid dividends are to be paid with the final payment. If the Company has insufficient funds to fully pay the redemption, then subsequent funds shall be applied to the redemption. This redemption shall be at the option of the Investors.

Conversion: The holders of the Series B Convertible Preferred Stock shall have the right to convert the Series B Convertible Preferred Stock at the option of the holder, at any time, into shares of Common Stock of the Company at the conversion rate of one-to-one or the conversion rate then in place. Any accrued but unpaid dividends will also have the right to be converted at the option of the Company.

Automatic Conversion:	The Series B Convertible Preferred Stock shall be automatically converted into Common Stock, at the then applicable conversion rate, in the event of an underwritten public offering of shares of the Company's Common Stock at a per share public offering price (prior to underwriting commissions and expenses of not less than $5.00 per share (adjusted for stock splits, dividends and combinations) and for a total offering of not less than $10 million.
Anti-Dilution Provisions:	The conversion price of the Series B Convertible Preferred Stock shall be subject to appropriate adjustment in the event of a stock split, stock dividend or similar event; and shall be adjusted on a weighted average basis to prevent dilution, in the event that the Company sells additional shares of Common Stock, preferred stock or convertible debt convertible into Common Stock or preferred stock (other than shares which are presently authorized and, which may be issued from time to time to employees, consultants or directors) at a purchase price less than the applicable conversion price of the Series B Convertible Preferred Stock.
Voting Rights:	Except as set forth herein, each holder of Series B Convertible Preferred Stock shall have the right to that number of votes equal to the number of shares of Common Stock issuable upon conversion of the Series B Convertible Preferred Stock held by such holder and shall vote with the Common Stock.
Protective Provision:	So long as at least 50% of the issued Series B Preferred Stock is outstanding, except as otherwise required by law and as described below, the holders of a majority of the outstanding shares of Common Stock, Series A Preferred Stock, and Series B Convertible Preferred Stock (voting together as a single class on an as-converted to Common Stock basis) shall be required to approve matters which require stockholder vote; provided, however, that, on the following matters the holders of Series B Convertible Preferred Stock, voting together as a single class, will have a separate class vote requiring majority approval of the total number of votes:

    (i)   the creation of any senior or pari passu security;

    (ii) payment of dividends on Common Stock;

    (iii) repurchase of stock;

    (iv) an increase or decrease in the number of authorized shares of Series B Convertible Preferred Stock;

    (v) any adverse change to the rights, preferences and privileges of the Series B Convertible Preferred Stock;

Protective Provision (cont.):	(vi) any other action materially affecting only the Series B Convertible Preferred Stock;
	(vii) any redemption, repurchase, or other acquisition for value of any of the Company's equity securities, other than from present or former consultants, directors, or employees pursuant to the terms of a stock option plan of the Company; and
	(viii) any change in the Company's line of business.

RIGHT OF FIRST REFUSAL:

Right of First Refusal: In the event that any of the existing shareholders, managers, employees or other shareholders propose to sell to a third party or parties a number of shares of their stock, then the stock to be sold will be offered first to the Company to purchase the shares on the same terms as the third party offer. If the Company does not purchase any, or all, of the available shares, then the Series A Preferred Stock and Series B Convertible Preferred Stock shareholders shall have the right to purchase the remaining portion at the same terms. If the Series A Preferred Stock and Series B Convertible Preferred Stock shareholders and/or the Company do not purchase all of the shares, then they may be offered to the third party.

Pre-Emptive Rights: Each purchaser of Series B Convertible Preferred Stock in this financing will have a right of first refusal to purchase a pro rata amount of any Common Stock or securities convertible into Common Stock offered for sale by the Company, on the same terms and conditions and at the same price as offered to third parties, in order to maintain their pre-existing percentage interest in the stock of the Company. This right shall extend for a period for 15 days after the notification by the Company to the Series "B Convertible Preferred Stock shareholders. Such right shall expire upon and shall not apply to an initial public offering of Common Stock, and shall not apply to: (i) shares issued under stock option plans approved by the Board of Directors; or (ii) shares exchanged for assets or securities of another corporation in any acquisition of assets, merger, or other reorganization.

Co-Sale Rights: Each purchaser of Series B Convertible Preferred Stock in this financing will have a co-sale right to sell shares in the event that any of the existing shareholders propose to sell to a third party or parties a number of shares of their Common Stock or securities convertible into Common Stock. This co-sale right also extends to the Company and existing shareholders if Series B Convertible Preferred Stock shareholders sell any of their stock. This clause does not apply to any holders of less than 10,000 shares of stock

Co-Sale Rights (cont.):	or any manager, board member, or employee selling less than 10,000 shares of stock in any 12 month period. This number of shares will be adjusted for any stock splits, combinations, etc. authorized by the Company.

REGISTRATION RIGHTS:

Demand Registration:	Any time after the earliest of two (2) years after the Closing or three (3) months after initial registration (but not within six months of the effective date of a registration), Investors holding at least 40% of the Series B Convertible Preferred Stock or at least 40% of the Series A Preferred Stock (or Common Stock issued upon conversion of the Series A Preferred Stock or the Series B Convertible Preferred Stock, as the case may be) may request that the Company file a Registration Statement for their shares for a registered offering of the Company. The Company will use its best efforts to cause such shares to be registered. The Company shall not be obligated to effect more than two registrations under these demand right provisions.
S-3 Registration:	After two years from the signing of this Agreement and when Form S-3 (or a successor form) is available, holders of at least one-third of the total amount of Series B Convertible Preferred Stock or at least one-third of the total amount of Series A Preferred Stock issued (or Common Stock issued upon conversion of Series A Preferred Stock or Series B Convertible Preferred Stock, as the case may be, or a combination thereof) wishing to sell a minimum of $500,000 worth of Common Stock may demand registration of such shares on Form S-3 (or a successor form). Such registration shall be kept effective by the Company until the earlier to occur of such time as (i) all shares registered thereunder have been sold, (ii) the holders whose shares are registered thereon agree to terminate the registration, (iii) the registration rights of all such holders terminate, or (iv) ninety days. The Company shall not be obligated to effect more than three registrations under this provision and shall not be required to effect such a registration within the ten months following the effective date of any other registration statement (other than an S-8 or S-3 for employees' stock) or more than once in any fiscal year.
Piggyback Registration:	The Investors shall be entitled to "piggyback" registration rights on all registrations by the Company of its Common Stock, subject to the absolute right, however, of the underwriters to reduce the number of shares proposed to be registered on behalf of all selling shareholders (on a pro rata basis) in view of market conditions.

Expenses: The registration expenses (exclusive of underwriting discounts and commissions or fees of counsel to the selling shareholders) of the demand, S-3 and piggyback registrations shall be borne by the Company.

Transfer of Rights: The registration rights may be transferred to a transferee (i) who acquires at least 50% of any Investor's shares and (ii) who is not, in the Company's reasonable opinion, a competitor of the Company or a party who is demonstrably hostile toward the Company, provided the Company is given written notice of such assignment within 30 days after the transfer of the shares. Transfer of registration rights to a partner or member of an Investor shall be without restriction.

Termination of Rights: All registration rights shall terminate as to a holder who holds 1% or less the outstanding shares of the Company's Common Stock (on an as-converted basis) when all of such holder's shares may be sold during a single three-month period under Rule 144.

Other Provisions: Other provisions shall be contained in the Stock Purchase Agreement with respect to registration rights as are reasonable, including cross-indemnification, the period of time in which the Registration Statement shall be kept effective, underwriting arrangements and the like.

Board Representation: Series B Convertible Preferred Stock shareholders will be entitled to and represented by one seat on the Board of Directors of the Company. This representation will be subject to the terms contained therein. The Board of Directors shall be indemnified by the Company, through the purchase of director's liability insurance, to the fullest extent of the law. All travel expenses in attending meetings and performing Company duties shall be borne by the Company. A Compensation Committee, consisting of Directors, majorities of whom are not officers or employees of the Company, will approve compensation packages for key managers of the Company, including the President. The number of Directors on the Board cannot be increased without the approval of a two-thirds majority of the Directors. The Board of Directors will initially be composed of the following: (i) two Series A Preferred Stock representatives; (ii) one Series B Convertible Preferred Stock representative; (iii) one management representative; (iv) the President and CEO of the Company; (iv) one Common Stock representative; and (v) two outside directors approved by the other Board members.

APPENDIX 7

THE STOCK PURCHASE

Agreement:

The investment shall be made pursuant to a Stock Purchase Agreement acceptable to the Company and the Investors, which agreement shall contain, among other things, appropriate representations and warranties of the Company, covenants of the Company reflecting the provisions set forth herein and appropriate conditions of closing which shall include qualification of the shares under applicable Blue Sky Laws, the filing of a Certificate of Amendment and/or Determination of Preferences to authorize the Series B Convertible Preferred Stock and delivery of opinions of counsel.

Covenants:

So long as an Investor continues to hold a minimum of 1,000 shares of Series B Convertible Preferred Stock or Common Stock issued upon conversion of the Series B Convertible Preferred Stock, the Company shall provide annual and quarterly financial statements. So long as an Investor holds at least 250,000 shares of Series B Convertible Preferred Stock (or of Common Stock issued upon conversion), such holder will be entitled to receive status reports and an annual business/operating plan. Such plan will have been approved by the Board of Directors. This right to financial information and plans shall terminate upon a public offering. The above-mentioned Investors will receive, upon request, financial statements and status reports including: cash flow statements; income statements; balance sheets; sales results; cash flow, income and balance sheet forecasts.

A mutually acceptable accounting firm will audit annual statements.

The Company will prepare an annual business plan, with financial projections, for Board approval.

There will be no material transactions with executive management or other shareholders without approval of the Board of Directors, including but not limited to salaries, bonuses, stock purchases and options.

PROPRIETY INFORMATION AND INVENTIONS AGREEMENT:

Agreement:

Each officer, director and key employee of the Company shall have entered into a proprietary information and inventions agreement in a form reasonably acceptable to the Company and the Board of Directors. As part of this agreement, the founders, managers, employees and consultants associated with the Company agree

Agreement (cont.):	to assign all of the technology, patents, etc. to the Company. The Company agrees to pursue the protection of all technology, including the pursuit of all appropriate patents, copyrights, trademarks, etc.
Expenses:	Upon the Closing of the financing, the Company will pay or reimburse the Investors for their reasonable legal expenses incurred in connection with the transaction. This reimbursement will not exceed $10,000 in total from all Series B Convertible Preferred Stock Investors. The Series B Convertible Preferred Stock Investors will be obligated to arrive at an agreed distribution between all parties prior to submitting any request or reimbursement to the Company.
Key Man Insurance:	The Company shall take out key man life insurance on key employees, made payable to the Company. This will be at the determination of the Company and when affordable by the Company.
Use of Proceeds:	The Company intends to use the proceeds of this offering to expand its software development, to purchase equipment, to expand sales and technical support channels including international distribution and for working capital.
Finders:	The Company and the Investors shall each indemnify the other for any finder's fees for which either is responsible.
Conditions of Closing:	Any closing of this financing will be contingent on (i) completion of due diligence, (ii) required shareholder approval, (iii) modification of the Articles of Incorporation and by-laws as noted in this term sheet, (iv) no negative material changes in the business or operations of the Company and (v) completion of legal documentation.

APPENDIX 8

Term Sheet for Crowdfunded Offering of Class B (Nonvoting) Membership Interests in a Limited Liability Company

_____ , LLC

TERM SHEET

FOR CLASS B (NONVOTING) MEMBERSHIP INTERESTS

Amount of Investment:	$_____
Type of Security:	Class B (Nonvoting) Membership Interests
Pre-Money Valuation:	$_____
Capital Structure:	Existing holders of previously issued Class A Membership Interests and Class B Membership Interests: ___%
	Holders of Newly Issued Class B Membership Interests: ___%
	Total: 100%
Use of Proceeds:	The Company shall use the proceeds for the development of [describe Company's principal product or service] from this financing, together with general business and operational purposes and working capital.
Holders of Class B Membership Interests:	Rights and Privileges of Holders of Class B (Nonvoting) Membership Interests have all of the rights of a Member in the Company, including a Member's: (i) economic interest in the Company (including the right to receive a percentage of distributions of cash flow or the proceeds of capital transactions), pari passu with the economic interests of the holders of Class A (Voting) Membership Interests; (ii) right to inspect the Company's books and records; and (iii) unless this Agreement or the Articles of Organization provide to the contrary, right to act as an agent of the Company. Holders of Class B Membership Interests, however, DO NOT have the right to participate in the management of and vote on matters coming before the Company.
Financial Statements and Reporting:	The Company will provide holders of Class B (Nonvoting) Membership Interests) with copies of all information and materials made available to the holders of Class A (Voting)

Financial Statements and Reporting (cont.):	Membership Interests from time to time, including, without limitation, all internal management documents, financial reports of operations, budgets, and unaudited monthly financial statements.
Expenses:	Each party shall be responsible for its own expenses associated with this transaction.
Conditions to Closing:	Closing shall be subject to the completion of due diligence, the delivery to the investors of a standard legal opinion of counsel to the Company, and a standard Membership Interests Purchase Agreement. Each Investor will also be required to sign a counterpart of the Company's Operating Agreement, a true and correct copy of which is attached to this Term Sheet.
Non-Binding:	This term sheet is non-binding on the parties.

_____ , LLC

By: _____

Print Name: _____

Title: _____

Signature of Investor: _____

Print Name: _____

Date: _____

APPENDIX 9

Sample Risk-Factors Section of a Crowdfunded Offering Statement

[Offering of LLC Membership Interests by
Limited Liability Company Formed To Develop and Market
a Mobile Smartphone Application Or "App"]

RISK FACTORS

Investing in the Company's Units is very risky. You should be able to bear a complete loss of your investment due to the general unprofitability of the mobile software application industry. You should carefully consider the following factors, including those listed in the accompanying business plan.

A. Development Stage Business

_____ , LLC commenced operations in [date of LLC's formation] and is organized as a Limited Liability Company under the laws of the State of Connecticut. Accordingly, the Company has only a limited history upon which an evaluation of its prospects and future performance can be made. The Company's proposed operations are subject to all business risks associated with new enterprises. The likelihood of the Company's success must be considered in light of the problems, expenses, difficulties, complications, and delays frequently encountered in connection with the expansion of a business, operation in a competitive industry, and the continued development of advertising, promotions and a corresponding customer base. There is a possibility that the Company could sustain losses in the future. There can be no assurances that _____, LLC will even operate profitably.

B. Product Development

The "_____" mobile software application product exists only as a conceptual model. The Company has engaged _____ [name of software developer] as the exclusive developer of the product, and has agreed to a preliminary project timetable for the development and testing of the product, but there can be no assurance that that timetable will be met, that the product will be ready to market within the agreed-upon time periods, that [name of software developer] will have sufficient personnel available at all times to develop the Company's product in accordance with the agreed-upon timetable, that the Company will be able to raise the capital necessary to pay the cost of developing and testing the product, or that the product when fully developed and tested will have all of the functionality and features described in the Company's business plan.

C. Inadequacy of Funds

Gross offering proceeds of a maximum of $_____ may be realized. Management believes that such proceeds will capitalize and sustain _____ , LLC sufficiently to allow for the implementation of the Company's Business Plan. If only a fraction of this Offering is sold, or if certain assumptions contained in Management's business plans prove to be incorrect, the Company may have inadequate funds to fully develop its business and may need debt financing or other capital investment to fully implement the Company's business plans.

D. Dependence on Key Individuals and Part-Time Management

In the early-stages of development the Company's business will be significantly dependent on the Company's management team. The Company's success will be particularly dependent upon _____ [name of LLC founder]. The loss of this individual could have a material adverse effect on the Company.

In addition, the Company will be significantly dependent on _____ [name of software developer] to develop and test the "_____" mobile software application product. _____ [name of president of software developer] has been awarded Class A Voting Units of membership interest in the Company in exchange for his software development services as described in the Company's Operating Agreement attached as Exhibit "B" to this Memorandum, and will also serve as an officer of the Company. The loss of this individual could have a material adverse effect on the Company and the execution of its business plan.

Until such time as the Company has sufficient revenue to pay compensation to its managers, officers and employees generally, the Manager and officers of the Company will be engaged in business and other activities in addition to the Company, all as more particularly described in the Company's business plan attached as Exhibit "A" to this Memorandum. There can be no assurance that these activities will not prevent or inhibit the Manager and officers of the Company from devoting sufficient time and attention to the business and activities of the Company.

E. Risks Associated with Expansion

The Company plans on expanding its business through the production of the "_____" mobile software application product. Any expansion of operations the Company may undertake will entail risks. Such actions may involve specific operational activities, which may negatively impact the profitability of the Company. Consequently, members must assume the risk that (i) such expansion may ultimately involve expenditures of funds beyond the resources available to the Company at that time, and (ii) management of such expanded operations may divert Management's attention and resources away from its existing operations, all of which factors may have a material adverse effect on the Company's present and prospective business activities.

F. Customer Base and Market Acceptance

The Company will generate revenue primarily from the restaurants, bars and brands that choose to have their menus featured on the "_____" mobile software application product. With a free membership, restaurants, bars and brands will be limited to uploading their menu, purchasing advertising, and receiving basic notifications when a customer engages with their profile on _____. For an additional fee, restaurants, bars and brands can list their daily specials and happy hour pricing so that their happy hour price on beer and cocktails will appear in searches for those beers or cocktails. The Company will also generate revenue by:

- selling service upgrades to the "_____" product for the managers and owners of participating restaurants, bars and brands;
- selling display, interactive and rich media ads to food service and beverage brands who wish to market to consumers who are about to make decisions about purchasing food, beer, wine or cocktails; and
- as the "_____" product becomes established in the marketplace, selling access to consumer analytics and back-end information to enable alcohol and other brands to monotor hyper-local trends and measure the real-time success of their local and national advertising and marketing campaigns.

While the Company's management has developed a strategy for achieving such revenue streams, as more particularly described in the Company's business plan attached as Exhibit "A" to this Memorandum, there can be no assurance that any or all of these revenue streams will materialize, that the restaurant, bar and brands the Company has targeted for the initial roll-out of the "_____" product in the New York City metropolitan area will participate in sufficient numbers to generate sufficient revenue for the Company to meet its business plan objectives, or that consumers will download the free version of the "_____" product in sufficient numbers to satisfy the marketing objectives of participating restaurants, bars and brands.

G. Competition

Management believes that the "_____" mobile software application product is demographically well positioned, top quality and unique in nature. The expertise of Management combined with the innovative nature of its project set the Company apart from its competitors. However, there are more than 350,000 mobile software applications currently available for download on Apple Inc.'s App Store alone, some of which purport to direct consumers to local restaurants and bars in their vicinity, and there can be no assurance that the Company will be successful in building a following for the "_____" mobile software application product on Apple Inc. App Store or any other online mobile software application platform. Further, there is the possibility that existing and new competitors could seize upon _____, LLC's business model and produce competing projects having a similar focus. Likewise, these new competitors could be better capitalized than _____ , LLC, which could give them a significant advantage. There is the possibility that the competitors could capture significant market share of _____ , LLC's intended market.

H. Trend in Consumer Preferences and Spending

The Company's operating results may fluctuate significantly from period to period as a result of a variety of factors, including purchasing patterns of customers, competitive pricing, debt service and principal reduction payments, and general economic conditions. There is no assurance that the Company will be successful in marketing any of its products, or that the revenues from the sale of such products will be significant. Consequently, the Company's revenues may vary by quarter, and the Company's operating results may experience fluctuations.

I. Risks of Borrowing

If the Company incurs indebtedness, a portion of its cash flow will have to be dedicated to the payment of principal and interest on such indebtedness. Typical loan agreements also might contain restrictive covenants, which may impair the Company's operating flexibility. Such loan agreements would also provide for default under certain circumstances, such as failure to meet certain financial covenants. A default under a loan agreement could result in the loan becoming immediately due and payable and, if unpaid, a judgment in favor of such lender, which would be senior to the rights of members of the Company. A judgment creditor would have the right to foreclose on any of the Company's assets resulting in a material adverse effect on the Company's business, operating results or financial condition.

J. Unanticipated Obstacles to Execution of the Business Plan

The Company's business plans may change significantly. Many of the Company's potential business endeavors are capital intensive and may be subject to statutory or regulatory requirements. Management believes that the Company's chosen activities and strategies are achievable in light of current economic and legal conditions with the skills, background, and knowledge of the Company's principals and advisers. Management reserves the right to make significant modifications to the Company's stated strategies depending on future events.

K. Management Discretion as to Use of Proceeds

The net proceeds from this Offering will be used for the purposes described under "Use of Proceeds." The Company reserves the right to use the funds obtained from this Offering for other similar purposes not presently contemplated, which it deems to be in the best interests of the Company and its members, in order to address changed circumstances or opportunities. As a result of the foregoing, the success of the Company will be substantially dependent upon the discretion and judgment of Management with respect to application and allocation of the net proceeds of this Offering. Investors for the Units offered hereby will be entrusting their funds to the Company's Management, upon whose judgment and discretion the investors must depend.

L. Control by Management

As of [date of offering statement], the Company's Managing Member owned approximately ___% of the Company's _____ outstanding units of membership interest, and ___% of the Company's _____ outstanding Class A Voting Units. Upon completion of this Offering, the Company's Managing Member will own approximately___% of the issued and outstanding units and will continue to own___% of the Company's Class A Voting Units, and will be able to continue to control _____ , LLC. Investor members will own a minority percentage of the Company and will have minority voting rights, while investors purchasing Class B Non-Voting Units will not have voting rights at all. Investor members will not have the ability to control either a vote of the Company's Board of Managers, Class A Voting Units, or any appointed officers.

In addition, certain holders of the Company's Class A Voting Units have been afforded the right to protect their ownership percentage in the Company from dilution in the event of a subsequent offering of Units, including the Offering represented by this Memorandum. For a full description of these rights, please see the Company's Operating Agreement attached as Exhibit "B" to this Memorandum.

M. Return of Profits

A member will be entitled to receive revenue profits proportionate to the amount of units held by that member. The Company's Managing Member will determine a profit distribution plan based upon the Company's results of operations, financial condition, capital requirements, and other circumstances. See "DESCRIPTION OF SECURITIES" section.

N. No Assurances of Protection for Proprietary Rights; Reliance on Trade Secrets

In certain cases, the Company may rely on trade secrets to protect intellectual property, proprietary technology and processes, which the Company has acquired, developed or may develop in the future. There can be no assurances that secrecy obligations will be honored or that others will not independently develop similar or superior products or technology. The protection of intellectual property and/or proprietary technology through claims of trade secret status has been the subject of increasing claims and litigation by various companies both in order to protect proprietary rights as well as for competitive reasons even where proprietary claims are unsubstantiated. The prosecution of proprietary claims or the defense of such claims is costly and uncertain given the uncertainty and rapid development of the principles of law pertaining to this area. The Company, in common with other firms, may also be subject to claims by other parties with regard to the use of intellectual property, technology information and data, which may be deemed proprietary to others.

O. Dilution

Purchasers of Units will experience immediate and substantial dilution of $____ in net tangible book value per unit, or approximately ___% of the assumed offering price of $____ per unit (assuming maximum offering proceeds are achieved). Additional Units issued by the Company in the future will also dilute a purchaser's investment in the Units.

P. Limited Transferability and Liquidity

To satisfy the requirements of certain exemptions from registration under the Securities Act, and to conform with applicable state securities laws, each investor must acquire his Units for investment purposes only and not with a view towards distribution. Consequently, certain conditions of the Securities Act may need to be satisfied prior to any sale, transfer, or other disposition of the Units. Some of these conditions may include a minimum holding period, availability of certain reports, including financial statements from _____, LLC, limitations on the percentage of Units sold and the manner in which they are sold. _____, LLC can prohibit any sale, transfer or disposition unless it receives an opinion of counsel provided at the holder's expense, in a form satisfactory to_____, LLC, stating that the proposed sale, transfer or other disposition will not result in a violation of applicable federal or state securities laws and regulations. No public market exists for the Units and no market is expected to develop. Consequently, owners of the Units may have to hold their investment indefinitely and may not be able to liquidate their investments in_____, LLC or pledge them as collateral for a loan in the event of an emergency.

Q. Broker-Dealer Sales of Units

The Company's Membership Units are not presently included for trading on any exchange, and there can be no assurances that the Company will ultimately be registered on any exchange due to the fact that it is a limited liability company and not a corporation. The NASDAQ Stock Market, Inc. has recently enacted certain changes to the entry and maintenance criteria for listing eligibility on the NASDAQ SmallCap Market. The entry standards require at least $4 million in net tangible assets or $750,000 net income in two of the last three years. The proposed entry standards would also require a public float of at least $1 million shares, $5 million value of public float, a minimum bid price of $2.00 per share, at least three market makers, and at least 300 shareholders. The maintenance standards (as opposed to entry standards) require at least $2 million in net tangible assets or $250,000 in net income in two of the last three years, a public float of at least 25,000 shares, a $1 million market value of public float, a minimum bid price of $10.00 per share, at least two market makers, and at least 300 shareholders. No assurance can be given that the Membership Unit of the Company will ever qualify for inclusion on the NASDAQ System or any other trading market until such time as the Managing Member deem it necessary and the limited liability company is converted to a corporation. As a result, the Company's Membership Units are covered by a Securities and Exchange Commission rule that opposes additional sales practice requirements on broker-dealers who sell such securities to persons other than established customers and accredited investors. For transactions covered by the rule, the broker-dealer must make a special suitability determination for the purchaser and receive the purchaser's written agreement to the transaction prior to the sale. Consequently, the rule may affect the ability of broker-dealers to sell the Company's securities and will also affect the ability of members to sell their units in the secondary market.

R. Long Term Nature of Investment

An investment in the Units may be long term and illiquid. As discussed above, the offer and sale of the Units will not be registered under the Securities Act or any foreign or state securities laws by reason of exemptions from such registration, which depends in part on the investment intent of the investors. Prospective investors will be required to represent in writing that they are purchasing the Units for their own account for long-term investment and not with a view towards resale or distribution. Accordingly, purchasers of Units must be willing and able to bear the economic risk of their investment for an indefinite period of time. It is likely that investors will not be able to liquidate their investment in the event of an emergency.

S. No Current Market For Units

There is no current market for the Units offered in this private Offering and no market is expected to develop in the near future.

T. Compliance with Securities Laws

The Units are being offered for sale in reliance upon certain exemptions from the registration requirements of the Securities Act, applicable Connecticut Securities Laws, and other applicable state securities laws. If the sale of Units were to fail to qualify for these exemptions, purchasers may seek rescission of their purchases of Units. If a number of purchasers were to obtain rescission, _____ , LLC would face significant financial demands, which could adversely affect _____ , LLC as a whole, as well as any non-rescinding purchasers.

U. Offering Price

The price of the Units offered has been arbitrarily established by _____ , LLC, considering such matters as the state of the Company's business development and the general condition of the industry in which it operates. The Offering price bears little relationship to the assets, net worth, or any other objective criteria of value applicable to _____ , LLC.

V. Lack of Firm Underwriter

The Units are offered on a "best efforts" basis by the Managing Member of _____ , LLC without compensation and on a "best efforts" basis through certain NASD registered broker-dealers, which enter into Participating Broker-Dealer Agreements with the Company. Accordingly, there is no assurance that the Company, or any NASD broker-dealer, will sell the maximum Units offered or any lesser amount.

W. *Projections: Forward Looking Information*

Management has prepared projections regarding_____ , LLC anticipated financial performance. The Company's projections are hypothetical and based upon a presumed financial performance of the Company, the addition of a sophisticated and well funded marketing plan, and other factors influencing the business of _____ , LLC. The projections are based on Management's best estimate of the probable results of operations of the Company, based on present circumstances, and have not been reviewed by _____ , LLC independent accountants. These projections are based on several assumptions, set forth therein, which Management believes are reasonable. Some assumptions upon which the projections are based, however, invariably will not materialize due the inevitable occurrence of unanticipated events and circumstances beyond Management's control. Therefore, actual results of operations will vary from the projections, and such variances may be material. Assumptions regarding future changes in sales and revenues are necessarily speculative in nature. In addition, projections do not and cannot take into account such factors as general economic conditions, unforeseen regulatory changes, the entry into _____, LLC market of additional competitors, the terms and conditions of future capitalization, and other risks inherent to the Company's business. While Management believes that the projections accurately reflect possible future results of _____ , LLC operations, those results cannot be guaranteed.

X. *General Economic Conditions*

The financial success of the Company may be sensitive to adverse changes in general economic conditions in the United States, such as recession, inflation, unemployment, and interest rates. Such changing conditions could reduce demand in the marketplace for the Company's products. Management believes that the impending growth of the market, mainstream market acceptance and the targeted product line of _____ , LLC will insulate the Company from excessive reduced demand. Nevertheless, _____ , LLC has no control over these changes.

APPENDIX 10

Sample Accredited Investor Questionnaire

IMPORTANT

Please Complete

INVESTOR NAME: _____

(Indicate the exact name in which you would like the Shares issued.)

_____ INC.

1. INVESTOR QUESTIONNAIRE

This Questionnaire is being distributed in connection with the proposed offer and sale of [describe securities to be offered] (the "Shares"), of _____ Inc. (the "Company"), in a private placement exempt from the registration req uirements of Section 5 of the Securities Act of 1933, as amended (the "Act"), and the securities laws of certain states. The purpose of this Questionnaire is to assure the Company that each investor meets applicable suitability requirements. The information supplied by or on behalf of the entity named above (the "Investor") will be used in determining whether the Investor meets such criteria.

By signing this Questionnaire, the Investor will be authorizing the Company to provide a completed Questionnaire to such parties as the Company deems appropriate in order to ensure that the proposed offer and sale of Shares will not result in a violation of the Act or the securities laws of any state. In making the determination that the proposed sale of Shares is exempt from registration, the Company will rely, in part, on the information supplied by or on behalf of the Investor in this Questionnaire.

All potential investors must answer all questions contained in this Questionnaire. If the answer to a particular question is "no," "none" or "not applicable," please so state. Please print or type all responses and attach additional sheets of paper if necessary to complete the answers to any item.

Completed Questionnaires should be sent to the attention of [name of company's legal counsel], by hand delivery, regular mail or overnight courier to the following address: [street address of company's legal counsel].

. . .

**THIS QUESTIONNAIRE DOES NOT CONSTITUTE AN OFFER TO SELL OR
A SOLICITATION OF AN OFFER TO BUY ANY SECURITY**

SECTION A. INDIVIDUAL INVESTORS. Each Investor who is an individual (and each individual equity owner of an entity required to provide such information) must answer the questions in this Section A where applicable.

1. NAME: _____

DATE OF BIRTH: _____

U.S. CITIZEN (check one) YES___ NO___

2. Residence Address and Telephone Number: _____

_____

_____

3. Business Address and Telephone Number: _____

_____

_____

4. Send correspondence to: Home: _____ Office: _____

   Other: _____

5. Social Security Number: _____

6. Email Address: _____

7. Please set forth the basis of or a description of your experience in any business or financial matters or investment experience that would help you evaluate the merits and risks of an investment in the Shares:

_____

_____

_____

_____

8. Do you (a) maintain an office, a house or apartment, (b) pay income taxes, or (c) hold a driver's license, or are you registered to vote, anywhere, other than as shown above in your answer to Question 2?

YES___ NO___

If the answer is "yes," explain in the space provided below.

_____

_____

_____

_____

_____

SECTION B. NON-INDIVIDUAL INVESTORS. Each Investor which is not an individual must answer the questions in this Section B where applicable.

1. NAME: _____

2. Address of Principal Place of Business: _____

_____

_____

3. Telephone Number: _____

4. Federal Tax I.D. Number: _____

5. Email Address: _____

6. Form of Entity (corporation, partnership, limited liability company or trust):

_____

7. Year of Formation or Incorporation: _____

8. Jurisdiction of Formation or Incorporation: _____

9. Nature of Activities: _____

_____

SECTION C. TYPE OF INVESTOR. Every investor must answer the questions in this Section C.

1. Indicate Type of Ownership Intended for the Share purchased:

____INDIVIDUAL OWNERSHIP (one signature required)

____JOINT TENANTS WITH RIGHT OF SURVIVORSHIP (both or all parties must sign)

____CORPORATION (an authorized corporate officer must sign)

____COMMUNITY PROPERTY (one signature required if Share are to be held in one name, i.e., managing spouse; two signatures required if the Share are to be held in both names)

____ TENANTS IN COMMON (both or all parties must sign)

____ OTHER—Trust, limited liability company, etc. (authorized individual must sign)

2. Please indicate which of the following categories applies to the investor by checking all those that apply:

(a) ☐ a natural person whose individual net worth, or joint net worth with that person's spouse, at the time of purchase exceeds $1,000,000.

(b) ☐ a natural person who had an individual income in excess of $200,000 in each of the two most recent years, or joint income with that person's spouse of $300,000 in each of those years, and who has a reasonable expectation of reaching the same income level in the current year.

(c) ☐ an organization described in section 501(c)(3) of the Internal Revenue Code of 1986, as amended, corporation, partnership, limited liability, Massachusetts or similar business trust or company, not formed for the specific purpose of acquiring the securities offered, with total assets in excess of $5,000,000.

(d) ☐ a trust, with total assets in excess of $5,000,000, not formed for the specific purpose of acquiring the securities offered, whose purchase is directed by a sophisticated person as described in Rule 506(b)(2) of Regulation D, promulgated under the Act.

(e) ☐ a bank as defined in section 3(a)(2) of the Act, or any savings and loan association or other institution as defined in section 3(a)(5)(A) of such Act, acting in either an individual or fiduciary capacity.

(f) ☐ a broker or dealer registered pursuant to section 15 of the Securities Exchange Act of 1934, as amended.

(g) ☐ an insurance company as defined in section 2(13) of the Act.

(h) ☐ an investment company registered under the Investment Company Act of 1940 or a business development company as defined in section 2(a)(48) of such Act.

(i) ☐ a Small Business Investment Company licensed by the U.S. Small Business Administration under section 301(c) or (d) of the Small Business Investment Act of 1958, as amended.

(j) ☐ a plan established and maintained by a state, its political subdivisions or any agency or instrumentality of a state or its political subdivisions for the benefit of its employees, if such plan has total assets in excess of $5,000,000.

(k) ☐ an employee benefit plan within the meaning of the Employee Retirement Income Security Act of 1974, if the investment decision is made by a plan fiduciary, as defined in section 3(21) of such Act, which is either a bank, savings and loan association, insurance company, or registered investment adviser, or if the employee benefit plan has total assets in excess of $5,000,000, or, if a self-directed plan, with investment decisions made solely by persons that are accredited investors.

(l) ☐ a private business development company as defined in section 202(a)(22) of the Investment Advisers Act of 1940.

(m) ☐ a director or executive officer of the Company.

(n) ☐ entity in which all of the equity owners meet at least one of the above criteria.

(o) ☐ none of the above.

SECTION D.REPRESENTATIONS AND WARRANTIES: The undersigned understands that the Company will be relying on the accuracy and completeness of the undersigned's responses to the foregoing questions, and the undersigned represents and warrants to the Company as follows:

(i) The answers to the above questions and the representations set forth in this Section D are true, complete and correct and may be relied upon by the Company in determining whether the offering in which the undersigned proposes to participate is exempt from registration under the Act and applicable state securities laws.

(ii) The undersigned will notify the Company immediately of any material change in any statement made herein occurring prior to the closing of the purchase or receipt of the Shares.

[Signature pages follow.]

INVESTOR QUESTIONNAIRE
SIGNATURE PAGE FOR INDIVIDUALS

IF THE SUBSCRIBER IS AN INDIVIDUAL, COMPLETE THE FOLLOWING SIGNATURE LINES TO THE INVESTOR QUESTIONNAIRE:

IN WITNESS WHEREOF, the undersigned has completed and executed this Questionnaire this _____ day of _____ , 20____ .

_____

Signature of Individual

_____

Print Name of Individual

_____

Signature of Joint Subscriber, if any

_____

Print Name of Joint Subscriber, if any

INVESTOR QUESTIONNAIRE
SIGNATURE PAGE FOR ENTITIES

IF THE SUBSCRIBER IS AN ENTITY, COMPLETE THE FOLLOWING SIGNATURE LINES TO THE INVESTOR QUESTIONNAIRE (only a representative of such Entity who is authorized to execute this document on behalf of such Entity should sign below):

IN WITNESS WHEREOF, the undersigned has completed and executed this Questionnaire this _____ day of _____ , 20____ .

_____

Print Name of Entity

_____

Signature of Authorized Representative

_____

Print Name of Authorized Representative

_____

Title of Authorized Representative

Exhibit A to

INVESTOR QUESTIONNAIRE
CERTIFICATE OF LIMITED LIABILITY COMPANY
OR PARTNERSHIP INVESTOR

CERTIFICATE OF _____

The undersigned, constituting the manager or general partner, as applicable, making the investment decision on behalf of _____ (the "Investor") with respect to the Company hereby certifies that:

1. The Investor commenced business on _____ and was established pursuant to a Partnership Agreement or an Operating Agreement (as applicable) dated _____ (the "Agreement").

2. A true and correct copy of the Agreement is attached hereto and, as of the date hereof, the Agreement has not been amended (except as to any attached amendments) or revoked and is still in full force and effect.

3. As the manager or general partner, as applicable, of the Investor, I have determined that the investment in, and purchase of shares issued by the Company is of benefit to the Investor and have determined to make such investment on behalf of the Investor.

IN WITNESS WHEREOF, I have executed this Certificate as the manager or the general partner, as applicable, of the Investor this _____ day of _____ , 20___ and declare that it is truthful and correct.

Print name / Signature _____

Exhibit B to

INVESTOR QUESTIONNAIRE
CERTIFICATE OF TRUST INVESTOR

CERTIFICATE OF _____
(Name of Trust)

    The undersigned, being the trustee or trustees making the investment decision on behalf of _____ (the "Trust") with respect to the Company hereby certify that:

    1. A true and correct copy of the Trust Agreement dated _____ the "Trust Agreement") is attached hereto and, as of the date hereof, the Trust Agreement has not been amended (except as to any attached amendments) or revoked and is still in full force and effect.

    2. As the trustee or trustees of the Trust, I (we) have determined that the investment in, and purchase of, shares issued by the Company is of benefit to the Trust and have determined to make such investment on behalf of the Trust.

IN WITNESS WHEREOF, the undersigned has executed this Certificate as the trustee of the Trust this _____ day of _____, 20____, and declare that it is truthful and correct.

Print Name / Signature_____

Print Name / Signature_____

Print Name / Signature_____

Print Name / Signature_____

SUGGESTIONS FOR FURTHER READING

As this book is going into print, the SEC has just approved the Title III crowdfunding regulations. Accordingly, there are not many how-to resources for issuers looking to take advantage of the new financing options created by the federal Jumpstart Our Business Startups (JOBS) Act of 2012.

Primary Source Materials

On April 5, 2012, President Barack Obama signed into law the U.S. Jumpstart Our Business Startups (JOBS) Act of 2012, Pub.L. 112-206, 126 Stat. 306, codified at 15 U.S.C. § 78a note, which can be found at www.gpo.gov/fdsys/pkg/PLAW-112publ106/pdf/PLAW-112publ106.pdf.

On July 10, 2013, the U.S. Securities and Exchange Commission (SEC) issued regulations implementing Title II of the JOBS Act in its Release No. 33-9416, which can be found at www.sec.gov/rules/proposed/2013/33-9416.pdf.

The SEC submitted its first draft of Regulation Crowdfunding—containing regulations implementing Title III of the JOBS Act of 2012—for public approval on October 23, 2013, in its Release No. 33-9470, which can be found at www.sec.gov/rules/proposed/2013/33-9470.pdf.

Comments on Regulation Crowdfunding submitted during the two-year period between proposal and adoption were collected by the SEC at www.sec.gov/comments/jobs-title-ii/jobs-title-iii.shtml.

The final version of the Title III crowdfunding regulations were issued by the SEC in its Release No. 33-9974, dated October 30, 2015, which can be found at www.sec.gov/rules/final/2015/33-9974.pdf. The regulations became effective on May 16, 2016, six months after publication in the Federal Register.

Funding Portals

Beginning January 26, 2016, after this book went to press, the SEC began allowing funding portals to register under Title III and Regulation Crowdfunding. Among the companies expected to register with the SEC as of December 15 are:

> Angel.co (the website of Angel List LLC, a social media company dedicated to identifying angel investor communities and creating angel investor syndicates for Title II accredited-investor only offerings).

EquityNet.com (billed as the "original equity crowdfunding platform," EquityNet boasts a patented software system that streamlines the business-planning process).

GrowVC.com (with offices in New York, London and Hong Kong, is positioning itself to be a player in international crowdfunded offerings).

SeedInvest.com (a technology platform that enables equity-based accredited investor crowdfunding).

Start.ac (changed the playing field for crowdfunding by letting members, who are potential investors, rank, rate, and suggest ways to improve a start-up idea).

IPOVillage.com (helped launch Crowdfunding-Website-Reviews.com, one of the Internet's top sites for getting information on crowdfunding platform websites).

Microventure.com (an angel investor Title II crowdfunding portal specializing in technology companies).

TruCrowd.com (focuses on serving nonaccredited investors).

Sprigster.com (focuses on providing crowdfunded financing for franchised businesses).

Start-upValley.com (focuses on start-ups and very early-stage companies).

SyndicateRoom.com (the United Kingdom's first equity crowdfunding platform that focuses on the investors and investor returns; requires that issuing companies must first have a lead business angle, or group of lead investors, on board providing a minimum of 25 percent of the funding round out of pocket).

Other Websites

Crowdfund Capital Advisors, CCA (www.crowdfundcapitaladvisors.com, a think tank for equity crowdfunding, run by the three entreprenerus who lobbied Congres to pass the JOBS Act).

The Crowdfunding Professional Association (www.crowdfundingprofessional. org).

The Crowdfunding Accreditation for Platform Standards Program (www. crowdsourcing.org/caps).

The Crowdfund Intermediary Regulatory Advocates (ww.cfira.org).

The National Crowdfunding Association (www.nlcfa.org).

Crowdfunding Abstracts (www.cfabstracts.com, up-to-the-minute news about crowdfunded investing).

The Crowdfunding Revolution: How to Raise Venture Capital Using Social Media, by Kevin Lawton and Dan Marom (New York: McGraw-Hill, 2012), $26.99.

Crowdfund Investing for Dummies, by Sherwood Neiss, Jason W. Best, and Zak Cassady-Dorion (New York: John Wiley & Sons, 2013), $26.99. The first book on this subject, written by the three entrepreneurs who successfully lobbied Congress to pass the JOBS Act but published before the SEC issued its Title II and Title III crowdfunding regulations.

Crowdfund Your Start-Up: Raising Venture Capital Using New Crowdfunding Techniques, by Rupert M. Hart (Houston: CordaNobelo, 2012), $9.95.

The JOBS Act: Crowdfunding for Small Businesses and Start-Ups, by William Michael Cunningham (New York: Apress, 2012), $14.99.

Resources for Writing a Business Plan

Books (with or without CD-ROMs)

Financial Intelligence for Entrepreneurs, by Karen Berman (Cambridge: Harvard Business Review, 2008), $29.95.

How to Write a Business Plan, by Mike McKeever (San Francisco: Nolo Press, 2014), $21.95.

How to Write a Winning Business Plan, by Joseph Mancuso (New York: Touchstone, 1992), $33.95.

The Complete Book of Business Plans, by Joseph Covello and Brian Hazelgren (Naperville: Small Business Sourcebooks, 2006), $19.95.

Writing a Convincing Business Plan, by Arthur DeThomas (Hauppage: Barron's, 2015), $12.95.

Software Programs

BizPlanBuilder (www.jian.com/business_plan_software/business_plan_solutions.html).

Business Plan Pro (www.businessplanpro.com/template_offer_lt/).

BizPlan.com (www.bizplan.com).

Others (http://business-plan-software-review.toptenreviews.com).

SUGGESTIONS FOR FURTHER READING

Business Plan Templates

www.bplans.com/samples/sba.cfm.

www.businessplanarchive.org (currently not available to the public).

http://www.sec.gov/edgar.shtml.

INDEX

ABOUT THE AUTHOR

Cliff Ennico (www.cliffennico.com, www.succeedinginyourbusiness.com), the author of *The Crowdfunding Handbook,* has more than thirty-five years of experience working with venture companies, venture capitalists, angels, and other professional investors, and start-up technology companies, and is a leading expert on the legal and financial issues that entrepreneurial companies face. He has advised corporate and limited liability company clients in dozens of private placement offerings of securities and hundreds of friends-and-family offerings.

Outside the legal profession, he is best known as the former host of *MoneyHunt;* on this fast-paced PBS reality television series (widely considered an inspiration for the hit ABC television series *Shark Tank*), entrepreneurs defended their business plans before America's toughest panel of experts—exactly what start-ups will be doing when seeking financing via crowdfunding. His weekly business advice column, *Succeeding in Your Business*, syndicated nationally by Creators Syndicate (creators.com), appears in dozens of major newspapers and on small-business websites throughout North America.

Mr. Ennico served his apprenticeship as a corporate and securities lawyer at two of Wall Street's leading law firms. Over the course of a thirty-five-year career, he has helped launch more than fifteen thousand entrepreneurial ventures, and he currently runs his own start-up law and consulting practice in Connecticut. Mr. Ennico has lectured on business and finance topics to business groups, venture capital clubs, and professional and bar associations throughout the United States and is the author of several leading books on small-business law and management, including *Small Business Survival Guide* (AdamsMedia), *MoneyHunt: 27 New Rules for Growing a Breakaway Business* (HarperCollins), *Forms for Small Business Entities* (ThomsonReuters), *Advising eBusinesses* (ThomsonReuters), *The eBay Seller's Tax and Legal Answer Book* (AMACOM), and *The eBay Business Answer Book* (AMACOM).

As a Wall Street lawyer turned successful entrepreneur, Mr. Ennico has seen both sides of a wide variety of legal and business problems, and is one of the few attorneys in America who can present this difficult material in a manner that is not only compelling but entertaining as well.

KIRKWOOD

KIRKWOOD

7-9-16

658.1522 ENNICO
Ennico, Clifford R,
The crowdfunding handbook :
R2003789043 KIRKWD

Atlanta-Fulton Public Library